How to Make Money *Make* Money

HOW TO MAKE MONEY
MAKE MONEY

PROFESSIONAL ADVICE ABOUT

STOCKS AND BONDS

By Henry Gellermann

THOMAS Y. CROWELL COMPANY NEW YORK

To Josef

Introduction

By Oliver J. Gingold,
Editor, "Abreast of the Market"
The Wall Street Journal

IT GOES WITHOUT SAYING that to get into the market a man must have money. Even more important to potential investors or speculators is to have some knowledge of what investment is all about.

For many years, before the turn of the century and well into this one, there were very few books available for students of the market. Knowledge of the machinery of the market place and its goings on was confined to the knowing few. Those not privy to the secrets of the pools, deals, and corporation affairs ("investment" was a word rarely heard in the Street in the early days) had a great deal of courage, if not downright foolhardiness, to try to break into that magic circle. And not many of them had much success; a famous broker around 1910 remarked to me that he had a complete turnover of customers at least three times a year.

Today, all who can read may learn what the new Wall Street is all about. Henry Gellermann, who has wide experience in financial affairs here and abroad, in this book offers those who wish to participate in investment in this country some facts they need if they are to do so with intelligence. Further, he tells his readers how to apply the knowledge the book contains.

There is little excuse today for an investor or speculator to buy or sell any security "with his eyes closed," as the old cliché has it. That sort of advice has always been dangerous, though frequently followed to a sorry end. But now, Wall Street brokers are spending millions of dollars annually to teach people about the market and are offering all sorts of information about investments. Most of this is free to the customers, and the result is that millions of security holders in the United States have knowledge about the Street and the merchandise it sells. Nevertheless, such education has really only begun; there is still much that governs the buying and selling of stocks and bonds that must seem like mumbo jumbo to the unknowing. Mr. Gellermann's book unveils some of these mysteries, too.

One does not have to read too much about some of the things that went on in Wall Street prior to the thirties to realize that such a regulatory body as the Securities and Exchange Commission was bound to appear sooner or later; as it was, the Commission took a hand none too soon. One mark of its success is easily noted; there are few brokers who would care to operate without regulation today.

It should be noted, though, that no manner of regulation and no amount of legislation can create good judgment in buying and selling securities, or in the timing of an investment. A great editor of *The Wall Street Journal*, Thomas F. Woodlock, used to say that there was no stock or bond so safe that it did not need vigilant watching.

Such care, of course, is up to the individual investor. But that, too, is all a part of the growing education of the investing public. Mr. Gellermann's excellent book contains a great deal of financial wisdom that, properly applied, can do a great deal to enhance the knowledge and fortify the decisions necessary to successful investment.

ACKNOWLEDGMENTS

Learning is a process that, for any individual, extends far into the past—so far into the past that it would be impossible for me to acknowledge the help and guidance I have received from teachers and books whose names and titles now slip my mind. Nonetheless I owe them a great debt.

In the immediate past, however, there have been a number of people who have directly aided me in the preparation of this book and whose thinking has had a profound effect on my own.

I should like to mention in particular Harold L. Bache and A. Charles Schwartz, whose steady encouragement over many years has made writing this book a rewarding task. G. Keith Funston and Ruddick C. Lawrence of the New York Stock Exchange, each of them a leader in promoting the concept of a broader shareownership, have been kind enough to contribute their own observations.

The staff of the New York Stock Exchange—notably Kenneth Hayes, Editor of the *Exchange Magazine,* and William D. Horgan, manager of the Exchange News Bureau—have made substantial contributions, not only by providing me with stimulating ideas but also by supplying a vast amount of statistical material and factual data about the operations of the Exchange. In addition, they have accepted willingly the laborious task of reading and commenting on the book in manuscript form. The author also wishes to thank Dow Jones and Company, Inc., Carlisle & Jacquelin, The National Association of Investment Companies, *The Commer-*

cial and Financial Chronicle, Filer, Schmidt & Co., and the Research Department of Bache & Co.

Finally my thanks to my loyal associates, Mrs. Helen Benson and Miss Margaret Brown. To these people, and many more, I am deeply grateful.

At the same time I must assume with some trepidation full responsibility for any part of the book that involves interpretation. Readers may take exception to my views on this or that matter. If that should be the case, the person to get in touch with is the author.

Contents

List of Tables

CHAPTER 1

What This Book Is All About

IT WOULD BE NICE to say that this book was written to help people who would like to make money in the stock market, a group that conceivably could embrace the entire adult population of the United States. In the interest of honesty, though, it would be more accurate to say it was written for people who want to increase their capital or their income or both.

The changing climate in the American investment scene is best explained by Mr. G. Keith Funston, President of the New York Stock Exchange, who has graciously consented to contribute the following to this book:

THE CONCEPT OF A PEOPLE'S CAPITALISM

A major development is shaping the American economy at mid-century. It is the gradual emergence of what we call a "People's Capitalism." It is evidenced, over the years, by the investment activities of millions of people—most of them in the middle and lower income ranges. In increasing numbers these average Americans are becoming the voting shareowners of the nation's publicly held corporations.

This effort to spread corporate risks and rewards is fulfilling the logic of capitalism in a democracy. There is no law that says capitalism must be dynamic or even humane. But our greatest progress has come as these qualities have been developed in our system of enterprise. That system has become more creative as it became more truthful, more fruitful as it became more responsive to the general public. Broader shareownership is thus deeply embedded in the American soil. It grows out of man's deep desire to own the tools with which he works.

The author has not attempted to prepare "A Simple Guide to Quick Profits in the Market" or "Easy Do's and Don't's for Making a Fortune in Wall Street." Such guides, of course, would be highly desirable and certainly would attract a large audience—but unfortunately human knowledge has not advanced to the point where such valuable literature can be prepared.

You may be an investor of long standing, or you may be one of the growing number of people who want to share in the profits of our capitalistic economy. But you also want to know exactly what you are doing with your money. Because different factors guide different individuals' judgment, you may be seeking a highly conservative investment program, or you may be looking for speculative opportunities, or perhaps a little of each. But whichever approach is emphasized, you want to make money—and, equally important, you want to avoid losing money.

First of all, then, you want to know about the mechanics of investment: how the market operates, what makes prices go up or down, how to select a stock, what a broker can do for you, how to speculate, and how not to do so. And you want to be able to translate all this information, and more, into a practical investment program.

This book does not guarantee to make you a financial wizard overnight, but it does contain a great deal of information and advice that should help you become an intelligent investor.

CHAPTER 2

Investment—Speculation—Gambling:

What'll It Be, Gentlemen?

YOU MUST HAVE MONEY to start out with, whether you consider yourself an investor, a speculator, or a gambler. This statement, I admit, may hit you with the same emotional impact as the solemn announcement that two plus two equal four. Still, it may well be desirable to restate this obvious fact, because overlooking it has resulted in a great many empty wallets and a great many broken hearts.

To put it another way, don't speculate with the rent money—and don't "invest" it either. All of us have probably shed a tear for, and marveled at the stupidity of, the unfortunate bank teller who has "borrowed" the bank's funds to bet on a sure thing in the fifth at Pimlico. You may not end up in Sing Sing if you cash in a couple of your U. S. government E bonds to buy 100 shares of a guaranteed uranium stock, but you almost deserve to.

It is my personal conviction that any purchase of securities should be made only on the assumption that you may incur

4

a total loss. What's more, you should know for certain that you can afford to take that loss without putting your family on a diet of oatmeal for six months. Perhaps that's a somewhat strict approach when you're buying, say, 100 shares of American Telephone or General Motors—but it's a safe one.

Just how much money the would-be investor should have available before he considers buying securities is entirely a matter of individual circumstances. It may be sound for a young and single man earning $5,000 a year to invest part of his income in securities, perhaps even speculative securities. But a man with a wife and three children and the same income might have no business buying any security except U. S. government bonds—if those.

Moreover, a family man earning $25,000 a year may be ill advised to embark on an investment program because his fixed commitments and living standard may regularly deplete his checking account.

It's up to you to decide whether you can really afford to invest or speculate. Here are suggestions:

First, have on hand a cash reserve for emergencies. This may be in the form of a savings account, a checking account, or a highly liquid asset such as a U. S. government bond. You may be one of those fortunate people who go through life unscathed by emergencies, but in case Suzy needs a fast appendectomy or a short-sighted boss throws you out of a job in favor of an incompetent nephew, you can fall back on your savings without being forced to sell your investments at a time when it seems wisest to hold on to them.

Second, protect your family with adequate life insurance. Your wife may be young, beautiful, and childless, in which case she has a lot of built-in insurance. More likely, she is no longer in her twenties, and in addition there are a handful of children of assorted ages to consider. So don't strain your conscience and jeopardize their future. Think about stocks after you've paid your bills—all of them.

If you have trouble making up your mind, ask a good broker. He'll give you the best advice he can, and it won't cost you a cent.

I remember that several years ago a middle-aged waitress, who worked in a restaurant where I often lunched, learned that I was in the securities business. Somewhat coyly, she first told me she had saved up enough money to buy some E bonds, not many but just "a few." This was at a time when the stock market had been advancing, and she asked me if I knew a really good stock she should buy. I told her to stick with her E bonds.

We got to know each other a little better, and each time we discussed her savings they had grown a little larger. Finally she admitted she owned between $3,000 and $4,000 worth of E bonds.

Soon after that I arranged for her to talk over her affairs with a neighboring broker, a member of the New York Stock Exchange; and the next time I saw her, I asked how she had made out.

"He was terrible," she told me, almost in tears. "He—he wouldn't take my money. Said to keep my bonds."

My estimation of this broker's good judgment increased still more.

The cardinal sin in the stock market is forced selling, selling against your better judgment because you must raise money in a hurry. More money has been lost in Wall Street because of emergency selling than for any other reason.

Few popular securities ever go straight up or straight down in price. At times the finest stock in the world will decline temporarily. Don't ever put yourself in the position of being forced to sell during one of these temporary setbacks—and you should never have to if you'll keep in mind

the fact that you have no business in the market without
an emergency cash reserve.

Does this mean that a sound approach to the market rules
out speculation? Not at all. This may seem like strange
advice, coming on top of what has just been said, but if you
want to speculate in securities, go to it. There's nothing
wrong with speculation from the viewpoint of the individual,
the economy, or society itself. Speculation is a bad word to
many people, either because they do not understand its nature or because they invariably associate speculation with
excess. Speculation has been one of the strongest driving
forces in this country, ever since the London Company
(chartered in 1606) paved the way for the founding of Virginia, and the Massachusetts Bay Company (incorporated in
1629) gave birth to New England.

Today's speculator is more apt to be interested in uranium
mines, atomic energy, Canadian oils, or transcontinental gas
and pipe lines. But he still performs a vital function—and
in the process sometimes, and I should like to stress the word
"sometimes," makes a neat profit on his willingness to take
a risk.

So forget any moral overtones you may find in the words
"investing," "speculating," or "gambling." Speculate if you
want to, but be sure you are undertaking an *intelligent* speculation, fully aware of the risks involved as well as the possible gains.

If you insist on putting a label on what you are doing in
the market, you'll frequently find it difficult to distinguish
between an investment and a speculation. A speculation has
been defined as a successful investment, and an investment
as a successful speculation. There's a lot of truth in each
of the definitions.

Let's say you know of a new company, soundly financed,
with highly competent management, which plans to exploit

a new invention commercially. You know there is no chance of this company paying a dividend in the foreseeable future, and it seems highly unlikely that stock in the company will increase in value for some time. Yet you are convinced that the company's future is unlimited. Are you speculating or investing when you buy stock in this company?

Or go back some years to the mid–1930's, when the bonds —not the stocks—of some of the country's major railroads were selling at fractions of their face value. Their stocks, incidentally, were virtually without market value at that time. One rail system after another went into bankruptcy in those days, and it seemed pretty clear that anybody buying rail securities was making an outright speculation and not a very smart one at that. Well, fortunes have been made by people who risked their money on rail bonds twenty years ago. Today, bonds that were selling then at less than $20 per $100 face value are now priced at above $100.

Or to take another example, in the early days of the automobile industry a man was a fool to waste his money helping to finance an outfit making horseless buggies—it was better to invest in a sound carriage or buggy whip company. A lot of people did lose money financing those early auto companies. On the other hand, General Motors has done pretty well for its stockholders.

Another rough gauge of the difference between speculation and investment is the time element involved. A man is often regarded as a speculator if he seeks quick profits, buying and selling within a few weeks or even a few days. The investor, on the other hand, buys a security to hold for months or years. This sort of reasoning doesn't stand up too well either. A successful speculation may not pay off for ten years—and an unhappy investor may watch his blue chip stock slowly slide downward for month after month after month.

In the long run, it seems to me that motive is the best

measure of the investor and the speculator. The investor is searching for the security of a company with a long and honorable dividend and earnings record, a company in a growing industry with proven management. He is not out to make a killing in the market but to find a security that will pay him an adequate dividend and slowly increase in value over the years.

The speculator is more likely to be a professional trader, a man who follows the market hour by hour and cautiously analyzes a given situation before making a commitment, a man who will take a small profit just as fast as he will accept a small loss. The nonprofessional, such as yourself, may also have a taste for speculative situations. But remember, whichever your attitude is, know what you're doing and get every ounce of information you can before you act.

I recommend gambling in securities only for those people who have a lot of money and want to get rid of it. If you insist on taking the gambler's approach to the market, there are only a few simple rules to follow: 1. Buy and sell only on the basis of tips and rumors; 2. Be sure to avoid acquiring any factual information about the security in which you are interested; 3. When the going gets rough, consult a good astrologer.

There's still one other factor to be considered before you decide to become an investor. You may be a loving husband and father, a ball of fire in your office, and a well-known clubman and raconteur. But stay away from the market if your temperament is such that every quarter-point change in a security you own causes you acute gloom or elation. If you're the type who will start pricing pianos and sables as soon as your stock goes up a point, or if you picture your wife in widow's weeds when your stock drops a point—then keep your money in the bank and brood about the merits of the FDIC, the government agency that insures bank deposits.

If you find yourself calling your broker every hour for the latest price on the ten shares of Puny Petroleum Inc. that you own, switch to government bonds. Think of the money you'll save if you don't have to treat a bad case of ulcers.

Investment in general, and speculation in particular, require a degree of emotional stability and a large dose of patience. A lot of people mistakenly fight the market. Don't make the additional mistake of fighting yourself.

CHAPTER 3

Corporations and Securities:

Where Stocks and Bonds Come From

BEFORE ATTEMPTING TO arrive at a practical investment program, let's look at the raw materials of investment—common and preferred stocks, bonds, debentures—and where
they come from in the first place.

The corporation, any way you look at it, is a strange animal that exists, believe it or not, largely in the minds of
lawyers and courts. A famous decision by the Supreme Court
described the corporation as "an artificial being, invisible,
intangible, and existing only in contemplation of law. Being
the mere creature of law, it possesses only those properties
which the charter of its creation confers upon it . . ."

The corporation is condemned by some as a tool of the
interests, lauded by others for its tremendous productive capacity and financial flexibility. Nevertheless, the corporation is one of the most brilliant concepts of modern society.
It has been directly responsible for the richness and strength
of our capitalistic economy.

11

The corporation owes its existence to the charter issued by the state in which it is incorporated—and, to put it mildly, most corporate charters confer rather broad powers. Some states offer unusually attractive features to the new corporation. This is one reason why so many companies incorporate in Delaware. I know of no state, however, that would permit the proposal made by a French gentleman some years ago. He formed a company and financed it by selling securities to the public, but the reason for the company's existence was so secret that he just couldn't tell anybody what it was. His reticence, however, did not deter a great many people from investing in his company.

The corporation emerged as a way of doing business mainly because it could raise large sums of money. Individual men, even those of great wealth, simply did not have enough money to finance such enterprises as transcontinental railroads or giant steel mills. The corporation provided for ownership by both large and small investors; it divided ownership into very small units or shares. Hundreds, and eventually hundreds of thousands of people in some cases, used their savings to raise the capital needed for a modern industrial enterprise.

Another prime advantage of the corporate form of business is the ease with which these small units of ownership can be bought and sold, particularly when they are traded on a national securities exchange.

Still another attractive feature of the corporation, from your own viewpoint as a stockholder, is that the corporation itself is responsible for its debts. You, one of the owners, are not. But if you are an owner of an unincorporated business, you've got to pay your company's bills, and your creditors don't much care where you get the money. And if you are a partner in an unincorporated business, you are fully responsible for the bills of the enterprise whether they were incurred by you or by one of your partners.

However, as one of the owners of a corporate enterprise, you can't be held liable for its debts. To put it another way, you cannot lose more than the amount you have paid for your ownership interest. Not too long ago, stockholders of national and state banks were subject to double liability. If a bank failed and the assets owned were not enough to pay the depositors, the value of stock in the bank not only dropped to zero but the stockholders could also be forced to pay an additional sum equal to the par value of their stock.

Common Stock

The basic security issued by a corporation is common stock. Some corporations—notably American Telephone & Telegraph Company—use the term "capital stock," but common and capital stock are considered identical when the company has no preferred stock.

Let's say that you have invented an electronic can opener which might well revolutionize the can-opener industry. You've patented your invention, but you need money to rent factory space, buy tools and equipment, pay wages to your employees. You had hoped you would be able to borrow enough money from a bank to get under way, but you found that bankers, who called your invention fascinating, were unwilling to finance such a speculative venture. After all, bankers are responsible for protecting their depositors' funds.

You figure you need about $20,000 to get into production. So you decide to form a corporation and sell enough common stock to raise that money. You have a couple of pretty wealthy friends, each of whom, you expect, will make a substantial investment in your new company. At the same time, you realize that a great deal of the money you need must come from other people of limited means. You more or less arbitrarily put a price of $20 each on 1,000 shares of common stock.

Three of your wealthy friends each buy 100 shares, which produce $6,000. You raise the remainder by selling anywhere from 1 to 50 shares to some 150 other people. Then the Electronic Can Opener Corporation is ready to start operations with a total capital of $20,000, 1,000 shares of common stock issued, and 150 common stockholders who are the owners of the company.

It is worth noting that you yourself are not an owner of the company unless you bought some of the common shares. But because the electronic can opener is your invention, and because you did all the work involved in raising the initial capital, the bylaws of the corporation probably give you an option to buy stock not yet issued, at a special price, at some future date.

Each owner of the corporation receives a certificate that shows the number of shares he owns and the par value of the stock, if any. The general tendency among larger corporations is to issue stock with no par value, although in the case of a newly formed corporation, par value may be the same as the price at which the stock is sold.

It's plainly impossible to expect that the 150 owners can direct the affairs of the corporation in person. So the owners vote to elect a board of directors who will be responsible to the common stock owners for the over-all policy of the corporation. These directors may be stockholders, or they may include local leaders in your community, such as a banker and outstanding businessmen.

The directors in turn select the company's top management, such as a president, several vice-presidents, a secretary, and a treasurer. These men will control the day-to-day operation of Electronic Can Opener Corporation and will report once a month to the board of directors on the results of their management and their plans for the future.

Let us suppose that at the end of one year's production the company has earned a net profit of $5,000. Up to that point no dividend has been paid, but the directors now feel that the stockholders are entitled to a small return on their investment. They realize, though, that the new can opener has been so well received by the public that a substantial amount of the profit should be used to increase production. So the board votes a dividend of $1 for each of the 1,000 shares, leaving a balance of $4,000, which is used to purchase additional machinery.

It's just possible, of course, that the electronic can opener turned out to be no more popular than the automatic gusset. At the end of the first year the corporation may have only broken even or even lost money. If the loss were substantial and the creditors insistent, the corporation might be obliged to go out of business. In either case, the common shareowners would be out of luck. No dividend could be paid, and their ownership interest in the business might turn out to be worthless.

There, in the simplest terms, is the story of a new corporation and its owners, the people who bought shares of common stock hoping that their income would be increased by dividends from their investment—but, at the same time, aware that their purchase of stock might result in a loss.

The people who bought shares of Electronic Can Opener Corporation were really speculating rather than investing. The company was a new one and the product unknown and untried; there was no record of earnings, dividends, managerial ability, competitive strength. Still, the common stockholder of Electronic Can Opener Corporation has just about the same rights and responsibilities as the common stockholder of General Motors Corporation or any other company with a long record of performance.

One of the most fascinating aspects of investment is the tremendous range of selection that is available—from small companies like this hypothetical can opener corporation to such well-known leaders as American Telephone & Telegraph, United States Steel, Union Carbide, Standard Oil Company (New Jersey), or American Gas & Electric.

Table 1 tabulates the 20 companies listed on the New York Stock Exchange with the largest number of common shareowners early in 1957.

TABLE 1

TWENTY LISTED COMPANIES WITH MOST COMMON SHAREOWNERS

Company	1957	1956	1952	1947	1942
American Tel. & Tel.	1,490,000	1,409,000	1,092,433	695,660	633,588
General Motors	640,473	537,751	447,188	408,408	389,520
Standard Oil (N. J.)	403,000	320,000	253,515	164,015	143,483
General Electric	366,524	354,703	254,180	248,424	218,356
Ford Motor	298,918	318,722	...	...	...
U. S. Steel	257,997	244,347	209,124	168,166	163,862
Socony Mobil Oil	181,605	174,301	156,904	140,268	114,382
Cities Service	174,496	171,003	...	...	...
Radio Corp. of America ..	158,397	158,311	171,941	201,320	222,322
E. I. du Pont	153,832	143,941	138,168	73,523	67,567
Pennsylvania R.R.	144,468	144,509	179,908	218,943	205,012
Standard Oil (Indiana) ..	143,225	132,800	116,800	97,240	97,353
Commonwealth Edison ...	143,009	138,895	123,359	116,128	103,636
Consolidated Edison	142,623	137,385	132,492	120,591	105,121
Westinghouse Electric ...	139,201	114,891	98,648	62,449	45,688
Pub. Serv. Elec. & Gas ...	137,404	130,765	121,423	76,905	36,080
Standard Oil of Calif. ...	137,381	120,839	104,854	89,313	74,567
Pacific Gas & Electric	135,454	129,501	103,559	73,466	39,362
Texas Company	131,035	120,377	113,642	92,865	90,141
Southern Company	121,954	122,181	115,417	...	...

As an investor—or a speculator—you have your choice of new and untried companies owned by a comparative handful of people or today's corporate bluebloods owned by tens of thousands of people.

Ownership of a corporation and control of a corporation should not be confused. In some cases, ownership of 90 per cent or more of a company's assets will not give control. In other cases, effective control may be exercised with no ownership or practically none.

One of the more devious devices of our earlier corporate entrepreneurs was to issue two or more classes of common stock, such as class A and class B. Voting control of the company was vested in, say, 1,000 shares of class A stock, while 500,000 shares of B stock—which also represented ownership of the company on a share-for-share basis with the A stock— had no voice in the management of the company. The public, naturally, was sold the B stock. The A stock, just as naturally, was reserved for a few friends of the family.

Largely through the efforts of the New York Stock Exchange, plus a steady strengthening of the ethical standards of the business world, this practice of disenfranchising the common stockholders has just about died out. Early in 1955, for example, one of the few remaining family corporations of large size moved into the public domain. In the biggest underwriting deal in financial history, a huge block of Ford Motor Company stock was sold to the public. For years control of this industrial empire had been tightly held by the Ford family. The public undoubtedly would have bought the Ford stock even if ownership carried with it no vote. However, in order to qualify for listing on the New York Stock Exchange, an arrangement was worked out whereby the publicly held stock exercised 60 per cent of the voting power, a percentage that would increase when and if additional Ford stock was sold to the public. The Ford family retained 40 per cent of the voting power, an arrangement that certainly gave the family effective control. Nonetheless, this was a significant step toward a broader corporate democracy. It may be noted in passing that the Ford family could have listed the stock on another exchange that does not have the strict requirements of the New York Stock Exchange.

In Europe the practice of retaining control of corporations through various classes of stock is still very much the rule, although even there a trend has developed toward broader share owner participation. Several years ago Royal Dutch Petroleum Company, one of the largest enterprises in the world, gave voting power to its stockholders in order to obtain a listing on the New York Stock Exchange.

Effective stockholder control of a company by the common shareowners is a thorny problem for a corporation's management and for the stockholders themselves. Some managements, to be sure, take the attitude that the stockholders are necessary pests who should be neither seen nor heard— "What do they know about running this business anyway?" Officers of other companies anticipate the annual meeting with the same enthusiasm they would show for a case of scrofula—they do attempt to placate unruly stockholders, but they do so with only partially concealed distaste.

But enlightened managements—and there are a great many of them—go out of their way to get the views of the stockholders on the sound theory that, after all, the stockholders really do own the company and the officers are simply hired hands.

The steady growth in the number of people who own the larger corporations, and the huge amounts of stocks issued by these companies, both make it extremely difficult for the stockholders to act cohesively. To acquire actual control of any of these companies—that is, control by ownership of 51 per cent of the stock—obviously would be beyond the reach of the wealthiest man. Even ownership of 10 per cent of outstanding stock would call for a huge investment. Table 2 lists the ten American companies with the largest amounts of stock outstanding, together with the price per share and total market value early in 1957.

TABLE 2

TEN COMPANIES WITH LARGEST NUMBER OF COMMON SHARES, 1957

	Shares	Market Price Per Share	Total Market Value
General Motors	279,922,000	$40	$11,196,880,000
Standard Oil (N. J.)	196,762,000	57	11,215,434,000
General Electric	87,150,000	56	4,880,400,000
Sears, Roebuck	74,887,000	28	2,096,836,000
Standard Oil Calif.	63,224,000	46	2,908,304,000
American Tel. & Tel. ...	62,902,000	178	11,196,556,000
Texas Co.	55,250,000	62	3,425,500,000
U. S. Steel	53,712,000	60	3,222,720,000
E. I. du Pont............	45,604,000	179	8,163,116,000
Socony Mobil Oil	44,390,000	53	2,352,670,000

At the same time, trying to persuade thousands of stockholders to speak with one voice—especially when that voice is opposed to management—is an arduous and costly process.

The net result is that management tends to perpetuate itself. There's nothing wrong with this—just as long as management remains responsive to the views of the stockholders and runs the company profitably. The advice of one school of thought is, "If you don't like the management, sell your stock!" That's a little like telling a father to get rid of his children if they don't obey him. Stockholders do get attached to companies in which they own a share, and their natural inclination is to persuade bad management to either resign or mend its ways.

Even with management encouragement, which is not always forthcoming, only a small proportion of the stockholders can attend the annual meeting in person. So once a year management sends to each stockholder a proxy statement.

The statement contains the names of directors to be voted on and other important matters on the agenda—perhaps the directors are asking for authority to issue additional stock, or maybe they are asking stockholder approval for a merger with another company. The proxy itself is a power of attorney that, if signed by the stockholder, gives another person named by the company the right to cast his vote for him. The results of most corporation voting closely resemble the results of political elections behind the Iron Curtain—950,000 in favor of management proposals, 50,000 against.

Nevertheless, a determined and well-heeled minority group of stockholders can be effective by waging a so-called proxy fight. Such a group may submit its own slate for the board of directors, plus other important changes in company policy, and solicit proxies just as management does. These contests for control of a corporation are strictly governed by the rules of the Securities and Exchange Commission, but only when the company's stock is registered on a national securities exchange.

Unfortunately, such contests sometimes run into considerable money. Robert R. Young is estimated to have spent more than $1,000,000 in his successful fight to throw out the management of the New York Central System and install his own people. On the basis of court decisions, management may use the resources of the company in these contests—and the *winner* of a proxy contest may also charge the costs of the contest to the company. Mr. Young first announced that he would not seek reimbursement from New York Central if he were successful. Later, he changed his mind.

Rather recently a technique known as cumulative voting, designed to give a minority stockholder group a stronger voice in a company, has received a good deal of attention. Normally, if you own 10 shares of stock, for instance, you are entitled to 10 votes for or against each director. If 12 directors are to be elected, you have a total of 120 votes. Under cumulative voting, you may cast these 120 votes for only one director and none for the others. Or you may split your vote any way you want to—60 votes each, say, for two directors, or 40 votes each for three directors.

Thus one or two or three directors could make a very handsome showing if they had the support of relatively few stockholders.

CHAPTER 4

Measuring the Value of a Stock:

Some Guide Lines

WHEN YOU COME right down to it, there's just one good measure of the value of a stock: What the market says it's worth.

You can assemble all the facts, use all the analytical techniques in the world to determine the "real" value of a company's securities. If the answer you arrive at disagrees with the answer you get in the market, you're wrong—as of that moment. Your calculations may indicate that the market is underpricing or overpricing a particular security, and sooner or later the market may agree with you. But a security is worth exactly what you can sell it for at the time you want to sell it. If you think the market price is low in relation to underlying value, that's too bad.

It's just as true that a stock is worth exactly what you can buy it for. If you think the market price is too low, that's fine. Buy it, and maybe the market will eventually reflect your judgment.

In 1953, Ernest T. Weir, chairman of National Steel Corporation, sent his stockholders one of the most unusual letters ever addressed by a major corporation executive to the owners of the company. The letter was unusual for several reasons. For one thing, the chairman of a leading company publicly took issue with the market valuation of his company's stock. He gave his stockholders some solid information as to just why he disagreed. And perhaps most interesting is the fact that he felt compelled to disagree at all. Mr. Weir said:

I am writing this letter to present some facts which I am sure will be of interest to you as an owner of capital stock in National Steel Corporation.

In the period beginning January 1, 1946, and ending December 31, 1953, we will have spent approximately $350 million on construction and development. As a result of this expenditure, our steelmaking capacity will have increased from 3,900,000 tons to 6,000,000 tons per year—an increase of 2,100,000 tons or 54%. In addition, there have been proportional increases in finishing capacity and in raw material reserves.

As of December 31, 1953, our total property account, including raw materials, will stand on our books at approximately $325 million, which is equal to about $55.00 per ton of ingot capacity. Compared with this valuation, the present actual cost of duplicating integrated steel plants such as ours would run, on a conservative estimate, between $250.00 and $300.00 per ton of capacity. Thus on the basis of the lower figure of $250.00 per ton, the replacement value of our property is *$1½ billion* although, as stated above, we carry it on our books at approximately *$325 million.*

At this writing, National Steel stock is selling on the market at a price which attributes to the company a total value of only $295 million—a figure which alone is substantially lower than the $350 million spent from 1946 through 1953 in expanding our capacity by 2,100,000 tons and which accords no value whatever to the previous property which, of course, was completely integrated with a production capacity of 3,900,000 tons.

In addition to the above, there are other pertinent factors. For instance, we estimate that net earnings this year will not be less than $6.00 per share [Mr. Weir was conservative; the company later reported earnings per share for 1953 at $6.84 despite a general decline in demand for steel during the last quarter of 1953.] So, on the basis of the present market price [about $41 in September, 1953], National Steel stock is selling for less than seven times its earnings. The present working capital of the company, alone, is equal to $19 per share. Our total funded debt is only $55 million and, as we have no preferred stock, the bonds representing this debt and our common stock are the only securities of National Steel Corporation. Steel is a great basic industry and National Steel is one of the industry's leading companies.

We believe these facts are interesting and of use in estimating the real value of National Steel stock.

ERNEST T. WEIR, CHAIRMAN
NATIONAL STEEL CORPORATION

Mr. Weir certainly had the facts right, but the market is not always interested in facts, or can painfully and stubbornly ignore them for extended periods. There's a good reason for that, too; the market is not preoccupied with past performance but is constantly trying to foresee the future.

It is an interesting footnote to Mr. Weir's letter that in early 1957 National Steel stock sold at around 77¾ a share, and 1956 earnings per share are estimated at the annual rate of $7 in spite of a strike that tied up the industry for five weeks.

In Mr. Weir's letter you noticed terms that undoubtedly had an unfamiliar ring. Many stem from two sources that are essential to the evaluation of a company and its securities, the balance sheet and the income statement.

The balance sheet is a financial photograph of a company

as of a given instant—usually as of the last day of the calendar year or the last day of the company's fiscal year. It lists everything the company owns and is owed; these are the assets. It also lists everything the company owes, such as taxes, wages, and interest on debt; these are the liabilities. Included in the balance sheet is a statement of the common stockholders' equity in the corporation, or the corporation's net worth—which is simply all the assets minus all the liabilities.

The balance sheet also shows the corporation's capitalization, which is a list of the securities that the company has authorized and the amount outstanding.

Table 3 shows a balance sheet for Eaton Manufacturing Company.

TABLE 3

CONSOLIDATED BALANCE SHEETS
EATON MANUFACTURING COMPANY AND SUBSIDIARIES

ASSETS

	Dec. 31, 1956	Dec. 31, 1955
Current Assets		
Cash	$ 8,731,549	$ 7,788,779
Marketable securities—at cost plus accrued interest (approximate market):		
Dominion of Canada bonds	442,746	447,878
Trade accounts receivable	$ 21,192,120	$ 23,958,652
Less allowance for doubtful accounts	115,000	115,000
	$ 21,077,120	$ 23,843,652
Inventories—at lower of cost (average or standard) or replacement market:		
Finished and in process	$ 22,398,399	$ 20,909,328
Raw materials	9,947,393	9,363,871
Manufacturing supplies	2,325,963	2,244,711
	$ 34,671,755	$ 32,517,910
Less allowances for shrinkage and obsolescence	1,733,583	1,626,020
	$ 32,938,172	$ 30,891,890
Prepaid expenses	1,012,141	474,146
Total Current Assets	$ 64,201,728	$ 63,446,345

	Dec. 31, 1956	Dec. 31, 1955
Other Assets	186,555	93,192
Property, Plant, and Equipment		
Major portion based upon cost:		
Land	$ 1,583,270	$ 1,504,522
Buildings and equipment	81,840,053	71,018,563
	$ 83,423,323	$ 72,523,085
Less allowances for depreciation and amortization	31,902,699	27,963,907
	$ 51,520,624	$ 44,559,178
Patents, Trade-Marks, Licenses, Etc.—		
at cost, less amortization	514,509	566,957
	$116,423,416	$108,665,672

LIABILITIES AND SHAREHOLDERS' EQUITY

	Dec. 31, 1956	Dec. 31, 1955
Current Liabilities		
Notes payable to banks	$ 5,000,000	$ 3,000,000
Accounts payable	12,606,910	12,840,701
Payrolls and additional compensation	2,856,573	3,022,972
Taxes other than taxes on income	467,452	512,674
Federal, state, and Canadian taxes on income		
—estimated	12,079,000	15,009,000
Total Current Liabilities	$ 33,009,935	$ 34,385,347
Shareholders' Equity		
Capital stock, par value $2.00 per share:		
Authorized 2,500,000 shares		
Outstanding 1,838,044 shares (1,789,942 shares		
in 1955) after deducting 2,578 shares in		
treasury	$ 3,676,088	$ 3,579,884
Capital in excess of par value	18,996,521	16,543,319
Earnings retained for use in the business	60,740,872	54,157,122
	$ 83,413,481	$ 74,280,325
	$116,423,416	$108,665,672

Current assets include cash on hand and U. S. government securities, accounts receivable, and finished or semifinished inventories which may be readily converted into cash, and investments in other companies, if any.

Fixed assets include land, buildings, machinery, and equipment owned by the company, shown at the prices they cost the company. This sum is reduced by allowances for depreciation and obsolescence or the amount of wear and tear on the company's plant and equipment.

Intangible assets include patents, processes, and good will; they are frequently given a nominal value, although their worth to the company may be substantial.

On the liability side of the balance sheet we have current liabilities, such as bills due in the normal course of running the business, payrolls, federal and state taxes, and dividends declared but not yet paid. A long-term liability might refer to a bank loan that does not fall due for, say, five years.

Long-term debt includes all the company's bonded debt, if any. Reserves may be established for a number of reasons, such as the possibility that the company may owe the government back taxes, the chance of a decline in the value of inventories, the need for money for the payment of pensions.

Under the stockholders' equity is included the number of preferred and common shares, both authorized and actually outstanding in the hands of the public. They are shown either at par or stated value, the latter an arbitrary value assigned the stock on the balance sheet.

The stockholders' equity is shown as the excess of the company's assets over its liabilities—also known as the company's net worth.

Standing by itself, the balance sheet for any particular year does not have too great significance, but when the balance sheets for a five- or ten-year period are compared, the company's picture is put into better focus.

Not long ago I was chatting with a young lady fresh out of college who had embarked with tremendous enthusiasm on her first job as researcher for a news publication. We were discussing the trend of corporate earnings when she interrupted the conversation and leaned toward me.

"You know," she said in a confidential manner, "what really impresses me about corporate earnings is not so much their size. It's the way these companies, even the very biggest, always manage to make their assets and liabilities come out exactly even, right down to the last penny. I think it's just marvelous."

She was thoroughly disillusioned when she learned that the assets and liabilities *had* to balance. If the assets exceed the liabilities, the company's bookkeepers should be fired because they can't add. If the liabilities exceed the assets, the company is bankrupt. In a solvent company, the variable figure that always enables the company to balance its assets and liabilities is the stockholders' equity. If a company has assets of $5 and liabilities of $4, the stockholders' equity is $1. On the balance sheet this will be reported as total assets $5, total liabilities $5.

The Income Statement

Most investors are inclined to show more interest in the income or earnings statement than in the balance sheet, which is understandable because the figures are easily comparable with prior periods, and out of earnings come dividends. Table 4 shows an income statement issued by Eaton Manufacturing Company.

The income statement shows briefly the total sales of the company and dividends received from subsidiary companies or other investments, if any. From this sum are deducted the cost of making the company's products, wages and salaries, research expenses, interest expenses. The result is income before taxes. Taxes are estimated, and the next figure is net income.

TABLE 4

STATEMENTS OF CONSOLIDATED INCOME AND RETAINED EARNINGS
EATON MANUFACTURING COMPANY AND SUBSIDIARIES

INCOME		
	1956	1955
Net sales	$227,196,703	$218,116,159
Other income:		
Cash discount and interest earned	386,225	421,856
Other income	385,798	347,529
	$227,968,726	$218,885,544
Less:		
Cost of products sold	$193,597,935	$184,041,375
Selling, advertising, administrative, and general expenses	6,588,835	5,827,064
Other charges	434,128	315,609
Taxes on income—estimated:		
Federal	$ 14,242,500	$ 15,262,000
Canadian and state	124,500	154,000
	$ 14,367,000	$ 15,416,000
	$214,987,898	$205,600,048
Net Income	$ 12,980,828	$ 13,285,496

Allowances for depreciation and amortization:
1956—$5,603,245;   1955—$5,325,124

EARNINGS RETAINED FOR USE IN THE BUSINESS		
Balance at beginning of year	$ 54,157,122	$ 46,241,452
Net income for the year	12,980,828	13,285,496
	$ 67,137,950	$ 59,526,948
Cash dividends paid—$3.50 a share in 1956, $3.00 a share in 1955	6,397,078	5,369,826
Balance at end of year	$ 60,740,872	$ 54,157,122

Annual income as reported in a company's yearly statement is a reasonably exact figure. However, the great majority of companies listed on registered securities exchanges also report income on a quarterly basis, and these figures are frequently subject to later revision. The reason for this is a good one—it is virtually impossible for a multimillion-dollar corporation, with scores of subsidiary operations that may circle the globe, to gather at short intervals all the information necessary to produce a completely accurate report. Almost invariably you will note that corporations report "estimated" quarterly earnings.

Now, how are these basic statistics used? There are dozens of ways; the experts have figured out more ratios, percentages, relationships, and tests than you want to bother with. Certain fundamental yardsticks, however, are used in almost any effort to measure the value of a common stock. They are yield, earnings per share, price-earnings ratio, book value, and leverage.

Actually these terms are a lot more ominous than the calculations involved, which you can do in a few minutes, if you can add, divide, and subtract.

Yield is the amount of money your investment earns for you. Your savings bank probably tells you that your deposit receives interest (which it may call "dividend") of 3 per cent a year. In other words, if you have $100 on deposit on January 1 of this year, at the end of the year—assuming you have made no additional deposits—you will find $103 to your credit in the bank. The extra $3 is the interest earned by your deposit.

The yield on common stocks is figured a little differently, but the general idea is the same. Let's say you want to figure the yield on a common stock that you are considering buying. The stock today is selling at $100 a share. You look up the total amount of cash dividends paid on this stock during the past 12 months, which come to $5 a share. The yield is simply the current price divided into the total of cash dividends during the preceding year.

$$\frac{\$100}{\text{Price}} \qquad \overline{)\$5.00} \qquad = \qquad \frac{5 \text{ per cent}}{\text{Yield}}$$
$$\text{Cash Dividends}$$

Is 5 per cent a *good* yield? Well, compare it with the yield on your savings bank deposit—or the yield on a good-grade preferred stock, which runs around 4 to 4.5 per cent—or the yield on a top-grade bond, which is around 3.5 to 4 per cent.

There are a great many common stocks that yield less than 5 per cent, and a great many yielding more. But here are a few signs to watch for.

The common stock of one of the most progressive and enterprising chemical companies in the country is now yielding about 1.6 per cent. The company is well established, has a fine earnings record, and has paid a cash dividend in every year since 1911. Something wrong? Well, not exactly; but here is one enterprise, clearly a growth company, that investors expect will go far in the future. There is such a thing, though—to use one of Wall Street's pithier adages—as buying not only the future but the hereafter. The stock of this particular company appears to be priced so that the investor is offered at least a touch of the hereafter.

Or take the case of a leading manufacturer of rayon and nylon yarn, whose shares recently sold at a price to yield a little more than 7 per cent. Is that too high a yield? Could be—or this may be a case of a stock that for one reason or another is underpriced. Too high a yield may be a danger signal, and any high-yielding stock should be given a thorough check.

This point is worth exploring. Consider the case of a stock paying an annual dividend of $5 a share and selling at $50 a share. This would be the equivalent of a yield of 10 per cent. (Five divided by 50 equals one-tenth, or 10 per cent.) A 10 per cent yield is certainly unusual. So the possibility must be considered that the market is pricing the stock in anticipation of a reduced dividend. If 5 per cent were roughly the current yield on an average stock, the 10

per cent yield could well indicate that the market anticipated a 50 per cent reduction in the dividend. A price of
$50 a share for a stock paying $2.50 annually in dividends
would indicate a yield of 5 per cent.

There are two ways in which a yield may be misleading.
Directors of a company, when they decide on a dividend, usually designate it as a quarterly payment; they expect that
quarterly rate to be maintained for at least the foreseeable
future. Let's say directors of XYZ Corporation declare quarterly dividends of 25 cents a share each for the first and
second quarters of the year. Then in the third quarter they
declare a quarterly dividend of 40 cents a share, and the same
amount in the final quarter. Yield would be figured on
total payments for the year, or $1.30. It probably would
be more realistic to calculate the yield on the basis of four
quarterly dividends of 40 cents each, or $1.60, on the theory
that the directors, when they boosted the quarterly dividend
from 25 to 40 cents, figured the company could continue to
pay the higher rate in the future.

Similarly, if the quarterly dividend is reduced, it might
be wiser to figure the yield on the basis of four payments
at the reduced rate.

It is highly important for the investor to bear in mind
that yield is based on past performance. There is no guarantee of any kind that the company will maintain the same
dividend rate in the future, or, for that matter, that any
dividends will be paid.

The owner of a share of stock—as distinct from the person
considering an investment—computes yield on another basis.
The price he paid is always the basis for his computation,
but the dividend total used is arrived at by adding dividends
paid in the 12 months preceding his calculation. Let's say
you paid $100 a share for XYZ Corporation at the beginning
of 1952. You figure your yield at the end of 1956 by dividing

cash dividends paid in 1956 by your original purchase price —although the price in the meantime may have doubled. Table 5 lists the yields as of the close of 1956 of 20 stocks listed on the New York Stock Exchange that have paid a cash dividend each year for 25 years or more.

TABLE 5

TWENTY COMPANIES LISTED ON NYSE WHICH HAVE PAID A CASH
DIVIDEND EVERY QUARTER FOR 22 TO 93 YEARS

Common Stock	Quarterly payments began	Cash dividend per share paid in 1956 incl. extras	Closing price 12/31/56	Yield
American News	1864	$1.60	$ 31½	5.1%
American Tel. & Tel.	1882	9.00	171⅜	5.3
Boston Edison	1891	2.80	49⅞	5.6
Coca-Cola	1921	5.00	98½	5.1
E. I. du Pont de Nemours.	1905	6.50	192¾	3.4
General Motors	1923	2.00	44	4.5
Green (H. L.) Company ..	1935	2.25	26¼	8.6
International Harvester ...	1910	2.00	38½	5.2
Liggett & Myers Tobacco ..	1912	5.00	64¾	7.7
Link-Belt	1913	3.15	71½	4.4
Morris (Philip) Inc.	1928	3.00	42⅛	7.1
National Biscuit	1899	2.00	35	5.7
Olin Mathieson Chemical..	1926	2.00	49⅜	4.1
Pepper (Dr.) Company	1930	0.60	10⅛	5.9
Safeway Stores	1927	2.40	69½	3.5
Sterling Drug	1913	2.70	52¾	5.1
Sunshine Biscuit	1927	4.00	69⅝	5.7
Texas Gulf Sulphur	1921	2.00	30⅜	6.6
Union Carbide & Carbon..	1918	3.15	115¾	2.7
William Wrigley, Jr. Company	1911	5.00	88¼	5.7

Earnings Per Share

Earnings per share is the amount of earnings available to the common stockholders—that is, the net earnings after all expenses have been paid by the corporation, divided by the shares outstanding. Start out with the gross profit of the company; deduct all operating expenses, cost of materials, depreciation, interest on bonds and bank loans, and the amount due in preferred dividends whether or not the dividends have been paid. Divide this total by the number of common shares outstanding (not authorized shares but those actually in the hands of the public). The result is the earnings per share.

Table 6 shows how earnings per share were computed in 1955 and 1954 for General Motors Corporation.

TABLE 6

TWO-YEAR COMPARISON OF GENERAL MOTORS CORPORATION'S
COMMON SHARE EARNINGS

	1955	1954
Net sales, plus equity in earnings of unconsolidated subsidiaries and other income	$12,532,489,247	$9,905,869,297
Deduct: Cost of sales and other operating charges; selling and administrative expenses; interest and amortization of discount on outstanding 3¼% debentures; depreciation and obsolescence of real estate, plant, and equipment; employes bonus; and U. S. and foreign income taxes	11,343,012,165	9,099,895,400
Net income	1,189,477,082	805,973,897
Deduct: Dividends paid on outstanding $5-dividend and $3.75-dividend preferred stocks	12,928,305	12,928,309
Net income available to common stock..	1,176,548,777	793,045,588
Amount earned per common share (achieved by dividing the average number of common shares outstanding— 273,512,806 in 1955 and 262,031,334 in 1954—into the net income available to common stock in each year)	4.32	3.03

Earnings per share, which may be computed quarterly, semiannually, or annually, represent the amount available for dividends on the common stock—*not* the amount that will be paid in dividends, but the amount the directors may draw on for a dividend payment. For instance, XYZ Corporation earned $3 a share on its common stock in 1956 but paid out in dividends only $1.75 a share. The balance of $1.25 a share was plowed back into the business for such uses as expansion, plant modernization, and development of new products and services.

Table 7 shows the amount of earnings available for common stock dividends, and the amount actually paid, for the major groups of companies listed on the New York Stock Exchange.

Somewhat surprising is the relatively high proportion of earnings paid out in dividends by the chemical industry, a group that is commonly regarded as among the lustiest of growth industries. The rubber industry, on the other hand, is not usually regarded as an outstanding example of aggressive growth; yet the proportion of rubber company earnings paid out in dividends is proportionately small.

Table 8 illustrates the dividend policies of a handful of companies over the past few years. The wide variation in corporation dividend policies is readily apparent.

In some cases you will find a company reporting a deficit of so much per share on the common stock. If XYZ Corporation, with 100,000 shares of common stock outstanding, fell short of meeting preferred dividend requirements by $50,000, the deficit per share would be computed by dividing the $50,000 by the 100,000 common shares; in this case a deficit of 50 cents a share would result.

Oddly enough, a corporation may report a net deficit but the board of directors may still vote a dividend on the common stock. Pennsylvania Railroad, for instance, has one of the finest dividend records of any company in the world. Each year since 1848, Pennsy has paid a cash dividend to its common stockholders, although in one year the company

TABLE 7

PAY-OUT RATIOS IN LATEST CALENDAR OR FISCAL YEAR OF COMMON STOCKS
OF COMPANIES LISTED ON THE NEW YORK STOCK EXCHANGE
(AS OF END 1956)

By Industry Groups

Number of Companies and Industry	Net Income Available for Common	Common Dividends	Per cent
	(in millions of dollars)		
29 Aircraft	$ 323	$ 122	37.8
23 Amusement	148	74	50.0
65 Automotive	1,972	927	47.0
32 Building Trade	244	113	46.3
85 Chemical	1,550	907	58.5
26 Electrical Equipment	382	242	63.4
6 Farm Machinery	113	56	49.6
37 Financial	246	148	60.2
70 Food Products & Beverages	474	267	56.3
9 Leather & Its Products	33	22	66.7
106 Machinery & Metals	543	284	52.3
40 Mining	604	285	47.2
9 Office Equipment	96	35	36.5
40 Paper & Publishing	340	163	47.9
48 Petroleum & Natural Gas	2,700	1,118	41.4
79 Railroad & R.R. Equipment	842	363	43.1
9 Real Estate	33	16	48.5
68 Retail Trade	538	310	57.6
9 Rubber	205	71	34.6
9 Shipbuilding & Operation	50	21	42.0
39 Steel & Iron	1,031	381	37.0
43 Textile	160	74	46.3
14 Tobacco	154	90	58.4
107 Utilities	1,944	1,316	67.7
26 Miscellaneous	121	53	43.8
23 U. S. Companies Operating Abroad	108	67	62.0
1051 TOTAL U. S. COMPANIES	$14,954	$7,525	50.3
20 Foreign Companies	750	264	35.2
1071 TOTAL	$15,704	$7,789	49.6

did not earn a profit. To accomplish this, the directors of the company were forced to draw on the company's earnings stored up from better years.

Per-share earnings, particularly their trend, are highly regarded as a sound guide not only to a company's current performance but to its ability to produce earnings for the common stock over the years, in good times and bad. Again, it must be emphasized, the past is merely a guide to the future, not a guaranty.

TABLE 8

DIVIDEND POLICIES OF SOME LEADING CORPORATIONS

Company	Earned Per Common Share		Dividends Paid Per Common Share		Per Cent of Earnings Paid in Common Dividends	
	1955	1954	1955	1954	1955	1954
Allied Chemical & Dye	$5.44	$4.50[1]	$2.86[1]	$2.86[1]	52.6	63.6
American Tel. & Tel.	12.27	11.42	9.00	9.00	73.3	78.8
Atchison, Topeka & Santa Fe	14.70	12.35	7.00	7.00	47.6	56.7
Bethlehem Steel	18.09	13.18	7.25	5.75	40.1	43.6
Chesapeake & Ohio	7.25	5.01	3.13	3.00	43.2	59.9
Chrysler Corp.	11.49	2.13	4.00	4.50	34.8	211.3
Commonwealth Edison	2.62	2.70	1.90	1.80	72.5	66.7
duPont de Nemours	9.26	7.34	7.00	5.50	75.6	74.9
Eastman Kodak	4.66	3.80[1]	2.14[1]	1.90[1]	45.9	50.0
General Electric	2.31	2.30	1.60	1.47[1]	69.3	63.9
General Motors	4.26	3.02[1]	2.17[1]	1.67[1]	50.9	55.3
Goodyear Tire & Rubber ..	5.90	5.04[1]	2.00	1.63[1]	33.9	32.3
Int'l. Business Machines ...	13.63	11.07[1]	3.90[1]	3.71[1]	28.6	33.5
Kennecott Copper	11.60[2]	7.20[2]	7.75	6.00	66.8	83.3
Pacific Gas & Electric	3.32	2.88	2.20	2.20	66.3	76.4
Sears, Roebuck	2.15	1.94[1]	1.00[1]	1.01[1]	46.5	52.1
Standard Oil Co. (N. J.) ...	10.83	8.94	5.25	4.55	48.5	50.9
Union Carbide & Carbon ...	4.83	3.10	3.00	2.50	62.1	80.6
U. S. Steel	6.45	3.23[1]	2.15[1]	1.50[1]	33.3	46.4
Westinghouse Electric	2.46	4.78	2.00	2.50	81.3	52.3

[1] Adjusted for stock dividends or split-ups.
[2] Before depletion.

Incidentally, you don't have to worry about computing per-share earnings yourself. Most of the larger companies, particularly those listed on the New York Stock Exchange, report their earnings quarterly as well as annually and include the per-share earnings in their report.

Price-Earnings Ratio

The price-earnings ratio of a stock—another esoteric piece of financial jargon that is really no more complicated than your telephone number—is merely the relationship between the per-share earnings of a common stock and the current market price. If XYZ Corporation's latest report showed annual earnings at the rate of $5 per share and the market price is $60 a share, the price-earnings ratio is 12.

Wall Street uses the price-earnings ratio, perhaps more than any other single gauge, as a quick measure of the worth of a company stock. But if you try to pin down a dozen securities analysts on just what a high or low ratio is, you're likely to get a dozen different answers.

To put the matter in some perspective, let's take two extreme examples: XYZ Corporation is currently selling at $100 a share, earned $5 a common share last year, thus the price-earnings ratio is 20. ABC Corporation, on the other hand, is currently selling at $10 a share, earned $2.50 a share last year, thus the price-earnings ratio is 4. Is one good and the other bad?

A high price-earnings ratio is usually interpreted as an optimistic market appraisal of a security. Investors are willing to pay a relatively high price on the theory that the company faces a prosperous future and that earnings will increase substantially.

A low price-earnings ratio is commonly regarded as a pessimistic market appraisal of a security. Despite relatively high earnings, investors are willing to pay only a relatively low price for the security. Evidently there is some concern over the company's ability to maintain or increase its earnings in the future.

Generally speaking, a ratio of between 10 and 15 is regarded as normal, although there are some important deviations from this range. It is possible that a stock with a price-earnings ratio of 48.2, which was the 1955 ratio for International Business Machines, is entirely reasonable or even low. On the other hand the price-earnings ratio of Avco for 1955 was 137.5, which appears to be far too high.

Book Value

Book value, also known as net asset value per share, should be handled somewhat gingerly, like the contributions to charity in your income tax return.

In effect, book value is an attempt to determine the assets of a corporation that are working for the common stockholder. The figure is usually computed by taking the total of tangible assets as shown on the corporation's balance sheet, deducting everything the company owes (including the face value of bonds and preferred stock), and dividing the result by the number of common shares outstanding.

Table 9 shows how book value is computed.

TABLE 9

DETERMINATION OF A COMMON STOCK'S BOOK VALUE

Assets		Liabilities	
(in millions of dollars)			
Fixed assets	$300	Funded debt	$120
Current assets	100	Preferred stock	80
Other assets	30	Current liabilities	20
	$430		$220

$430,000,000 — $220,000,000 = $210,000,000.
$210,000,000 ÷ 8,250,000 common shares = $25.45 book value per share.

Book value as an indication of what a stock should be worth sounds fine in theory, but in my opinion it is a highly overrated guide.

A recent study by the Stock Exchange of 1,055 issues showed a tremendous variation in the relationship between market prices and book values—and, curiously, not a single one of the 1,055 stocks were selling at exactly its book value. Table 10 shows the results of the study.

TABLE 10
RELATIONSHIP OF MARKET PRICES TO BOOK VALUES

Market Price: Book Value	Number of Issues
200% or more above	72
100–199% above	130
80–99.9% above	62
60–79.9% above	76
50–59.9% above	38
40–49.9% above	48
30–39.9% above	49
20–29.9% above	59
10–19.9% above	48
0– 9.9% above	78
0– 9.9% below	68
10–19.9% below	80
20–29.9% below	64
30–39.9% below	63
40–49.9% below	48
50–59.9% below	30
60% or more below	42

If the book value is far above the market value, we might assume the security in question is attractive—but let's not assume that or we'll get into trouble. The book values of the common stocks of most railroads—all, so far as I know— are higher than the market values, and in many cases by a considerable margin. Unfortunately, a railroad's assets, as indicated on its balance sheets, are far from indicative of the road's earning power.

Or take the book values of stocks of chemical companies. You'll find generally that the market price of a chemical stock is far higher than the book value—which is just as misleading as the relatively low book value of a rail issue.

There are several factors to be considered in appraising book value: first, a corporation usually values its assets at cost rather than replacement value; second, a corporation's assets may be as productive as their dollar value indicates— or they may not; third, intangible assets are not used in computing book value. However certain assets—such as valuable patents, good will, trade names—may be far more productive from an income viewpoint than, let us say, a spur railroad that has not earned a penny in the last fifty years.

I'm inclined to believe that the only valid use of book value is as a measurement of the amount of earnings a company has plowed back into the business over a period of years. In other words, a more or less static book value over a ten-year period would indicate a company that, at best, is merely holding its own. A steady increase in book value would indicate that the management has steadily raised the potential earning power of the company. It could be useful to check such a trend with the earnings and market price trends over the same period.

Leverage

This is another financial jawbreaker and an important one —important to the investor because of the sharp difference in the way in which larger or smaller earnings may affect a high-leverage common stock and a no- or low-leverage stock.

In some corporations all of the net earnings are directly available for dividends on the common stock because no interest needs to be paid on preferred shares or on bonds, and interest charges and preferred dividends, if any, are relatively small. In the first instance the common stock has no leverage. In the second case the leverage is low.

But take a company that must pay out a great deal in preferred dividends and interest charges before the common stockholder has a crack at the earnings. In that case the common stock is said to have a high leverage.

Check the balance sheet to find this information—the balance sheet will show clearly the company's fixed obligations, and whether they are preferred stocks, bank loans, bonds, or a combination of all three.

In general, a no-leverage or low-leverage capitalization is regarded as more conservative than a high-leverage capitalization from the viewpoint of the common stockholder—particularly if the stockholder is interested primarily in dividend income rather than capital appreciation. When a company does not have to pay interest on bonded indebtedness or on one or more preferred issues, the earnings are all available to the common stockholder. Even if earnings are poor, there may be just enough left to pacify the common stockholder with a small payment.

If a company has a hefty amount to pay out in interest or preferred dividends—which, of course, are deducted from earnings before the common stock can be considered—it's quite possible that little or nothing may be left over for the common stockholder. But there's a consolation prize for the investor or speculator who owns a high-leverage issue. Per-share earnings on his common stock will increase at a faster rate than on a no-leverage stock, even if earnings on both issues increase by the same proportion. For this reason a high-leverage stock is considered more speculative than a low-leverage issue; the stockholder has more of an opportunity to profit from rising corporate income, but also more of an opportunity to lose out when the company's income declines.

The following tabulations show what happens to the per-share earnings of common stock in a no-leverage company and in a high-leverage company when earnings advance and decline.

	No-leverage	High-leverage
Shares outstanding	1,000,000	1,000,000
Income before interest and taxes..	$5,000,000	$5,000,000
Bond interest	——	1,500,000
Income before taxes	$5,000,000	$3,500,000
Federal taxes (52%)	2,600,000	1,820,000
Net income	$2,400,000	$1,680,000
Earnings per common share	$2.40	$1.68

The high-leverage company, you can see, is helped along by a smaller tax bill, but nevertheless that bond interest charge of $1,500,000 certainly shrinks per-share earnings.

Let's say these same two companies in the next year increased their earnings before taxes and interest by 50 per cent. Here's what happens to per-share earnings:

	No-leverage	High-leverage
Shares outstanding	1,000,000	1,000,000
Income before interest and taxes..	$7,500,000	$7,500,000
Bond interest	——	1,500,000
Income before taxes	$7,500,000	$6,000,000
Federal taxes	3,900,000	3,120,000
Net income	$3,600,000	$2,880,000
Earnings per common share	$3.60	$2.88

Again, the high-leverage gets an assist from a proportionately lower tax bill, but look at what's happened to per-share earnings. For the no-leverage company, per-share earnings rise in the same proportion as income before taxes, or 50 per cent. But in the high-leverage company, per-share earnings jumped 71.4 per cent.

Now, what happens when earnings before taxes and interest decline? Let's assume earnings for each company decline by 50 per cent.

	No-leverage	High-leverage
Shares outstanding	1,000,000	1,000,000
Income before interest and taxes..	$2,500,000	$2,500,000
Bond interest	—	1,500,000
Income before taxes	$2,500,000	$1,000,000
Federal taxes (52%)	1,300,000	520,000
Net income	1,200,000	$ 480,000
Earnings per common share	$1.20	$ .48

In this case, the charge for bond interest really hurts, despite the fact that the blow is softened somewhat by a smaller tax bill. Per-share earnings for the no-leverage company have declined 50 per cent; for the high-leverage company they have dropped 71.4 per cent.

CHAPTER 5

Preferred Stocks:

Are They Really Preferred?

"PREFERRED STOCKS" sounds as though they might be quite out of the ordinary—like the soap that is preferred by reigning beauties or the automobile that is preferred by the inmates of five-level ranch-type homes.

Some preferreds are just about in the same class as a gilt-edged bond; others have the same attraction as the common stock of a bankrupt corporation. It all depends.

In the simplest terms, a preferred stock represents an ownership interest in a company and usually is entitled to a fixed dividend. Preferred dividends must be paid before the common stockholders get their cut of the earnings. The price for this preferential treatment, however, is that the preferred stockholder normally cannot share in a company's prosperity beyond the stipulated amount of the fixed annual dividend.

Preferred stock outranks common but, in turn, is outranked by any bonds issued by the company. Interest on bonds must be paid before the preferred stockholders receive a dividend.

The preferred stockholder, too, is usually without a vote in the affairs of his company—despite the fact that the preferred represents an ownership interest—except in matters that have a bearing on the preferred stockholder's interest. For instance, preferred stockholders would probably be entitled to a vote if the company proposed issuing additional preferred shares. And, if enough preferred dividends are omitted, the preferred stockholders might even take over control of the company.

There are two theories regarding the issuance of a preferred stock. One school says that the issuing corporation is trying to satisfy the demands of an investor who is looking for a security that does not carry the full risk of a common stock but does have more earning power than a bond. The other theory claims that the company that sells a preferred stock has not got enough assets, or a high enough credit standing, to sell a bond, nor good enough prospects for the future to sell a common issue.

A majority of preferred stocks have a par value of $100, which—unlike the par value of common stock—is of some significance because the dividend is expressed as a percentage of par. For instance, a 4½ per cent preferred issue is supposed to pay the owner $4.50 a year for each $100 par share he owns. Some preferreds have a par value of $50 or $25. In the case of a 7 per cent preferred issue (don't get excited; just finish reading the sentence) the owner is supposed to receive $3.50 a year for each $50 par share he owns.

If you find that you can buy a $100 par, 5 per cent preferred issue at $70 a share, don't rush out and buy it on the theory that you have unearthed a rare bargain. True enough, the stock at that price would yield you 7.1 per cent on your $70 investment. But make a few discreet inquiries as to the possibility that the company may have trouble paying the preferred dividend.

Let's look at some of the major characteristics of preferred stock. They are multiple, not to say intriguing.

Most preferred stocks being sold to the public today are cumulative. That means that when poor earnings force the company to omit one or more preferred dividends, the unpaid dividends accumulate or pile up and *must* be paid before the common stockholders are entitled to receive a cent. This is plainly a worthwhile protection for the preferred stockholders—but also a protection that has led to some curious situations. The arrears on some preferred issues, for instance, have been accumulating for upward of ten years with not a cent paid.

Then there are noncumulative preferreds. An omitted dividend on a noncumulative preferred issue is lost to the stockholder forever—he is preferred, but not preferred enough. This particular type of preferred raises a rather interesting point in management policy. If earnings do not justify a dividend on the common stock, the common stockholders are just out of luck. But what about the preferred stockholders? The company may earn enough to pay the preferred dividend but, inasmuch as it is under no legal compulsion to do so, may decide to omit the preferred dividend in order to strengthen the company's financial position *for the benefit of the common stockholder.* This has happened in the past and could happen again, which is a good reason to regard noncumulative preferreds with at least mild suspicion. It must be admitted, at the same time, that some of the highest-rated preferreds are noncumulative.

Another type of preferred—and this one is in the minority —has an interesting gimmick because it promises the owner a share of the profits after a specified amount has been paid to the common stockholders. Let's say XYZ Corporation has

a 4½ per cent participating preferred ahead of the common. The company has a good year, and the preferred earns
its 4½ per cent. There's enough left over to pay the common $1.25 a share, and more. Suppose the "more" amounts
to $1 a share on the common; in that case the $1 a share
would be evenly divided between the participating preferred
and the common. Usually there is a limit to the amount
that a participating preferred can share in the earnings, but,
whether there is a limit or not, be a little wary when you
consider this category of stock. All you have to do is find
out how much the preferred has participated in past earnings: and don't be surprised if the answer is zero.

Some preferred issues, and they may be cumulative or
noncumulative or participating, have a feature that makes
a lot of sense from the viewpoint of the corporation but
does the investor little or no good. These are the callable
preferreds, which means that the corporation can pay the
owner of the issue a specified amount and demand that he
surrender his preferred for that sum. Normally the call
price is slightly above the par value—say $105 for a $100 par
preferred, or even $110.

Callable preferred stock is issued because it gives a company the opportunity to redeem a preferred issue that carries
a high dividend rate and replace it with a preferred with a
lower dividend or eliminate it entirely. That's fine for the
company, but, so far as the investor is concerned, it simply
sets a ceiling above which the price of the stock is unlikely
to advance. If the call price of a preferred is $110 a share,
why pay $115 if it's possible that you may be forced to sur-
render your stock to the company at $110?

Perhaps the tastiest preferred dish served by corporations
to stockholders is the convertible preferred, particularly
when the issue is cumulative as well as convertible. This

type of issue is regarded by many analysts as the *crème de la crème* of preferreds.

A convertible preferred stock may be swapped for the company's common stock, at the option of the stockholder, under specific terms. The theory here is that the owner of a convertible preferred issue has the opportunity, if he wishes to exercise it, to participate in the earnings of a prosperous company—and note the word "prosperous."

Let's say that an issue of convertible preferred stock may be converted into common stock at the rate of two shares for one. You own one share of preferred for which you paid $100. The common is selling at $60 a share. Obviously it would be to your advantage to convert into common—you automatically make a profit of $20.

In practice, though, it works out a little differently, because the price of a convertible preferred very closely reflects any price appreciation in the common. In the illustration above, the preferred most likely would be selling at $120 a share. In either case, though, you stand to benefit from the company's prosperity.

CHAPTER 6

Bonds and Debentures:

Corporate IOU's

IF YOU HAVE $500 or $1,000 to invest, you won't find much practical use for the information in this chapter. If you have $5,000 or $10,000, you may want to flirt with the idea of buying one or two bonds. If you have $25,000 or more, there are some bonds that exactly match your financial complexion.

Bonds and debentures are often considered the jewels of the investment world, although it must be admitted that some have more than a touch of paste in them. Bonds are not automatically excluded from the consideration of the small investor because they are prime-grade investments, but because they are usually issued in multiples of $1,000. Also, if you're an investor who is looking for growth, in income or capital, bonds offer you a rigid rate of return on your investment and little chance for capital appreciation. However, I'd like to emphasize that there are some highly interesting exceptions to this general rule.

Bonds and debentures represent the debt of a corporation.

As a bondholder, you are a creditor. You have no ownership interest in the company, and you can't so much as voice a whisper in running the company unless you have the misfortune to be a bondholder in a bankrupt concern.

When a company sells bonds, it is really borrowing money just as you borrow money when you go to a savings and loan association to finance the purchase of your home. In that case, you mortgage your property—which, in effect, is just what a corporation does when it issues bonds.

In return for lending your money to a business, you are promised that the company will pay you rent, or interest, for the use of your money. The company also promises to pay back to you at a specific time—five, ten, twenty, or even more years away—the face amount of the loan. These promises to pay interest and to repay the principal amount of the bond are backed up either by specific assets of the company—perhaps a dozen new diesel locomotives—or by the company's general credit rating.

Oddly enough, the bondholder does not deal directly with the corporation issuing the bond but with a trustee appointed by the corporation. The trustee, normally a bank or trust company, is appointed by the corporation and paid by it. But the trustee, by law, must be independent of the corporation and is supposed to act in the best interests of the bondholders. The trustee carries out a number of purely mechanical functions, such as making interest payments, redeeming bonds when they fall due, and keeping an eye on property that is pledged to insure payment of the bonds. The trustee also is required to exercise the same vigilance on behalf of the bondholder as any prudent man would in taking care of his own affairs. In the case of a company that cannot meet its obligations, such as interest payments on bonded indebtedness, it is the trustee who steps in and takes legal action on behalf of the bondholder.

Maturity and Interest

Bonds are issued in a fascinating variety, but they all have some characteristics in common. For instance, they all have a par value, also known as face value. Most companies issue bonds with a par value of $1,000, but bonds in units of $500, $5,000, $10,000 or more are not uncommon.

The market price of a bond is always expressed as a percentage of a $1,000 par value bond. If a bond is quoted at 90, that means a bond with a par value of $1,000 is selling in the market at $900. A price of 92 means the bond is selling at $920 per $1,000. A price of 95¼ means the bond is selling at $952.50.

The interest rate on a bond is always specified and is expressed as a percentage of par. The owner of 3½ per cent bonds has the company's promise to pay $35 in interest annually on each $1,000 bond. A 4 per cent bond pays the owner $40 annually in interest. Assuming the company is solvent, you will receive the specified interest no matter what you paid for the bond; so—unless you paid par for the bond —you will really receive more or less on your investment than the percentage specified on the bond.

Bonds also have a maturity date or term—with one interesting exception. XYZ Corporation in 1956 may have issued a bond that matures in 1976, which is the year when the company promises to pay back the face value of the bond. The term of this bond is 20 years. The term of a bond may range from 5 years, which is usually regarded as a minimum, up to —believe it or not—infinity.

One of the most intriguing companies in existence from an investor's viewpoint is the Canadian Pacific Railroad. The company operates the largest privately owned railroad in the world, a trans-Canada and transatlantic airline, ocean-going ships, and hotels. It owns mineral rights to millions of acres of land and has a substantial interest in a highly profitable mining and smelting company. The company keeps its books in a way that may be loosely described as conservative; some of its debt is expressed in terms of undevalued pounds sterling (the company claims it owes $4.80 per £, the official price of sterling before it was devalued, instead of $2.40).

But Canadian Pacific—along with a handful of other companies—has still another claim to fame. CP has outstanding $292,548,888 in 4 per cent perpetual bonds. That has always struck me as a really notable example of ingenuity and faith in the future. Here is a company that has borrowed millions of dollars that it never has to pay back—and if you don't think that's unusual, try it on your neighborhood bank. As this is written, by the way, CP perpetuals are selling at a premium over their par value—the amount per bond the company never has to repay.

Several domestic corporations have also displayed a similar faith in the future, a faith shared by the people who bought their bonds. While not quite on the grand scale of the perpetual loan, these companies have still shown a certain flair for thinking in big terms. One of the longest of all railroad obligations outstanding is West Shore Railroad first 4 per cent bonds, due 2361. These bonds were issued in 1885, and the interest is guaranteed by the New York Central Railroad. Lehigh Valley Railroad at one time had perpetual bonds outstanding, but in this company's recapitalization plan the bonds were exchanged for debt with a fixed maturity date. Then there's the New Jersey utility company, which in 1938 sold a noncallable issue of $750,000,000 in 8 per cent bonds that do not mature until 2037. This is a matter that scarcely concerns the average investor, though, because most of the bonds, it is said, were sold *en famille*. The original buyers still receive their 8 per cent annually, but if you want a mild shock, take a look at today's newspaper and note the high price of this issue.

Bankruptcy

Every now and then a corporation finds that it is not earning enough money to pay the interest on its bonded indebtedness. This sad condition may be temporary or may show signs of becoming permanent. You and the other bondholders, if you're real tough and want to try to get back every last cent you loaned the company, are in a position to force the firm into bankruptcy. The assets of the company may be put on the auction block and everything sold. As a bondholder, you have the first claim on the money that is raised from the auction. If there is any left over, the preferred stockholders get a whack at it; and if there are still a few cents left in the corporate kitty after that, the common stockholders are next in line.

Speaking realistically, though, the assets of most corporations, particularly if the company is of any size, might be a little difficult to sell. I can count on the fingers of one hand the people I know who would be interested in buying 5,000 miles of trackage in the Southwest or who would even care to pick up half a dozen used cabooses at a bargain price.

It would probably be to your advantage to follow the usual procedure and participate in the reorganization of the company—or, to use a well-known graphic phrase, "put the company through the wringer." Back in the 1930's corporate bankruptcy, especially among railroads, was so prevalent that going into 77–b carried no more stigma than selling apples on the street corner. Section 77–b of the bankruptcy laws pertains to corporate reorganizations.

Corporate reorganization, in essence, is an attempt to protect the company's creditors—as a bondholder, you are one— and to issue new securities that are geared to the real earning capacity of the company. Corporate bankruptcy today is probably more the result of mismanagement than of any other single factor, but many years ago, notably in the case of railroads, it was another story. In those days, it was an inept entrepreneur indeed who could not inject a little water into a company's capitalization. Actually, watering the capitalization was a simple operation. It consisted merely of selling to an eager public stocks and bonds far in excess of the company's earning power. Going through the wringer was just squeezing the water out.

In reorganization, the bondholder may do quite well for himself—or he may come out poorly. In exchange for his beautifully engraved bond, he may be offered so many shares of common or preferred stock, or perhaps an ingenious form of bond that is not a bond at all. Or he may be offered a new lien on the company's property. In any case, the bondholder has a decisive voice in just what new securities may be issued by the semidefunct company.

Some people made small fortunes buying the securities of bankrupt railroads in the late 1930's and early 1940's. At that time it was evident to the "experts" that railroads were in their last throes and perhaps even headed for government ownership. Whether the people who bought rail securities at that time were foolish investors or speculators with faith and vision, I leave to the reader's judgment.

The Varieties of Bonds

Bonds have three elements in common—they are evidence of debt, they have a maturity, and they have an interest rate. From there on, we can branch out.

Bonds vary in a number of ways—the amount and kind of collateral behind them, the order of precedence when there are several bonds issued by the same company, methods of repaying the principal, the call provisions of the bond, the possibility of converting the bond into another security issued by the same company, the investment caliber of the debt. That last factor is important because the bond, despite the rich, mellow connotations of the word, may be as speculative as a second-rate common stock. But let's look at the varieties of bonds.

DEBENTURES

Debentures represent corporate debt that is secured not by a lien on any specific property but by the general credit rating of the corporation. Years ago a debenture was considered somewhat of a second-rate bond—after all, if you buy a bond that is secured by a specific asset like a four-story brick factory, you know exactly what to do in case of bankruptcy. General credit rating, though, has a somewhat nebulous sound. What is your security if the bond defaults? The answer is that a corporation might have trouble selling debentures to the public unless it were in the strongest financial position.

Nowadays debentures are coming into more and more favor among the financially fastidious, and there's no reason why they shouldn't. Some of the soundest companies in the country favor debentures for their debt financing—Standard Oil Company (New Jersey) and Texas Company, for example —and these companies assure the holders of their debentures that they will not issue mortgage bonds to outrank the debentures.

MORTGAGE BONDS

Normal corporate practice is to issue a bond that is secured by a mortgage on some or all of the company's property. The bonds may be open-end, which means that the corporation may issue additional bonds under the same mortgage with due allowance for the rights of the original bondholders and the size of the company. Or the bond may be closed-end, which means the corporation is prohibited from selling more bonds under the same mortgage. Currently the trend is toward open-end bonds, largely because of the flexibility this type gives to the issuing company.

Top rating among mortgage bonds goes to the first mortgage bond, since it has precedence over all other claims against the company. The first mortgage bond is known as a senior lien because of this priority. The same company may also issue junior liens, which are, in effect, second mortgage bonds, although "second mortgage" is a term not too well liked in financial quarters. Usually second mortgage bonds are given a fancier title, such as "general mortgage" or "consolidated mortgage" bonds.

A junior lien is not necessarily a second-rate investment. The first mortgage bond may be so amply secured by assets and earning power that the junior lien is as well covered as the senior lien. Also, the senior lien may be retired, in which case the junior lien becomes in effect a first mortgage.

COLLATERAL TRUST BONDS

Instead of being secured by the assets of a corporation, the collateral trust bond is secured by securities deposited with the trustee. The collateral is usually bonds or stocks in a subsidiary company, or may be stocks and bonds held by the company as an investment. The market value of the collateral is usually larger than the face value of the bond issued against it—and the quality of the collateral trust bond is judged by the quality of the collateral.

EQUIPMENT TRUST CERTIFICATES

ETC's are among the elite of the investment world, often ranking ahead of top-grade first mortgage bonds. Probably no other class of security has treated its owners so well over the years. They offer the investor a comparatively low yield but are still greatly in demand among institutional investors.

Equipment trust certificates are used almost solely by railroads for purchasing new equipment, although lately airlines have shown an interest in adopting the ETC to their own needs. If you travel by train, you may have noticed the small metal plate, riveted to the side of the new diesel engine, that states that such and such bank is the owner and lessor of the engine.

A railroad wants to buy, say, a dozen new locomotives. The order is placed with the manufacturer and a substantial down payment is made, often as much as 25 per cent of the cost. Title to the equipment is vested in a trustee—a bank or trust company—who rents it to the railroad in return for an issue of equipment trust certificates. The annual rental is enough to pay interest charges and also to retire a certain amount of the certificates every year. The debt is paid off—usually in 15 years—before the equipment depreciates appreciably, and then ownership of the equipment passes to the railroad.

There have been few defaults on equipment trust certificates—possibly for the good reason that you can't run a railroad without locomotives.

INCOME BONDS

Income bonds may seem attractive—"income" is a word with a solid sound—but they were originally issued as the result of rail reorganizations. Some, as a matter of fact, have turned out quite well from the investor's viewpoint.

Income bonds are also called adjustment bonds, but, whatever you call them, they aren't really bonds at all but a sort of high-grade preferred stock. The company pays interest only if interest is earned; or payment of a part of the interest must be made and the balance is contingent upon earnings.

The income bond does have the advantage of ranking ahead of all preferred and common stock issued by the company—and, if earnings are large enough, the income bond may enjoy considerable stature.

PARTICIPATING BONDS

This type of security carries with it the provision that the owner will receive his stipulated interest, say 5 per cent, and may also share in the earnings up to another 2 or 3 per cent if earnings are large enough. Management of a sound enterprise wouldn't dream of issuing participating bonds because the bonds would participate at the expense of the common shareowners—who, after all, are the owners of the company. The device may be used by companies with poor credit standing as an inducement to get people to buy the bonds.

GUARANTEED BONDS

A parent company, particularly in the railroad industry, may guarantee bonds issued by a subsidiary or operating division. The guarantee enables the subsidiary to borrow on better terms than would be possible on the basis of its own credit.

When one railroad leases the property of another, the guarantee may be part of the leasing agreement.

CALLABLE BONDS

Any type of bond may be callable, and they frequently are—but a callable bond is certainly no boon to the investor. A bond that may be paid off in part or in full before maturity, at the discretion of the issuing company, is a callable bond. Thus a callable bond issued in 1956 and due in 1976 may be callable in whole or in part in, say, 1957 and any year thereafter—whenever the company decides to act. The bondholder is usually given 30 days' notice that all or part of the issue may be called, and normally the owner is paid a small premium. For instance, the owner of a $1,000 bond issued in 1956 and called in 1957 may receive as much as $1,050. The premium steadily becomes smaller as maturity approaches, until at maturity it is zero.

All these details, of course, are spelled out in the bond certificates. If a bondholder should happen to be spending three or four years in Tahiti at a time his bond is called, no damage is done. He won't receive any interest, but he can always turn in his bond for the call price.

A bond issue is usually called during a period of low interest rates. Thus a company that had sold a $50,000,000 bond issue with a 5 per cent coupon would find it advantageous to call the issue if the same amount of money could be raised at 3 per cent. At 5 per cent, the annual interest payments would total $2,500,000; at 3 per cent, interest would be $1,-500,000. Immediately after the end of World War II, scores of companies took advantage of an unusually low pattern of interest rates to call in outstanding bonds and refund them at a lower interest rate—to the benefit, of course, of the common stockholder.

The call price of a bond is in effect a ceiling on its market price. Thus, if XYZ 4's of 1970 were callable today at 105, the investor would be considered soft in the head if he paid 110—*unless* the bond were convertible.

SINKING FUND BONDS

Any type of bond may have a sinking fund provision, which is quite similar to the amortized mortgage used in buying a home. Years ago the mortgage on a house fell due with a thud; you paid the entire amount at the end of 15 or 20 years. Bankers eventually caught on to the idea that foreclosing mortgages was not popular with the public, so they figured out a way of paying mortgages off a little at a time. Today, your monthly payment to the bank not only takes care of the interest charge but also nibbles away at the principal. If you live long enough to make all your payments, at the end of the term of the mortgage the house is yours, debt free.

Similarly, a corporation may decide to set aside each year a certain amount to retire a portion of an outstanding bond. An industrial bond with a sinking fund provision may be considered more palatable by the investor on the theory that the company may be out of business in 25 years. And, of course, the more bonds are retired, the less the company must pay in annual interest charges.

The company may retire its bonds in two ways—either by buying them in the open market if the price is advantageous, or by calling them. Thus, from the investor's viewpoint, a sinking fund bond has the same disadvantage as a callable bond.

SERIAL BONDS

A serial bond is simply one that matures in installments over a period of years; the entire issue does not fall due in a specific year. In a way, serial bonds are a substitute for sinking fund bonds, because the borrower, or the issuer of the bond, does not have to repay the full principal amount in one lump sum. Yorktown Heights, for instance, might want to sell a $10,000,000 bond issue. The Town Board decides it will be easier to pay off the loan in installments. So Yorktown issues serial bonds. Series A, with a face value of $1,-000,000, is due in 1960; Series B, face value $1,000,000, is due in 1962; Series C, face value of $1,000,000, is due in 1964, and so on.

A serial bond may have the same coupon for all series; in

which case each series—A or B or C—will be sold at a different price, or each may be sold on a yield basis.

The serial bond offers to the investor a wide range of maturities and coupon rates or yields.

CONVERTIBLE BONDS

Convertible bonds—good ones, that is—are in a sense the investor's dream. They offer the owner safety of income plus the opportunity to share in the fortunes of a prosperous company.

The owner of a convertible bond has the privilege, at his discretion, of exchanging his bond for a specific number of shares of stock in the same company. Usually the bond may be converted only into common shares; in a few cases the conversion privilege is for preferred stock. The conversion may be on a straight bond-for-stock basis or, less frequently, bond-plus-cash-for-stock.

When a convertible bond is first sold, in most cases, it is not to the owner's advantage to convert it into stock—that is, the price of the stock is low in relation to the bond. The conversion privilege, in other words, is in the nature of a lure; if things go all right, and the common stock advances in market value, the company tells its bondholders, you'll be sitting pretty.

One of the oddities of the securities market is that the price of a convertible bond, under certain circumstances, has no relation to the value of the bond *as a bond*. The price of the bond is tied directly to the price of the common stock into which it may be converted.

Let's say that a bond selling at par, or $100, is convertible into two shares of common stock, and the market price of the common is $50. At this stage there's not much point in the bondholder converting into the common. But suppose the common advances to $75 a share. Theoretically, there would be a mass rush to convert a security worth $100 (the bond) into another security worth $150 (two shares of stock). In actual practice, the bond in this case would move up as the stock moved up, so that the ratio would always be about the same. If the stock advanced to $100, the bond would advance to $200.

But maybe the stock does not advance, perhaps it even declines. Still assuming that you bought a good bond in the first place, the stock can decline sharply without affecting the value of the bond as a bond. If the bond is a good one with a coupon of 4 per cent, it will probably sell around 105 no matter how low the price of the stock goes.

The best time to buy a convertible bond in a promising company, in my opinion, is when the bond is first issued. A 4 per cent convertible bond might sell today at issuance for around 100. You pay $1,000, in other words, to earn an annual interest return of $40. But suppose the same issue had been sold five years ago at par and the price had advanced today to 150, reflecting an advance in the common. If you wanted to buy the bond today, you would have to pay $1,500, although your annual interest would still be $40. Then suppose that the common declined and kept on declining. You would have the choice of converting immediately into a stock that might be steadily declining in market value, or hanging on to your bond. If the stock declined to a price at which conversion would give you an outright loss, you would be stuck with a bond that had cost you $1,500 and on which you continued to earn $40 a year—a return on your money of 2.6 per cent.

There is one other hitch to a convertible bond—it seems that every dream has a ghost in the background. Most convertibles are callable, which means that the issuing company is in a position to force conversion, a course that a company might find most desirable. Take the case we mentioned in which a convertible bond advanced to $150 to reflect an advance of the common to $75. This bond, though, is callable at $110—and the company calls it. There isn't much of a choice for you. You can accept the call price of $110 and take a loss of $40 on your bond—or you can convert at a profit. Naturally, you convert.

When convertible bonds were first offered to investors, the bonds weren't quite nice—they didn't come from the right side of the investment track. In some cases they evolved out of a reorganization plan, in other cases the conversion privilege was a sweetener to stimulate sale of the bonds. Convertibles today, though—good convertibles, of course—have a truly aristocratic standing.

A classic in the field of corporate financing is the consummate skill with which American Telephone & Telegraph Company has used the convertible debenture to raise hundreds of millions of dollars to finance growth and expansion.

MUNICIPAL AND AUTHORITY BONDS

If you're in the upper income brackets—say $25,000 a year or more—or if you have a sizable amount of money to invest, municipal issues certainly deserve a place in your portfolio. Interest received on corporate bonds is taxable by the federal government at the usual individual income tax rates. But interest received from the great majority of municipal bonds —and this term is used to include the swelling number of bonds issued by various state-created authorities for the construction of bridges, roads, and terminals—is exempt from federal taxation.

Municipals are really debentures, because they are not secured by specific property but by the general faith and credit of the issuer. Authority bonds are somewhat similar, but the revenues of a specific project—such as income from a toll bridge—are usually pledged to insure payment of principal and interest. In addition, authority bonds may be guaranteed by a state government.

Any way you look at it, though, this type of security is in a class by itself. Unfortunately most are so good that their yield is normally quite low—but when taxes are taken into consideration, the low yield may be more profitable than appears at first glance.

Taxes and securities are discussed in more detail in Chapter 20.

Are Good Bonds a Good Investment?

This is a reasonable question, and it should be given a clear-cut answer. Unfortunately—and this applies to virtually every question about investment in securities—there is no such thing as a clear-cut answer. It depends: if this trend should develop . . . or if this new development doesn't upset the apple cart . . . or assuming the economy continues to expand . . . or perhaps world affairs may take a turn for the worse. . . .

If you are looking for an investment that will safely give you a comparatively low rate of return over a long period of time, a prime bond is the answer. If you are looking for an investment that will enable you to get back the full amount you paid whenever you want it, be leery of bonds. If you want an investment that will return your original payment to you at a specific time some years in the future, buy a bond. If you are looking for an investment that will protect the purchasing power of your dollars, shy away from bonds.

These are important considerations, so let's look at them in a little more detail. Any prime bond may be expected to give you a small but safe return over the years. The number of companies that have maintained the interest payments on their bonds for decades is almost beyond counting. Just look up any bond that Moody's rates as AAA, or Standard & Poor classes as A1+, or Fitch as AAA, and you have the answer.

There's no such animal as a bond that can be sold whenever you wish to sell it, at approximately the price paid. The finest security in existence, the bonds of the United States government, have often fallen below par. For instance, in 1956 long-term governments, the 2½ per cent 1967–72, sold below 90. In other words, a government bond that would inevitably (or at least as inevitably as federal taxes) be redeemed at its $1,000 face value sold for less than $900. Was that an indication of lack of faith in the government's credit? No connection whatsoever. The government's credit was good then, is still good as this is being written, and, I suspect, will continue to be good for some time to come. The answer lies in the fact that any top-grade bond is sold on the basis of yield rather than price—and yield, in turn, reflects the going price of money.

The yield on a bond may be figured in two different ways, the current yield and the yield to maturity. Investors who are interested in holding a bond for a limited length of time will be most interested in current yield. If you plan to hold the bond until it matures, then you'll be more interested in yield to maturity. For the sake of simplicity, let's stick with current yield.

Current yield is figured in very much the same way you would figure the current yield on a stock. A bond selling at 110, or $1,100, paying 4 per cent annual interest, would yield about 3.64 per cent. Divide the annual interest—in this case $40—by the price, and you have the current yield.

Now, let's say there is a shortage of lendable funds all over the country. Banks have been lending so much money—to individuals, to corporations, to municipalities, and to the federal government—that they are just about loaned out. Borrowers who are anxious to raise money—and this includes the federal government—step up the amount they are willing to pay in interest to get the money they need. For the sake of exaggeration, let's say the interest rate on long-term prime loans goes from 3 per cent to 5 per cent. This is the figure that the U. S. government is willing to pay, and that ultimately determines the price of loans for other borrowers—who, of course, will have to pay slightly more than the government.

Why should you buy at par, or $1,000, a government bond issued a couple of years ago, which pays 3 per cent a year in interest, when the government is currently willing to pay 5 per cent? The answer is, you shouldn't—and the market place figures out the answer for you. The interest rate on this particular government bond will not change—but the yield will. If the price of the bond advances, the yield to you declines. If the price of the bond declines, the yield to you advances. This is fundamental.

It boils down to this: How far must the price of the bond drop so that I will get a 5 per cent return on my investment?

The answer is, to about 60.

In short, if you want an investment that will return you the full amount you paid *whenever you want it,* stay clear of bonds. You're at the mercy of the money market, a market in which supply and demand is measured in billions of dollars, and in which your own opinion or good judgment has a regrettable lack of influence.

This same logic applies to corporate bonds. If it costs more to borrow money, bond prices go down; if it costs less, bond prices advance.

The third question raised is whether a bond will return your original investment to you at a specific time. The answer is yes, if the bond is any good at all—and there are a great many bonds that are fine investments for this purpose. Your choice is narrowed considerably, however, if you insist on buying a noncallable bond.

How about bonds as a method of protecting the purchasing power of your dollars? No good at all! A bond offers you elasticity of neither income nor principal. The bond you buy today for $1,000 will be worth exactly $1,000 when it matures in 20 years, but whether that $1,000 represents the same amount of purchasing power is another question. Based on the record, the purchasing power of the dollar has been declining for years and will continue to decline in the future.

If you're looking for a hedge against inflation, there's just one answer: common stocks.

CHAPTER **7**

The Investment Banker:

Capitalism's Midwife

THE INVESTMENT BANKER is probably one of the most misunderstood and most important men in the nation.

In the public mind he is a top-hatted tycoon of vast wealth and power—yet I know of two of these gentlemen who have appeared at their annual convention in frayed suits with buttons missing. The typical investment banker is commonly regarded as one of a handful of men of great power who casually manipulate the affairs of scores of giant corporations, if not the entire economy, for their personal gain. Investment banking, actually, is one of the most competitive businesses on earth, and a notable number of investment bankers have performed ably and selflessly in the public service.

When we were discussing the hypothetical newly formed Electronic Can Opener Corporation, the possibility was considered that the new device might revolutionize the can opener industry. Well, let's suppose that it did—that the new can opener eliminated drudgery in the kitchen and even opened the way toward emancipating the housewife. The company finally grew large enough so that substantial additional capital was needed to build the factories and buy the machinery necessary to keep up with demand.

Now, it's quite likely that the can opener company's bank would be delighted to lend it enough money to finance current needs, such as inventories and materials. The bank, though, would undoubtedly take a very dim view of lending the company $5,000,000 on a long-term basis.

So the company seeks the advice of a banker who really isn't a banker at all in the traditional sense of the word. The president of Electronic Can Opener Corporation may feel confident that he has a good grasp of his own business, but after the investment banker gets through probing the company, he may think differently.

The function of the investment banker is to raise money for businesses that need capital for any one of a dozen reasons —to buy an automated assembly line, to construct a research laboratory, to acquire the assets of another company, to increase production from 1,000 units daily to 5,000. In order to raise that money, the company must issue a brand new security, such as a stock or a bond, or additional amounts of an outstanding security. But issuing the security is one thing; persuading individual and institutional investors to buy it is another. That is one of the problems of the investment banker.

In the case of Electronic Can Opener, the investment banker will not take the word of the president that the company owns four plants, that earnings last year amounted to so many dollars, that orders on hand amount to six months' production. In fact, the banker most likely will not take *anybody's* word for *anything*. His job is to sell securities, and he wants to know exactly what lies behind those securities. The company's physical assets will be inspected, management will be evaluated, the company's books will be inspected with the detached thoroughness of a certified public accountant. Then, too, the company's place in the industry and its prospects for the future will be meticulously analyzed.

The banker may take months to do his job. The result will be a specific recommendation; perhaps an issue of first mortgage bonds, or so many shares of common stock, or maybe a suggestion to defer new financing for the time being in view of the general state of the securities market.

The management of Electronic Can Opener may ignore the advice offered and go to another investment banker—in which case the first banker has spent a lot of money for nothing. More likely, though, management will go along with his recommendation.

Let's say the recommendation is to sell 50,000 shares of a new issue of convertible preferred stock. The investment banker and management agree that the company does not want to saddle itself with a bond issue on which interest must be paid in good times or bad. They agree, too, that since the company is a relatively new one, investors would be more interested if they had a prior claim at a fixed ratio in the company's earnings—which a preferred issue provides —and, at the same time, were offered through the conversion privilege the chance to share in the company's future if it turns out to be prosperous.

The underwriter at this point contracts with Electronic Can Opener to buy the 50,000 shares of preferred. If the underwriter does not sell even one share of the preferred stock to the investing public, the company still gets its money. Sometimes, when there is a glut of new issues or the market is kicking up its heels, the underwriter may run into real trouble in selling a security. Then he has on his hands what is known to the trade as a sticky issue. Eventually he will dispose of the issue, even though he may be forced to reduce the price drastically and take a large loss in the process. On the other hand, the issue may go out of the window, to use another trade expression. This means that demand is so strong that the issue is sold out within a few minutes after the offering price to the public is announced.

Price and timing are the two variables for which the underwriter has full responsibility. If the underwriter sets too high a figure, he may price the issue out of the market. If he sets too low a price in order to attract as much demand as possible, he costs his client—the issuing company—money and establishes a reputation as a man of dubious judgment. For instance, if he agreed to pay the issuer $10 a share, sold the stock to the public at $11, and then the market price jumped to $20 a share, the underwriter obviously misgauged the market. He could have paid the issuer as much as, say, $18 or $19 a share.

In some cases the issuing company, such as a utility, is required by law to ask for competitive bids on a new issue. The bid most advantageous to the company must be accepted. The competition is so keen in competitive bidding that frequently the difference between the best bid and the second-best bid amounts to only a few cents per $1,000 bond. And sometimes, if market conditions are adverse, no bids at all will be submitted to the company.

If the underwriter's timing is wrong, he may find himself with an issue that will take months to sell—a rather expensive operation, because the underwriter has borrowed the money to pay the issuing company in the first place, and it costs money to borrow money.

The price of the convertible preferred issue of Electronic Can Opener Corporation will be influenced largely by the current yield on similar securities, the conversion privilege, and the fact that the company is a relatively new one. If top grade preferreds are selling in the market to yield, say, 4¼ per cent, then the investment banker would probably arrive at an offering price that would yield as much as 5 per cent. But the preferred does have the conversion feature, so the yield might be shaded to 4.9 per cent.

This particular issue will probably have a par value of $100 a share and a dividend rate of 5 per cent, or $5 a year for each share. If the investment banker figures that this security will be attractive to an investor at a yield of 4.9 per cent, he will set the price at slightly above par. If he figures that he must offer a higher yield, say 5¼ per cent, he will fix the offering price at slightly below par.

The importance of the difference between yield and the specific dividend rate on a preferred stock, or coupon rate on a bond issue, was well illustrated by a question put to me by an elderly lady a few months ago. She had bought ten $1,000 bonds of an obligation guaranteed by the New York Central. The bond carried a 5 per cent coupon and was due in 2013. The market price at the time she questioned me was 85, or $850 per $1,000 bond, which would give a new investor a yield of about 6 per cent. Her own yield, of course, was 5 per cent because she had bought the bonds at par. But she was disturbed because of the market price of the bonds and wondered if she shouldn't sell. I suggested that she hold on to her bonds. The yield, 5 per cent, was good, and, in view of the fact that New York Central common stock was selling around $40 a share, was paying a dividend, and was apparently going to keep on paying a dividend for some time to come, the chances of the Central defaulting on the interest payments seemed remote.

The relatively low price of the bonds—which had disturbed her in the first place—was merely the market's appraisal of the Central's ability to pay off the bonds at maturity, plus, of course, the state of the money market. After all, in 50-odd years the New York Central may be in the brassière business or not in business at all; but, as I said, my friend was an elderly lady whose principal concern was assured income for the next 10 or 15 years.

There are a number of variations in the relationship between the investment banker and his client. A large corporation may wish to sell a $50,000,000 issue of bonds, but to avoid legal requirements relating to full disclosure of its affairs, may not want to offer the bonds to the public. In this case the underwriter may act as an intermediary between the corporation and an institutional investor such as an insurance company.

Or an established company may want to sell a large amount of common stock in addition to the total already outstanding. Normally, the company will give its present stockholders the right to buy the additional stock under stipulated conditions, but there is always some stock left over. The underwriter will contract to market those shares that the stockholders do not buy.

Or an underwriter may take over an issue on a "best effort" basis, a method often used when the stock is highly speculative. Instead of paying the issuer outright for the security being sold, the underwriter agrees to use his best efforts to market the stock; but if the stock cannot be sold, then that is the company's problem, not the underwriter's.

The underwriter's profit is derived from the so-called spread between the price paid to the issuer and the price paid by the public. If the price of a common stock offered to the public is fixed by the underwriter at $50 a share, the company might receive $49.25 a share; the spread of 75 cents a share is the underwriter's profit.

Except in the case of relatively small issues—perhaps $5,-000,000 or $10,000,000—the usual practice of the underwriter is to form a buying syndicate. To spread the risk, the underwriter may call in half a dozen other firms for the job, who jointly agree to purchase the new issue. The buying syndicate, in turn, will form a selling syndicate, which may include fifty or a hundred or even more firms which are given the job of actually selling the issue to the investor.

One of the tougher jobs the investment banker is likely to have tossed to him is the sale to the public of the common stock of a company that has never been publicly owned. Some of these companies are literally being forced on the market because of the impact of inheritance taxes, which force the heirs to sell stock to raise money to pay the tax. Other companies reach a stage in their development that requires such large sums of money for further growth that public sale of the company's securities is imperative.

An outstanding example of a privately owned company moving into the public domain is the Ford Motor Company. Campbell Soup is another, and Firth Carpet a third. From the investment banker's viewpoint, the problem of marketing stock in such companies is price. From the investor's viewpoint, there may be a lush opportunity for profits.

Take Firth Carpet Company, for decades a family enterprise in New Jersey. A large block of the stock was offered to the public in 1946 at a price of $20 a share—a price arrived at, I am sure, after a good deal of soul-searching by the investment banking syndicate that handled the issue. The same day that the stock was offered to the public at $20, it sold in the over-the-counter market at $25.25. The investor who bought Firth Carpet at the offering price had an immediate profit of about $5.25 a share. Somebody had made a bad mistake, but a mistake that was apparent only with the benefit of hindsight.

Or take Campbell Soup. Public offering of 1,300,000 shares of Campbell Soup was made in mid-November 1954 at a price of $39.25 a share. This was generally regarded in the financial press as a price that, if not an outright bargain, was low enough to attract the investing public on a large scale. And it did. Almost every investor worth his salt tried to get a few shares of Campbell at the offering price, and naturally a great many were disappointed.

But their disappointment, it turned out, was easy to bear. For months Campbell Soup did not move more than a dollar or two from the offering price. Visions of quick and easy profits were laboriously dispelled by the relentless decision of the market that the stock was worth so much and no more. In 1956, the stock closed more than $2 a share below the offering price. Here was an example—again using hindsight as a yardstick—of superb pricing judgment by the underwriters.

But the real classic is Ford Motor. The Ford Foundation, richly endowed by the Ford family, was the major owner of Ford stock—stock, by the way, that carried no voting rights. Voting power was concentrated in a small number of shares held by the Ford family. The Foundation, reasonably enough, felt that it would be desirable to diversify its investments; so the Foundation, the Ford family, the Bureau of Internal Revenue, and the New York Stock Exchange worked out a recapitalization plan for the company.

That recapitalization plan deserves at least passing mention as a masterpiece of financial legerdemain—and a very desirable transfer from private to public ownership of one of the largest enterprises in the world. At the time of the recapitalization, the Ford Foundation started out with no voting rights in the company, although it was the largest stockholder, and ended with no voting rights; the Ford family started out with 100 per cent voting power and ended with 40 per cent; the public started out with no stock and no voting power and ended with some 10,000,000 shares of stock and 60 per cent of the voting power. The 60 per cent of the voting power in the hands of the public, even though it represents a majority, has about as much chance of controlling the Ford Motor Company as I have of controlling the outcome of the Irish Sweepstakes. Still, the recapitalization was a step in the right direction—and it should be pointed out that the voting power retained by the Ford family will be cut down still more if the family disposes of another amount of its stock.

The investment bankers who underwrote the Ford stock had the almost impossible task of determining a price that would reflect not only the stock's earning power but also the public's state of mind about the stock. The price had to bear a reasonable relationship to the price of General Motors and Chrysler stocks. The price had to reflect to some degree the company's earnings and prospects for the future. The price had to be low enough to make sure the stock would be quickly bought by the public—and high enough so that the Foundation would realize the maximum possible amount from the sale of its holdings. King Solomon, with the help of a Univac, might have arrived at the right price, but I personally believe there was no such thing as a right price.

The Ford stock was offered to the public at $64.50 a share and was a quick sellout. The very day the stock was offered, it sold in Canada at more than $70 a share. Free riders— people who bought the stock in the belief that the price would advance sharply and immediately, so they could take a quick profit—may have had a field day, despite the efforts of the underwriters to get the stock into so-called firm hands —people who would buy the stock and hang on to it.

Actually, the price quickly dropped well below the offering price, and in 1956 it closed at around $59 a share. In that same period between the first offering of Ford stock and the year's end, General Motors common declined from $44.62 a share to $40.25 a share, while Chrysler dropped from $81.12 to $64.875 a share. The last chapter, of course, has not been written, but you might like to mull over in your mind the problem of whether the underwriters' price was too high or too low.

New issues of stock, in short, may be a bonanza for the investor, or they may result in a stalemate. Or, less frequently, they may result in a temporary or even permanent loss. I think it's worth bearing in mind, however, that the investment banker tends to underprice an issue rather than overprice it. He does this not for altruistic reasons, but because he wants to be sure to dispose of the stock and protect his own investment, to say nothing of making a profit.

One of the most famous antitrust suits in history was brought by the United States government against a group of leading investment bankers, who were charged, among other malefactions, with conspiracy to restrain and monopolize the securities business of the country. The case was tried before Federal Judge Harold R. Medina who, in 1953, threw it out of court. In his decision, which is a classic appraisal of the investment banking business, Judge Medina said:

It would be difficult to exaggerate the importance of investment banking to the national economy. The vast industrial growth of the past fifty years has covered the United States with a network of manufacturing, processing, sales and distributing plants, the smooth functioning of which is vital to our welfare as a nation. They vary from huge corporate structures such as the great steel and automobile companies, railroads and airlines, producers of commodities and merchandise of all kinds, oil companies and public utilities, down to comparatively small manufacturing plants and stores. The variety and usefulness of these myriad enterprises defy description. They are the result of American ingenuity and the will to work unceasingly and to improve our standard of living.

But adequate financing for their needs is the lifeblood without which many if not most of these parts of the great machine of business would cease to function in a healthy, normal fashion.

CHAPTER 8

Where Securities Are Bought and Sold:

Supermarkets for Investors and Speculators

STOCKS AND BONDS are probably the most liquid form of wealth in the world. Liquidity means simply the ease with which property can be converted into cash at a fair price. For the investor, that last point is an important one. Almost any kind of property can be sold quickly *at a price,* but a quick sale may entail heavy financial loss.

Take your house, which has just been appraised at $25,000. That's a reasonable price in today's real estate market. But finding a buyer at that price—if, indeed, you ever do—may take weeks or months of individual negotiations with potential buyers.

When you want to sell a stock which is traded on a stock exchange, though, the transaction is usually completed within a matter of minutes—and normally at a price that shows only a small variation from the last previous transaction in the same stock. The reason for this is that all the orders to buy or sell certain securities converge in one place, the stock exchange.

79

Not all exchanges perform their function—which, essentially, is to provide a market place for specific securities—with the same efficiency. And, as a matter of fact, one market for securities, the over-the-counter market, is not, properly speaking, a market place at all.

The New York Stock Exchange

The largest organized securities market place in the world today is the New York Stock Exchange. The Exchange boasts that the securities traded in its market represent the cream of American industry—and the boast is a sound one. About 1,100 companies have qualified to have their stocks traded on the New York Stock Exchange. These companies earn about half the net profits reported by all United States companies and pay their stockholders about half of all dividends paid.

These corporations provide jobs for more than 12,000,000 workers. They produce virtually all of the automobiles and trucks made in this country, ship around seven-eighths of all the finished steel, produce three-quarters of all the electric power, refine 90 per cent of all oil produced, and transport 95 per cent of rail traffic and air-passenger travel.

High prestige goes with a listing on the New York Stock Exchange, which is one reason the Exchange refuses to accept for listing a great many more securities than it does. Listing a stock—that is, meeting certain standards in order to qualify the security for trading on the Exchange—requires a good deal more than paying a fee.

THE EARLY DAYS

The Stock Exchange started life in 1792 when a group of 24 merchants, brokers, and auctioneers agreed to meet daily at a particular spot—only a block or so from the site of the present Exchange—to buy and sell securities. The investors and speculators of those days had a pretty meager fare, although there was a great deal of speculative interest in the newly issued stock of the government and in Alexander Hamilton's first United States Bank. Shares in a few other banks were also bought and sold.

A year later, in 1793, the brokers moved indoors, but after the public interest in government securities and stock of the United States Bank died down, business did not amount to much. Following the War of 1812, commercial and industrial activity picked up and more securities reached the market. In 1817 the Exchange adopted a formal constitution and elected a president, who had the job of calling off the list of securities traded. As each security was named, the assembled brokers made their bids to buy or offers to sell.

The president was also empowered to fix commissions and to levy fines for violations of procedure and for nonattendance. Fines ranged from 6 to 25 cents. Absences were excused if the brokers had been sick or were out of the city.

The New York Stock and Exchange Board, as it was known then, moved more than a dozen times before finally settling down in a permanent location. The building at 18 Broad Street, completed in 1903, contains most of the trading floor as it is today. In 1922, the adjoining office building at 11 Wall Street was added. Completing the block bounded by Wall Street, Broad Street, New Street, and Exchange Place, a new building was finished in 1957, so constructed that an entire floor can be removed to allow for expansion of the present trading floor when and if that becomes necessary.

Following the end of the Civil War, the work of the Stock Exchange rapidly expanded as the nation's industrial growth started to snowball. Railroad securities were the Exchange's main staple for many years, but eventually industrial issues, and later utilities, were added to the list. By 1871 volume had increased to the point where the call market gave way to the continuous auction market, a system still in effect. A broker did not have to wait for a particular stock to be called, but could buy or sell it immediately. Installation of the first ticker in 1867 added to the Exchange's efficiency, as did the use of the first telephones in 1879.

The year 1886 was a somewhat notable one in Exchange history, because then for the first time the daily volume of trading topped 1,000,000 shares. Fifty years later, 1886, could be recalled with some nostalgia, because for a while during the 1930's the volume of trading shrank to less than 500,000 shares daily. Average daily volume in 1956 ran a bit over 2,100,000 shares.

THE EXCHANGE TODAY

In 1938, after some pointed prodding by the Securities and Exchange Commission, the New York Stock Exchange graduated from the status of a private club to that of a public institution. Management of the Exchange is headed by a paid president, G. Keith Funston, who directs a professional staff and is responsible to the Exchange's Board of Governors. The board of 33 Governors includes the president and three governors having no connection with the securities business, who are chosen to represent the public interest. The latter provision was an outgrowth of the 1938 reorganization; some very distinguished businessmen and educators have served as Public Governors.

Membership in the Stock Exchange now stands at 1,366. There's no rule against a woman being a member of the Exchange, but it just happens that no lady has managed to achieve that distinction. If a member is a partner in a brokerage firm, that firm is known as a member firm—as an investor, you will probably do business with a member firm of the New York Stock Exchange. Quite recently, the Exchange broke with tradition and permitted corporations to become members, so you may do business with a member corporation.

About half the individual members are partners or officers in firms doing business with the public—in the trade, they are known as commission houses. Members of these firms execute customers' orders to buy or sell listed securities on the trading floor of the Exchange. Only a member has the right to do this. The member firm charges the customer a commission on each transaction. The Exchange itself prescribes minimum commissions that must be charged, and a firm may charge more than the minimum, although I do not know of any firm that does. Table 11 shows how to figure New York Stock Exchange commissions.

TABLE 11

COMMISSIONS ON STOCKS, RIGHTS AND WARRANTS TRADED IN
100-SHARE AND 10-SHARE UNITS

Selling at $1.00 and Above

Commissions shall be based upon the money involved in transactions for 100 shares or less and shall be computed as follows:

Amount of Money Involved	Commission
Under $100	As mutually agreed
$ 100 to $1,999	1% plus $ 5.00
$2,000 to $4,999	½% plus $15.00
$5,000 and above	1/10% plus $35.00

Odd-lot—$2 Less

Notwithstanding the foregoing:

(1) when the amount involved in a transaction is less than $100, the minimum commission shall be as mutually agreed;

(2) when the amount involved in a transaction is $100 or more, the minimum commission charge shall not exceed

$1 per share or $50 per 100-share or odd-lot transaction, but in any event shall not be less than $6 per transaction.

About a quarter of the Exchange's members are so-called specialists, key men in the efficient functioning of the market whose work will be discussed in more detail in another chapter.

Some members are odd-lot dealers, who have the responsibility of executing orders to buy or sell small quantities of stock. An odd lot is normally any amount from 1 to 99; in the case of stocks in which the round lot is 10 shares instead of 100, an odd lot is 1 to 9 shares.

A handful of members are known as floor traders. These men have no connection with the public, but buy and sell on the trading floor for their own account. The floor trader, also known as an "in-and-outer," is strictly a speculator, frequently completing his transactions within one day. He has been subject to severe criticism on a number of grounds, such as the claim that he has an unfair advantage over the public because he is right on the scene of action and also because it is presumed that he tends to ride with the market, buying as prices advance and selling as prices decline, thus aggravating price movements. His defenders claim that he makes a real contribution to the liquidity of the market by constant buying and selling. Also, it is said, he helps to stabilize the market by buying when prices are too low and selling when prices are too high.

Still another type of member is the floor broker, also known as the $2 broker. When a commission broker has more business than he can take care of, he will ask a $2 broker to help out by executing some of his orders for him, a service for which the $2 broker receives part of the other broker's commission.

The partners in a member firm—or, in the case of a member corporation, the officers—who are not actually members of the Exchange are known as allied members. They are not allowed to execute transactions on the floor of the Exchange, but they are subject to Exchange regulations just as members are.

All of the partners of a member firm are subject to unlimited liability for the firm's obligations.

Next in line to a member firm's partners are the registered representatives, once known as customers' men. Before they are allowed to do business with the public, they are given appropriate training and must pass a written examination administered by the Exchange to prove their qualifications.

Just in passing, mention should be made of the New York Institute of Finance. The Institute was formerly administered by the Exchange itself but is now in private, and capable, hands. Wall Street takes a good deal of pride in the Institute, which gives courses in every phase of the securities and brokerage business, and many of today's leaders in the field got their start with the help of the Institute's professional training.

Buying a membership in the Exchange is not too difficult, provided you can afford it. In 1957 the price of a membership—or seat, to use the popular term—was around $100,000. The price, which depends in large part on the level of activity in the market, has gone above $600,000 in the past and was as low as $17,000 in 1942.

A man applying for membership must be at least 21 years old, a citizen by birth or naturalization, and of excellent reputation. His application must give his complete history, and final action on his application requires the approval of the Board of Governors. In addition to the cost of the membership itself, there are an initiation fee of $4,000 and annual dues of $750. A member may also incur various other charges, such as the 1 per cent levy on his commissions that is a major source of Exchange revenue.

The Board of Governors has broad powers to discipline members for violating Exchange regulations or the Securities Exchange Act of 1934, or for committing any act against the welfare of the Exchange. A member may be fined as much as $5,000 and may be suspended from the Exchange for a period running up to five years. In the worst cases, a member may be expelled from the Exchange, and expulsion is irrevocable.

It speaks well for the high ethics of Exchange members that suspension is a rarity and expulsion all but unheard of. Off hand, the only expulsion I can recall in recent years happened in the case of a fairly new member who made the unforgivable mistake of lying to the Exchange about his financial affairs. That just isn't done.

There are roughly 650 member firms. Many have branch offices throughout the country, raising the total of member firm offices to more than 2,000.

The functions of member firms are as varied as individual members. Some—the commission houses, also known as "wire houses" because of their extensive communication facilities —do a large-scale business with the general public. In many cases the operation of this type of firm is highly mechanized, and they handle an order involving 5 or 10 shares of stock with the same courteous routine as a 1,000-share order. At the other extreme are firms that prefer not to do business with the public at large, and instead concentrate on large accounts, individual as well as institutional.

Members and member firms of the Exchange are subject to a staggering number of rules, regulations, and laws. The bible of the membership is the *Director and Guide,* a loose-leaf book about four inches thick. The print is small and there are no pictures. There are also the Securities Exchange Act of 1934 to consider, regulations and rulings of the Securities and Exchange Commission, regulations of the Federal Reserve Board, statutes of the various states pertaining to the securities business, and numerous provisions of civil and criminal law. Running afoul of this mass of regulatory material merely by inadvertence would seem to be a fairly easy misstep—but ignorance of the law is no defense.

The Stock Exchange also prescribes minimum capital requirements for member firms and requires three audits a year of member firms that carry customers' accounts. One must be made by an outside auditing firm, and it must be a surprise audit. The other audits may be made either by the firm's own staff or by an outside firm.

The Exchange boasts that the solvency record of its members is better than that of the nation's banks and mercantile establishments—and the record proves the truth of the statement. A member firm of the Exchange has not gone broke since 1938.

Customers of member firms, in short, are protected against virtually everything except Acts of God and their own cupidity.

The Stock Exchange looks over its listed companies—and companies applying for listing—with the same loving kindness it gives to its members and member firms. Roughly 100 companies ask to be listed each year, and about 20 are chosen. Not only that, but once a company has been listed there is no guarantee that it will hold its listing as long as it chooses. As a matter of fact, in recent months there have been indications that the Exchange is getting tougher about its delisting policy. Delisting is a serious matter, which may involve depriving investors of the Exchange's market place, when the mere fact that the stock was listed may have influenced the purchase of the stock in the first place.

To qualify for listing, a company must be a going concern with substantial assets and proven earning power. The rules are not ironclad, but the Exchange favors a company with net income of $1,000,000 or more annually. Great emphasis, though, is placed on the degree of national interest in the company, its standing in its own industry, and the relative stability and character of the market for its products. The company should have at least 300,000 shares of stock out-standing, owned by at least 1,500 stockholders. These pro-visions are designed to make sure that there will be enough shares distributed among enough people so that an adequate auction market in the stock is possible.

The company applying for listing must agree to publish quarterly earnings unless the seasonal nature of the business would make such reports misleading. At least 15 days before the annual meeting of stockholders, the company must agree to supply stockholders with copies of its annual report.

A somewhat esoteric portion of the listing agreement, al-though of passing importance to the stockholder, is the re-quirement that the company must have a transfer agent and registrar in New York City. The transfer agent, usually a bank or trust company, keeps a record of the name and ad-dress of each stockholder and the number of shares owned, and makes sure that when ownership of the security changes hands, the stock certificate is properly endorsed. The regis-trar sees to it that the number of shares of stock issued does not exceed the authorized amount—and the company agrees that no additional stock will be issued without Exchange approval.

And, as a bit of lagniappe to the stockholders, the Exchange has rigid standards regarding the engraving of stock certifi-cates in order to prevent forgeries.

Delisting a stock may be done only with the approval of the Securities and Exchange Commission. The Exchange, though, does have the power to suspend trading in a stock and then apply to the SEC for permission to delist—permission which, if my memory is not faulty, has never been denied.

The Exchange will consider delisting a common stock issue when (1) the total outstanding stock is held by less than 250 holders of record; or (2) the size of the company has been reduced, as a result of liquidation or otherwise, to below $2 million in net tangible assets *or* aggregate market value of the common stock, *and* the average net earnings after taxes for the last three years have been below $200,000.

The Exchange may start delisting proceedings for a number of reasons. For instance, if the outstanding amount of a common stock, exclusive of concentrated holdings, has been reduced to less than 5,000 shares, the Exchange may take the view that not enough stock is in the hands of the public to maintain an adequate market. Or if the Exchange is informed by an authoritative source that a security is without value, dealings will be suspended.

The Exchange has also taken steps to block the so-called backdoor listing, which constitutes a really serious menace to the maintenance of Exchange standards. A listed company may dispose of its physical assets, may plan outright liquidation, or may shrink in size because the competition has become too tough. An unlisted company anxious to acquire the prestige of an Exchange listing might want to merge with such a company. Up to quite recently, the company surviving the merger automatically became a listed company. Now, however, the surviving corporation must meet the same standards as any company applying for listing for the first time.

Just in the past few years, the New York Stock Exchange has taken an active interest in encouraging the listing of the larger foreign corporations. One such company, Royal Dutch Petroleum, which is among the largest corporations in the world, made drastic changes in its corporate setup to comply with Exchange regulations and thus qualify for listing. Others that have followed suit include Rhodesian Selection Trust and the Montecatini Company.

Some new foreign listings appear to have considerable profit possibilities because of the different accounting methods used by United States and foreign corporations, among other reasons. Royal Dutch, as an illustration, used more conservative methods of accounting for certain assets than an American oil company usually does. When more information about the company became available as a result of the listing, this was soon reflected in the price of the stock.

When Royal Dutch was first listed on the New York Stock Exchange, around mid-1954, the opening price was $58.625 a share. In early 1957, the price was about $43.50 after a two-and-one-half-for-one split, a gain of 86 per cent. During the same period, Standard Oil Company (New Jersey) rose 95 per cent, Standard Oil of California advanced 347 per cent, and Cities Service 92 per cent.

The American Stock Exchange

One of the most colorful market places in the world passed out of existence when the old Curb Exchange decided to become dignified. In 1921 the members of the curb market left the streets of New York forever and started to do business in their own new building across Trinity Church yard from the New York Stock Exchange. In 1953 dignity was carried a step further when the membership of the Curb Exchange voted to change the name to the American Stock Exchange.

For years—nobody is quite sure how many, but a fair guess is around 70—the Curb did business, rain or shine or snow or sleet, on the streets of New York. Communications between a milling crowd of brokers on the streets and the outside world were maintained through the clerks perched in the window sills of the buildings lining the street. A good window-sill location frequently commanded a premium rental. To help their clerks identify them, Curb brokers resorted to strange and eye-catching costumes, and even stranger hand signals were employed to rise above the din of many voices.

The mechanics of trading are somewhat different in the American Exchange than in the New York Stock Exchange. Brokers on the floor of the ASE still use curious hand signals to communicate with clerks sitting in banked rows above the floor. ASE brokers claim that this system enables them to pare a few seconds from the time it takes to execute an order on the floor of the New York Stock Exchange—and, if you're in a monumental hurry, a few seconds can be mighty important.

From an organizational viewpoint, the two exchanges are quite similar. Each has a board of governors to establish policy and a paid president to carry out these policies and attend to the actual operation of the market place. The President of the ASE is Edward T. McCormick, variously known to his friends as Ed, Ted, or Mac. McCormick, a man with an engaging grin who seldom lets the dust settle on him, believes the ASE can do as good a job for many corporations as the NYSE, or better. He has been particularly successful in getting foreign corporations—almost all, it should be noted, are in or close to the penny-stock category—to list their securities on the ASE, and has waged an aggressive campaign to move smaller domestic corporations from the over-the-counter market to his exchange. He has the advantage of observing the securities markets from two widely separate viewpoints. Unlike Funston, who came to the NYSE from the presidency of Trinity College, McCormick came to the ASE as a former commissioner of the Securities and Exchange Commission.

The NYSE takes the view that the ASE is mainly a seasoning exchange for companies that eventually may qualify

for listing on the Big Board, and it's true that many successful corporations have moved from the ASE to the NYSE.
Two of the ASE's prize companies have made the move in
recent years—Aluminum Company and Cities Service—but
the ASE still has on its list a number of outstanding corporations.

Listing standards on the ASE are considerably more flex-
ible than on the NYSE. Even companies without proven
earning power or enterprises that are in the developmental
stage may be accepted for listing. There's good logic to
bolster the ASE's position. Such companies, the ASE points
out, must comply with SEC regulations pertaining to disclosure, and the security is lifted from the comparative ob-
scurity of the over-the-counter market to a public market
place.

But the ASE does have one practice that is of questionable
value from the investor's point of view—that is, trading in
unlisted stocks. This represents a considerable portion of
total ASE trading. At one time, on both the New York and
American Exchanges, a security could be traded upon the
request of a member, rather than upon application by the
corporation issuing the security. Such issues were unlisted;
the company did not pay a listing fee, was not obliged to
comply with any listing regulation, and in effect was not required to make public any of its affairs. The NYSE abandoned this practice in the 1920's. Today a stock must be
fully listed or it can't be on the NYSE.

The Securities Exchange Act of 1934 threw out this gimmick for unlisted trading, but the law—and Congress de-
bated this possibility—was not made retroactive. Now all
stocks that are listed on a national securities exchange must
also register with the Securities and Exchange Commission,
which requires that the company supply detailed information
about itself. However, stocks that had unlisted trading priv-

ileges prior to passage of the act were allowed to continue on an unlisted basis—a sort of limbo in the securities world, which allows a company to eat its corporate cake and have it too. Such a company has a market place for its securities and need divulge little of its activities.

Time and the law are against unlisted trading—the number of such issues on the ASE is steadily declining.

The ASE has the same system of establishing minimum commissions as the NYSE, but the scale is not the same. ASE commissions are larger for lower-priced issues, smaller for higher-priced stocks.

Table 12 shows ASE commissions.

TABLE 12

AMERICAN STOCK EXCHANGE

Commissions on stocks, rights and warrants traded in 100-share units

Unit price of stocks	Rate per 100 shares
$1 and under $2	$ 7.00
$2 and under $3	8.00
$3 and under $4	9.00
$4 and under $5	10.00
$5 and under $6	11.50
$6 and under $7	12.50
$7 and under $8	13.50
$8 and under $9	15.00
$9 and under $10	16.00
$10	17.00
Over $10 and under $142	14.50[1]
$142 and above	50.00

[1] Plus 1/4 of 1 per cent of the total amount involved in the transaction.

Note: To compute the minimum commission on a transaction of 100 shares selling at $10 and over to and including $142 a share, add $58 to the price per share and divide the result by 4. To compute the minimum commission on a transaction in less than 100 shares, selling at $10 and over to and including $142 per share, multiply the applicable 100-

share commission by the number of shares in the transaction and divide by 100.

Notwithstanding the foregoing rates, when the amount involved in a transaction is less than $15, the commission shall be as mutually agreed; when the amount involved is $15 or more but less than $100, the minimum commission shall be not less than 6 per cent of the amount involved or the prescribed rate, whichever is greater; and when the amount involved is $100 or more, the minimum commission shall be not less than $6 or the prescribed rate, whichever is greater.

Between them, the ASE and the NYSE account for more than 90 per cent of the market value transactions on all United States exchanges. The NYSE itself accounts for about 87 per cent.

There is a heavy overlapping between the memberships of the two exchanges—roughly 85 per cent of the member firms of the ASE are also member firms of the NYSE.

Regional Stock Exchanges

There are eleven other exchanges in the United States registered with the Securities and Exchange Commission as national securities exchanges: Boston Stock Exchange, Cincinnati Stock Exchange, Detroit Stock Exchange, Pacific Coast Stock Exchange, Midwest Stock Exchange, New Orleans Stock Exchange, Philadelphia-Baltimore Stock Exchange, Pittsburgh Stock Exchange, Salt Lake Stock Exchange, San Francisco Mining Exchange, and Spokane Stock Exchange.

Four other exchanges are exempt from registration with the SEC: Colorado Springs Stock Exchange, Honolulu Stock Exchange, Richmond Stock Exchange, and the Wheeling Stock Exchange.

The Philadelphia-Baltimore Exchange, by the way, united two of the oldest exchanges in the country. The Philadelphia Exchange started in business in 1790, two years before the NYSE.

Regional exchanges for the most part were organized to trade in securities of local interest only. If the local enterprise made good on a national scale, it was expected that the company would move on to one of the big New York City markets. Functionally, that's a sound theory—but in the past 20 years or so the theory has been given a reverse twist. Local issues are still traded locally. But, more and more, volume on most of the regional exchanges includes transactions in securities listed on the NYSE and ASE.

Volume on American out-of-town exchanges is minute by New York City standards. In a recent issue the *Wall Street Journal* reported NYSE volume at 2,530,000 shares. The same issue reported Midwest volume at 131,000 shares, San Francisco volume at 51,361 shares, Los Angeles at 63,611, Detroit at 21,304, Salt Lake at 30,800, Boston at 20,666, Pittsburgh at 5,363, Cincinnati at 1,275 shares. Toronto, on the other hand, reported 4,050,000 shares.

Listing standards of the regional exchanges are prominent by their absence. New securities usually are accepted on their merits, a policy that allows for the same elasticity as using a rubber band for a ruler.

A friend of mine, a New York City broker, recently returned from a trip to a city—which shall be nameless—in which one of the smaller regional exchanges is located. He was sitting in the office of a member of the local exchange when another member of the same exchange called him and told him he had 45 shares of stock to sell—as it happened, an issue also listed on the NYSE. My friend said he was tied up at the moment but asked if it would be convenient to meet him in the exchange in half an hour. Apparently this arrangement was satisfactory. Half an hour later they met in the exchange, a room in the same building in which the two brokers had their offices.

"What's the market?" my friend asked.

The other broker said that the last transaction as reported by the New York Stock Exchange's ticker was $45 a share.

"Done," said my friend.

I feel sure this was not a typical transaction on a regional exchange, but it does illustrate two facts. Most of these exchanges base their prices on New York, and the volume of business in local securities is not heavy enough to swamp their facilities.

The Securities Exchange Act of 1934 provides that a security which is fully listed on a national securities exchange may have unlisted trading privileges, subject to SEC approval, on one or more other national exchanges.

Theoretically, therefore, any stock listed on the New York Stock Exchange could be traded on an unlisted basis on the American Stock Exchange. I have always admired the ASE for its studied aloofness—no single stock is traded on both New York exchanges. The regional exchanges have been less finicky, and, as a result, dual-traded or multiple-traded issues are common. What's more, the number is on the increase.

To the investor, does it make any difference whether the American Telephone stock he wants to buy is purchased in New York City, Chicago, or San Francisco? So far as price is concerned, probably not. The regional exchanges will base their price on that established in the New York Stock Exchange's auction market. However, the regional exchange does have one selling point. Transactions executed in New York are subject to New York State's stock transfer tax. Transactions executed in Chicago, to name one city, are not subject to such a tax.

There is one instance in which out-of-town exchanges do not follow—at least temporarily—New York City prices. The publication of news that may have an immediate effect on the price of a company's security is sometimes near the close of the New York market at 3:30 P.M. An unexpected dividend increase by U. S. Steel, though, might be reflected immediately in a higher price on the Pacific Coast Exchange, which, because of the time differential, stay open several hours later than New York. The price difference, of course, is ironed out as soon as the New York market opens the next day. Somewhat amusingly, the New York market sometimes evaluates the news quite differently than the West Coast, and the regional exchange has to move fast to catch up—or down.

The three regional exchanges with the strongest local flavor are Midwest, Salt Lake, and Pacific Coast. The Far Western exchanges, as might be expected, specialize in local mining and oil stocks. Midwest, headed by shrewd, articulate Jim Day, provides a market for regional issues and also takes no sass from the New York Stock Exchange. Midwest is out to get all the dual listings it can.

Canadian Exchanges

The Toronto Stock Exchange is one of the largest exchanges in North America and one of the most efficient and modern exchanges in the world. The *share volume* of business on Toronto frequently exceeds that on the New York Stock Exchange, and in *dollar volume* Toronto is topped only by the NYSE and ASE. The large share volume is explained by the fact that the unit of trading is larger than that of any other exchange.

The volume of shares traded on Toronto, though, can be brought down to size because of the large number of issues selling at less than $1 a share, or at $2 or $3 a share. Trading volume can pile up fast when the unit of trading is 500 shares, which is customary in stocks selling below $1 a share.

Other Canadian exchanges include the Montreal Stock Exchange, which has just arranged to merge with the Canadian Stock Exchange; the Vancouver Stock Exchange; the Calgary Stock Exchange; and the Winnipeg Stock Exchange.

On Toronto you'll find the securities of Canada's soundest corporations, as well as a rich assortment of highly speculative mining, oil and other stocks. Listing requirements on Toronto are decidedly skimpy when compared with the New York exchanges, and naturally they also handle unlisted trading in Toronto.

This is not said in righteous indignation. Canada is a nation bursting at the seams with natural resources that, in the end, may make the United States look like a country cousin. Exploiting the wealth of a nation evidently is a job for men, not boys, and needs an enthusiasm, a certain liberalism in interpreting the law, that more settled economies have outgrown. In fact, it takes considerable time for the law—and the public conscience—to catch up with the facts, which is very well illustrated by the growing pains our own country underwent in the past century.

And plainly enough drilling for oil, or sinking a shaft for gold or uranium, is an almost completely speculative operation. Look at it this way. United States oil companies are engaged in a ceaseless hunt for new sources of oil. It's axiomatic in the oil business that dry wells will outnumber productive wells by a comfortable margin. Each of those dry wells costs thousands of dollars, sometimes hundreds of thousands of dollars. The only reason the major producers can successfully risk a series of dry wells is that they have the resources to keep trying until they reach oil. If one small company runs out of capital because it sank three dry wells in a row—well, that's too bad. Another penny stock disappears from sight.

Some of the penny stocks pay off; most do not. And, in view of the paucity of factual information regarding most of these speculative issues—and I'm speaking only of honest speculations, which is not a contradiction in terms—it's difficult to make an intelligent selection. You are not only buying a pig in a poke, but you and the poke are in a coalblack room.

I have noticed, too, that many stocks traded on the Canadian exchanges sometimes display an almost extraordinary agility on the price scale. Guaranteed Uranium, Inc., for instance, may jog along sedately at around 25 cents a share for months on end. Then, all of a sudden, the price starts moving up, doubles, then triples. A rich uranium find? Possibly—but the same issue may sink back to 25 cents a share or less within a matter of days. I suppose the answer lies in speculative enthusiasm—and, again, it may not.

The Canadian exchanges, in general, function as their counterparts in the United States do, although there are some variations. The Toronto Exchange has 113 members, against the NYSE's 1,366, but a member in Toronto has the right to designate as many as five "attorneys" to execute orders for him. The limited number of actual members has had the effect of lifting the price of a membership on Toronto to a level close to that of a New York Stock Exchange membership.

In Toronto, odd lots of stocks are bought and sold by negotiations between individual brokers, rather than handled by the odd-lot dealer as on the NYSE or by the specialist as on other United States exchanges.

Round lots in Canada vary according to the class of the stock. On the New York Stock Exchange, as we know, the standard round lot is 100 shares. On Toronto a round lot in penny oil and mining stocks is 500 shares. For industrial stocks the round lot is 100 shares.

On the Vancouver Stock Exchange, mining shares under 30 cents are traded in round lots of 1,000 shares. From 30 cents to a cool $1 a share, the round lot is 500 shares; from $1 to $10, it is 100 shares; from $10 to $25, it is 25 shares. When you get to shares selling at $100 and over, the round lot is 5 shares.

CHAPTER **9**

Over-the-Counter Market:

Shop by Phone

WHATEVER YOU WANT TO CALL the over-the-counter market—
the off-board market, the unlisted market, the telephone
market—it's a strange creature. The name itself—over-the-
counter—goes back to the days when many securities were
traded over the counter, just as you'd buy a bolt of denim
or a bustle or two. Later variations on the original term were
apparently efforts at more precise terminology, which have
been none too successful.

For one thing, nobody knows how large the over-the-
counter market is—how many securities are traded over-
the-counter, the dollar or share volume of business.

A staff report to the Committee on Banking and Cur-
rency of the United States Senate—the so-called Fulbright
Committee—estimated that there are about 700,000 companies in the United States with one or more issues of stock
outstanding. The report, dated April, 1955, said that over
90 per cent of these are closely held and have no public

101

market. In at least 20,000 issues, though, the report stated that there is enough public interest to cause some trading. And for 2,500 to 3,000 unlisted stocks an active market exists. In addition, the report said, there are another 20,000 federal, state, and local issues with "at least a minimum market."

Speaking generally—very generally—the securities traded over-the-counter are those that are closely held or that have only regional interest. The exceptions to this generality are somewhat overwhelming. For instance, U. S. government bond issues are listed on the New York Stock Exchange, but the principal market for government issues—indeed, the only market worth mentioning—is over-the-counter. Trading in U. S. governments is concentrated among some half a dozen firms, known as government houses, that make the market and that deal principally with banks and institutional investors.

Dealers in governments sometimes trade in price variations of as little as $\frac{1}{64}$ of a point, which is the equivalent of about $15\frac{1}{2}$ cents per \$1,000 bond. When \$40,000,000 or \$50,000,000 face value of government bonds is involved in one transaction, though, $\frac{1}{64}$ of a point commands more respect. If by chance you get interested in U. S. government bond prices as a guide to the use of credit in the economy—some people find this a fascinating hobby—you'll notice that government prices are listed in the newspapers in a rather unusual way. The closing bid for Treasury 3's of 1995 was recently listed at 96.31, which means 96 and $\frac{31}{32}$ or, in dollars and cents, \$969.687 per \$1,000 face value bond—.9687 is the decimal equivalent of $\frac{31}{32}$. If a plus sign ($+$) were added to 96.31, it would mean an additional $\frac{1}{64}$ of a point or $96\frac{63}{64}$—in plain language, \$969.844 per \$1,000 face value bond.

The major, and often the only, market for state, county, city, town, and village bonds—as well as the increasing number of obligations issued by the so-called authorities—is also the over-the-counter market. These issues may range in size from the $1,000,000 worth of bonds sold by a village to pay for a small sewage system to $220,000,000 sold by the New Jersey Turnpike Authority to construct an express thruway.

Stocks of banks, insurance companies, and open-end investment companies are traded over-the-counter. In the case of banks and insurance companies, the reason is simply that these heavily regulated industries do not want to submit to the additional regulations that listing on an exchange calls for. Investment companies are taboo as far as the exchanges are concerned, because the amount of their outstanding shares varies from hour to hour.

Corporate bonds—industrial, rail, and utility—are frequently traded over-the-counter even though such issues are listed on an exchange. An institution, such as an endowment fund, may wish to dispose of a $100,000 block of Detroit Edison bonds. That's a fair-sized amount of money, and the institution does not want to take the chance of offering the bonds for sale on an exchange and taking the best price that may happen along. So a negotiated sale is made in the over-the-counter market.

Corporate stocks are also bought and sold in the over-the-counter market, but most such transactions are in stocks that are not listed on an exchange. This does not necessarily indicate that over-the-counter stocks have less merit than issues listed on the New York Stock Exchange; but, given my choice, I'd take an exchange-listed stock in preference to an unlisted one. There's something about a liquid market and a public price record—plus, of course, the listing standards of the Exchange and regulations of the SEC applying to listed stocks—that inspires confidence.

How do you go about buying and selling over-the-counter securities? You can deal either with a member firm of an exchange or directly with an over-the-counter firm. Let's say you select a nonmember firm and order 100 shares of ABD Corporation common stock. The firm may have an inventory of ABD Corporation common from which it will sell you 100 shares. Or, if the dealer does not have the stock, he will telephone several other firms that make a market in that issue and buy 100 shares at the best price he can get.

The over-the-counter firm will not, as a rule, function as your broker, who is an agent acting for you and charging you a specific commission for his services. The over-the-counter dealer is a principal in the transaction, and you are a principal. The price he charges you, if ABD Corporation is an actively traded stock, is fairly close to previous transactions. If ABD is an inactive issue, the price may be whatever you are willing to pay. In either case the price charged by the over-the-counter dealer will be a net price—no mention will be made of a commission, but you can be sure that the equivalent of a commission, or more, will be included in the price.

If you are selling 100 shares of ABD, the process is the same. The dealer himself may buy the stock, or he may find a buyer before he takes the stock off your hands. The price you receive will be a net one, with no apparent deduction for a commission—but the deduction has been made. The profit to the dealer, of course, is the difference between the price he pays you and the price he receives from a buyer.

There is no record of transactions in the over-the-counter market, which puts the individual investor at a strong disadvantage. The professional or institutional investor can transact business with an over-the-counter firm on some basis of equality, but the individual is more or less forced to rely on the integrity of the firm with which he is dealing. Almost all over-the-counter firms are members of the National Association of Securities Dealers, which has regulatory authority over its members. NASD has never ruled on what it considers a reasonable profit on a purchase or sale by one of its members, but is known to favor between 3 and 5 per cent. There have been some startling deviations from this policy, however.

Many newspapers publish prices for selected over-the-counter issues, but that is no guarantee that you can buy a stock at the price indicated. The prices are really bids and offers supplied by various over-the-counter firms to the National Quotation Bureau, which compiles them and distributes them to newspapers. The range between these bids and offers, as might be expected, is often substantial—$2 for a $20 issue, $4 for a $50 stock. As a matter of actual practice it is quite likely you will be able to buy an issue at or close to the published bid—but don't bank on it.

Some member firms of the New York Stock Exchange, well aware of this somewhat sticky pricing problem, execute orders in the over-the-counter market for their customers only on a commission basis. Your order to buy 100 shares of ABD will be accepted, and the member firm will go into the over-the-counter market and buy the 100 shares at the best price obtainable. The price to you will be the cost of the 100 shares plus the commission that would be charged for a similar transaction on the floor of the Exchange. Selling orders are executed on the same basis.

CHAPTER 10

The New York Stock Exchange:

$100,000,000 a Day

THERE ARE STOCK EXCHANGES all over the world, in London, Amsterdam, Frankfurt, Zurich, Paris, Rome, Bombay, Calcutta, Cairo, Johannesburg, Valparaiso, Melbourne—almost everywhere except Moscow.

The New York Stock Exchange, though, outranks them all—in the dollar volume of trading, in the stature of the companies listed, in the services it offers the public, in its importance to the economy. This is the market place you should know about, because, as an investor or a speculator, this is the market where most of your business will flow.

The Exchange is a huge room connected to the outside world by one of the most complicated communications systems in existence. The room is about five stories high. Banks of windows on the east and west walls filter in an adequate amount of light—an amount of light that is the bane of professional photographers unless they are equipped with high-speed lenses and the newest and fastest film.

106

Dotting the trading floor are a dozen horseshoe-shaped counters known as trading posts. Each is numbered, and each is rimmed at the top with the symbols and current prices of the stocks traded at that post. Inside the posts is a conglomeration of clerks, pigeonholes, pneumatic tube carriers, and specialists' books. All transactions take place outside of the posts. Each post, on the outside, is ringed with jumper seats where weary brokers can sit down and mull over the state of the market and the world.

Lining the walls of the floor are telephone booths with direct connections to the offices of member firms in New York City and elsewhere.

On the north and south walls of the trading floor there are huge identical annunciator boards—remember, these are five-story walls. Each broker on the floor is assigned a number, and when his clerk in a telephone booth wants to get hold of him, the clerk flashes his number on the board and he comes running—well, not running, because there's an Exchange rule against running on the floor, but he gets there in a hurry.

In each corner of the trading room, well above the level of the floor, is a lighted projection of the ticker tape, a moving band of stock symbols and prices that is the inexorable record of the market. On the east and west walls at the same level are projections of the bond ticker tape, which loafs along—transactions in bonds are fewer than in stocks—and frequently takes long rests while the stock tape steadily grinds out the day's business.

On the south side of the trading room, some twenty feet above the floor, is a small rostrum containing an electrically operated gong that signals the opening and closing of the market at 10:00 A.M. and 3:30 P.M.

And on the west wall is a curious clock with one hand. The lapse of time between the execution of an order and the report of the transaction on the ticker tape is normally around two minutes. Sometimes, though, the volume of business becomes so large that it is impossible to report each transaction on the tape immediately. When that happens, the tape is said to be late, and each minute of lateness is recorded on the one-handed clock. When the tape becomes as much as five minutes late, a "flash" system of reporting prices automatically goes into effect. Prices of some 30 key stocks are telephoned directly from the floor to the ticker room and are printed immediately on the tape.

You Buy a Share of Stock

Let's see what happens to your order to buy 100 shares, from the time you walk into your broker's office in Cleveland until word gets back to you that your order has been executed. You have decided to buy 100 shares of XYZ Corporation common. Before you do, though, you want to have a fairly precise knowledge of what the stock will cost you. If the stock is an active one, you can simply wait until the next sale is reported on the ticker tape. If the stock is infrequently traded, you ask your broker to get you a quotation, or "quote." He wires or telephones his New York office for the quotation. In the New York office, a quotation clerk dials a code for that stock over a direct wire to the quotation department of the New York Stock Exchange. All day long quotations are being phoned directly from the trading floor to the quotation department, so that the very latest price information is always available to you.

The quotation clerk immediately relays back to his Cleveland office the information you requested. In the securities market a quotation has a very precise meaning. It is not really a price, but the highest bid and the lowest offer present in the market—in other words, the highest price per share anybody is willing to pay for a stock and the smallest amount anybody will sell the stock for. The quotation you are given for XYZ may be 24 to $\frac{1}{4}$, which means that the highest price anyone would pay for XYZ is $24 a share and the lowest price anyone would accept is $24.25 a share. There is no guarantee that you can buy XYZ at $24.25 a share, but you will undoubtedly be able to buy it at that price or very close to it.

The quotation suits you, so you tell your broker to buy 100 shares of XYZ "at the market," an important term that means that you will pay the best price the floor broker can get for you when he executes your order.

Your order is sent to your broker's New York office over the firm's own wire network and quickly telephoned to the trading floor. A clerk in one of the telephone booths that line the walls of the floor makes a record of the order and summons the floor broker, who is a partner in the brokerage firm you are dealing with. When the broker receives the order from his clerk, he takes off for the post where buy and sell orders in XYZ converge from all parts of the country.

If the clerk knows that the floor broker is busy handling another order, he enlists the help of a $2 broker. The latter will use the same diligence in executing your order as your own floor broker would—or he won't get any more business from your brokerage firm. In any case, your order is handled with the utmost dispatch—speed can be a highly important factor in the market.

When your broker reaches the right trading post, he glances at the price indicator at the top of the post, which shows the price of the preceding transaction in XYZ. The indicator also shows whether the preceding transaction was higher or lower than, or the same as, the transaction preceding it. The indicator shows that the last transaction in XYZ took place at $24\frac{1}{8}$, or 24.12½ cents a share. Your broker mingles with the XYZ crowd, which includes every broker who has an immediate interest in buying or selling XYZ. The crowd may contain a dozen people or only one man, the specialist in XYZ.

"How's XYZ?" your broker calls out. At this point he does not disclose his identity as a buyer or a seller; he is merely looking for information.

Someone in the crowd, most likely the specialist, replies, "An eighth to three eighths." He does not bother to give the number of dollars, because that figure is shown on the price indicator. His answer, translated into English, means there is someone who is willing to pay $24.12½ cents a share for XYZ and someone who is willing to sell for $24.37½ a share.

At this point the broker who is representing you could take the easy way out and say, "Three eighths for a hundred."

He won't, though, if he's a good broker. His job is to buy 100 shares of XYZ for you at the best price possible. He knows it would be useless to bid 24⅛ because that bid has already been made and nobody was willing to sell at that price. So—for the first time disclosing that he is a buyer—he sings out, "A quarter for a hundred." He may be forced to go higher—he knows there is an offer to sell at 24⅜—but he will at least try to do better.

Now, the man who offered to sell at 24⅜ has the choice of waiting in hopes that your broker will raise his bid or deciding that someone else may come along and offer to sell at 24¼. Chances are he'll settle for 24¼, in which case he says, "Sold."

If your broker had been offering to sell XYZ at 24¼ a share, another broker would have made the purchase merely by saying, "Take it."

Your broker and the broker representing the seller of 100 shares of XYZ have completed a transaction. Neither one summons his lawyer to draw up a contract complete with penalty clauses, cancellations, and writs of attainder. The two brokers have agreed on the amount, price, and stock. Whether the transaction involves 100 shares or 10,000, that's all there is to it. And, in the long history of the Exchange, no broker has gone back on his word. Each broker merely jots down on a slip of paper the number on the badge worn by the other, the number of shares, the price, and the stock.

The selling broker gives the details of the transaction to an Exchange employee, who transmits the information on a slip of paper via pneumatic tube to the ticker room. A couple of minutes later, while you are sitting in your broker's office in Cleveland, the report of your purchase will appear on the ticker tape, like this: $^{XYZ}24\frac{1}{4}$. The price is reported on transactions of 100 shares. If you had bought 200 shares, the transaction would be reported like this: $^{XYZ}2s\ 24\frac{1}{4}$. And if you had bought 1,000 shares, the purchase would be reported like this: $^{XYZ}1000s\ 24\frac{1}{4}$.

When trading volume starts to tax the capacity of the ticker system, the first one or two digits of the price may be omitted, so that your 100-share purchase of XYZ would come out like this: $^{XYZ}41\frac{1}{4}$. And, as I mentioned, if the volume of business really piles up, the Stock Exchange resorts to its system of "flash" prices. (See appendix A for the ticker symbols of 200 of the most active issues traded on the NYSE.)

Probably most orders that reach the trading floor of the New York Stock Exchange are market orders—orders to get the best price possible, whether you're buying or selling, when your order reaches the floor. But there are other kinds of orders that you can use to your own advantage—only just be a little careful how you use them.

Do you recall that when your broker got a quotation on XYZ it ranged from 24 to $24\frac{1}{4}$? You might figure that XYZ is a good buy, but only at a lower price. So you place a *limit* order with your broker at 22, which means that your broker will buy XYZ for you only at that price or a lower one. Your order may be good for a day, a week, a month, or until canceled. The last is known more familiarly as a GTC (good till canceled) order, and, as a matter of practice, your broker will ask you to confirm a GTC order every three months if it has not been executed in the meantime.

XYZ, of course, may never decline to 22, and as a result you may miss out on a good investment. People who have placed limit orders just below the market are inclined to start conversations with, "If only I had . . ."

The same reasoning would apply if you had bought XYZ at, say, 15 and watched it climb to around 24. You decide the stock is good for a few more points and place a limit order to sell at 27. XYZ may reach 27, and your order will be executed; on the other hand, the price may never get that high.

A type of order sometimes used in an effort to protect or limit a loss is the *stop-loss* or *stop* order. Let's say you bought XYZ at 20, watched it go to 25—and then you took off on a fishing trip. While you're away you want to make sure that if the market should decline, you will be able to keep at least part of your profit, so you enter an order to sell at "23 stop." This does not mean that your stock will be sold at 23 if the market declines. It does mean that if the price drops to 23 or below, your stop order automatically becomes a market order and is executed at the best price obtainable.

Bidding for stock and offering stock for sale are carried out on the floor of the Stock Exchange with the precision of a ballet, and frequently the steps are just as complicated. But basically, the highest bid to buy and the lowest offer to sell take precedence over all other bids and offers.

Frequently, though, there are a number of bids in the market at the same price, but there is not enough stock offered for sale at that price to satisfy all bids. In such a case, bids that have clearly established time priority take precedence over all others. You may have entered your order to sell 100 shares of XYZ at 20 stop. Sure enough, while you are in your broker's office watching the translux—a device that projects the ticker tape as a moving band of light with symbols and prices in black—you see ^{XYZ}20.

"Fine," you think. "Joe's sold my stock for me at 20."

A little later, though, you discover that Joe has done no such thing. And, when you question him, Joe tells you there was *stock ahead*. One or more other people had the same bright idea of selling XYZ at 20—but their orders reached the trading floor before yours.

Or you might give Joe a market order to sell 100 shares of XYZ. Ten minutes later you see a sale of 100 shares of XYZ reported on the ticker tape. "That's me," you figure. But Joe has another answer.

Your broker on the floor has reported back to Joe, as he is required to in such cases, and Joe tells you that the floor broker has "matched and lost." This is what happened. Your floor broker and another floor broker with an order to sell 100 shares of XYZ at the market reached the trading post at the same time and made their offers to sell simultaneously. But there was only one bid to buy 100 shares of XYZ. So, in the interests of fairness, the two selling brokers flipped a coin to decide who would make the sale. Your broker lost. You'll never know, incidentally, when your broker wins the toss, because in that case he is not required to report back to the customer.

If and when you're in the market for preferred stocks, your order will be handled somewhat differently from a round lot order for a common stock. Right next to the main trading floor of the Exchange is another trading room of much smaller dimensions, which is known, with some lack of reverence, as "the garage." The garage contains 6 additional trading posts—there are a total of 18 posts—plus post 30, which occupies a special place in the intricacies of the Stock Exchange. Post 30 is also called the inactive post, and the unit of trading there is ten shares. A handful of preferred issues are traded in ten-share units at the other posts, but the great majority, along with some high-priced commons, are bought and sold at post 30.

Post 30 is manned by two firms of specialists. Some trading is conducted along the same lines as in the auction market at posts 1 to 18. Most trading, however, is done through filing cabinets. In these filing cabinets are stacks of cards which indicate whether the order is a buy or sell, the name of the broker offering or bidding for the stock, the name of the stock, the number of shares, and the price. Usually these cards represent GTC orders. When your order to buy ten shares of XYZ 5 per cent preferred reaches post 30, it may be filled out of the cabinet, it may become another order in the cabinet, or it may be filled by one of the specialists at the post.

Your broker, of course, will be delighted to explain to you in great detail the various types of orders and how you can best use them to your own advantage. There's another service offered by your broker which is not very well known, but which you may want to know about the next time you take a trip to Florida, California, or, if you're lucky, Paris or Rio. You may be a customer of Jones & Company and find yourself in a town or city where Jones & Company does not have an office. You have an immediate urge to sell 100 shares of XYZ, but the only member firm of the Exchange in that town is Brown & Brown. You could make a long-distance call to Jones & Company, but why not do it the easy way and save yourself money too? Stop in at Brown & Brown, tell them you have an account with Jones & Company and want to sell 100 shares of XYZ. They'll verify the fact that you have an account, and either execute the order for you themselves or wire it to your own broker. In either case, the only charge is the usual commission.

In the illustrations we've given of a purchase and a sale on the floor of the exchange, it has been assumed that when you wanted to buy, another broker was on hand who was willing to sell at a price acceptable to you. Or, if you wanted to sell, a broker was ready to buy your stock on behalf of another individual. But what happens if your broker arrives at the trading post where XYZ is bought and sold and no other broker shows up?

Your broker is still able to buy or sell XYZ for you, but to do so he deals with a unique kind of broker known as the specialist.

CHAPTER 11

The Specialist:

Maker of Markets

THERE IS PROBABLY no other individual in the securities business—except your own broker—who can do more than the specialist to get you the best price possible, whether you are buying stock or selling it.

I don't know of any case in which a specialist has actually gone broke in the course of his work, but sometimes they seem bent on doing just that.

The specialist is never a direct representative of the public, but he continually serves the best interests of the investing public. To say that he is a key figure in the smooth functioning of the Stock Exchange's market place is a mild understatement.

Legend has it that, toward the end of the last century, a member of the Exchange broke his leg. When he came back to the floor, still only semimobile, he stayed close to the post where Western Union was traded. Western Union was a highly popular issue at the time, and our apocryphal invalid did a thriving business, often executing orders for other brokers who were too busy to stay around the Western Union post. The specialist did not really come into his own, though, until World War I.

The specialist functions in two capacities. He may act as a dealer on the floor, buying and selling stocks for his own account; or he may act as a broker, executing orders on behalf of other brokers. He cannot act both as a dealer (a principal) and a broker (an agent) in the same transaction because of the obvious conflict of interests.

The specialist gets his name from the fact that he takes a particular interest in a small group of stocks, 1 or 2 to as many as 25 or 30. These stocks are always traded at one post, and the specialist stays right at that post. In a few of the most active issues, two or more specialists may compete with each other.

About 350 men out of the Exchange's membership of 1,366 are authorized by the Exchange to act as specialists after they have qualified as regular brokers. They are subject to higher capital requirements than other members, because of the large amounts of their own money they often must use to maintain a market, and their operations are kept under the Exchange's microscope and the SEC's too. There is a story to the effect that a specialist must have a high-speed computing machine in one part of his brain, but there's probably nothing to it.

First, let's look at the specialist as a broker's broker. You recall that you can direct your own broker to buy or sell for you at a limit price—that is, a specific price up or down from the market price at the time you place the order. For instance, you want to buy 100 shares of XYZ at a limit of 22— that is, you'll pay 22 a share or less, but not a cent more. The order goes to the trading floor, where your firm's broker takes it to the proper trading post. He discovers that the market in XYZ is currently about 24. He's too busy a man to stay at the post indefinitely waiting for XYZ to decline to 22—and, besides, it may never decline to 22.

Your order is turned over to the specialist, who enters it in his book—he writes down the price you will pay and the amount of stock you want to buy. If there are other limit orders already in his book at the same price, they will take precedence over yours. When and if the price of XYZ declines to 22 or lower, your bid to buy will become a market order. It's possible that other buyers may be ahead of you at a price of 22; actually, the market price may decline to 22 and then start moving ahead without your order ever being executed. If the price declines below 22, though, you can be pretty sure you will get your stock at a better price than you specified in your limit order.

Your broker on the floor will also turn over to the specialist your stop-loss order to sell XYZ at 22. You bought XYZ at 15, and you're simply trying to protect your profit. XYZ is selling at around 24 when your floor broker gets to the trading post, while your price is 22. The specialist enters it in his book. When and if the price declines to 22 or below, your order becomes a market order, which the specialist will execute at the best price available.

Stop-loss orders can be tricky—a great many investors who enter stop-loss orders have the mistaken idea that the price they specify is the price they will pay or receive. Not so—a fast-moving market may by-pass a stop-loss order before you know what's happened. For instance, XYZ closes at 24 on Monday. After the market closes Monday, highly unfavorable news about XYZ appears in the press. On Tuesday morning there is a glut of selling orders, with few buyers except at sharply lower prices. XYZ conceivably could open on Tuesday morning at 18, with nary a transaction taking place between 24 and 18. The investor who put in a stop-loss order at 22 is simply out of luck. Why? Because your broker must execute your stop-loss order at the first bid or offer below or above the price designated by you.

For his services to other brokers—and, of course, indirectly to you as an investor—the specialist is paid part of the regular commission that you pay. This commission is the same as a busy broker pays a $2 broker for his services.

The following is the amount paid to specialists and $2 brokers—and this does not represent an extra charge to you —on stocks selling at $1 or more per share:

Price of stock per share	Rate per 100 shares
$1 and above but under $5	$1.25
$5 and above but under $10	1.75
$10 and above but under $20	2.75
$20 and above but under $40	3.25
$40 and above but under $100	3.50
$100 and above	4.00

Market orders also are often turned over to the specialist, but only at the opening of the market when the floor broker has more than he can take care of.

Another function of the specialist is to stop stock, which is in effect a guarantee by the specialist that he will sell your broker a specific number of shares at a specific price.

Here's how stopping stock works. Your broker comes to the post with an order to buy 100 shares of XYZ at the market. The best offer to sell when he arrives is 24. Your broker, though, wants to get a better price for you if he can, maybe 23⅞ a share. At the same time, he does not want to take the chance of missing the market and being forced to pay a higher price. He asks the specialist to stop 100 shares for him at 24—hoping that, in the meantime, someone will come along and offer the stock at 23⅞ or less. If that does happen, your broker notifies the specialist that the stop is off. On the other hand, if the next transaction takes place at 24, the specialist sells you 100 shares from his book at 24.

Based on the importance of the information that it contains, you would expect the specialist's book to be built along the lines of the Domesday Book. Actually it is a slim, hard-covered, ring-binder volume measuring about 4 by 11 inches. Bids to buy are entered on the left-hand side, offers to sell on the right-hand side. Price and number of shares for each order are entered, the name of the broker placing the order, and the time limit. And nobody may inspect a specialist's book other than some authorized person, such as a governor of the Exchange.

The function of the specialist, as a broker's broker, while certainly important, is really mechanical in nature. He executes orders to buy or sell for other brokers under carefully specified conditions. But as a dealer, the specialist is required to exercise the highest skill and good judgment.

In the language of the Exchange, the specialist is required to maintain orderly markets, insofar as reasonably practicable, in the stocks in which he specializes. But exactly what is an "orderly market," and what does "insofar as reasonably practicable" mean? Whatever they mean, the specialist's judgment had better coincide pretty closely with the Exchange's interpretation or he won't be a specialist for long.

Going back to XYZ Corporation, you have just entered an order to buy 100 shares at the market. Your broker on the floor dutifully goes out to the trading post. However, at the moment, there are no other brokers interested in XYZ. But the specialist is—he's got to be. If the previous transaction in XYZ had been at 24 a share, your broker might make a bid at the same price. More likely he would bid 24⅛, and the specialist would probably offer to sell the stock at the same price, so the transaction would be consummated. If the stock were comparatively inactive, the specialist might not be willing to sell for less than 24¼; price changes between successive transactions are usually larger for inactive than active stocks.

Usually the specialist has an inventory of at least some of the stocks in which he specializes. In other words, he can sell you 100 shares of XYZ because he owns that much or more. His decision to sell—and this is an important point— is not based on whether or not he can make a profit by the sale. That is a subsidiary consideration. His responsibility is to supply the market with stock in order to "maintain an orderly market insofar as reasonably practicable."

It is axiomatic in any market that anything can be bought at a price. Your broker had instructions to buy 100 shares of XYZ at the market, knowing that the last transaction was at 24. If he raised his bid to, say, 30, it's a safe bet that word would have gotten around in a hurry that somebody was willing to pay that much for XYZ, and your broker could have bought 100 shares for you with celerity. A transaction at that price, however, could not occur in an orderly market—with a major exception which we'll come to—and your broker could reasonably be committed for observation for making such a bid.

When your broker bid 24⅛ or 24¼ for XYZ, it's just possible the specialist did not own any XYZ. He would still supply stock to the market by the simple expedient of going short the stock. That is, he would borrow 100 shares of XYZ from another broker—stock is frequently borrowed in the market in order to make a short sale—and sell those 100 shares to your broker. Eventually, of course, the specialist would have to buy the 100 shares to repay the loan, but in the meantime you were able to buy XYZ at a reasonable price.

The specialist not only sells stock to prevent wide fluctuations between successive transactions but he also buys for the same reason—whether he wants to or not, whether or not it is against his best business judgment to do so.

This is not, let me assure you, pure altruism on the part of the specialist. The specialist occupies an unusual and normally lucrative position in the securities business. And in return for the privilege of occupying that position he is required by the rules of the Stock Exchange to contribute to the smooth functioning of the market. The Exchange may not put this statement in so many words, but the net result is the same.

Getting back to XYZ, you may have 100 shares to sell—or 500 or 1,000—at the market. The preceding transaction was at 24 a share. When your broker reaches the trading post, he finds that no one is there with a bid to buy. Undoubtedly you could sell your stock if your broker were willing to take what he could get—20, 18, or 15. You can always find a buyer—at a price. However, the specialist will step in with an offer to buy at $23\frac{7}{8}$ or $23\frac{3}{4}$ a share—even if he is convinced that XYZ is overpriced at 20.

There is no other time than at the opening of the market, perhaps, that the specialist must walk the tightrope—"plank" might be a better word. This is when he is called upon to exercise the finest pricing judgment.

At the opening, there is an accumulation of so-called overnight orders, orders that have originated after the close of trading the previous day and before ten o'clock in the morning. The specialist has the delicate job of balancing market orders, limit orders, and stop orders, so that the price is the best possible expression of real supply and demand.

"Real" is the key word in that sentence, and I must admit it's not a very good one. Directors of a major corporation may announce a completely unexpected and large increase in the dividend rate after the close of the market. Almost invariably such an action would touch off a rash of orders to buy, which would hit the market at the opening the following day.

The specialist realizes, however, that this sudden demand for the stock is a little lopsided—lots of people, dividend increase or none, would probably be glad to sell the stock at a one-point advance over the previous close. So he tries to stimulate selling orders, through his own firm and through other brokers.

Sometimes supply and demand for a particular stock are so completely out of line at the opening of the market that the opening is delayed. This is serious business. The specialist calls for the assistance of a governor of the Exchange or a floor official, and between them they hammer out a price that seems to be the fairest possible. The opening may be delayed a few minutes, half an hour, or even hours. In the light of later events, the opening price may turn out to have been way off base. But nine times out of ten or oftener, the price is a good one, which means that subsequent transactions are close to the opening price. In opening the stock, of course, the specialist may feel obliged to buy or sell for his own account—not because he wants to, but because he has the responsibility of maintaining an orderly market.

One of the most quietly dramatic markets in the history of the New York Stock Exchange occurred one Monday, September 26, 1955. On that day, according to G. Keith Funston, President of the Exchange, the Exchange successfully met one of the most severe challenges faced in more than a quarter of a century. It was the Eisenhower "heart" market. On the Saturday preceding September 26, news of the President's heart attack had been announced.

Prior to that the market had been rising steadily to a record high as measured by the market averages. The Eisenhower administration had shown that it was kindly disposed toward business interests—the government, in fact, had been

called a businessman's administration. Then, without warning, the public was faced with the possibility that the President's strong and popular guidance might be lost.

The reaction of the investing public was swift and decisive.
Selling orders poured into the Exchange from all over the
country. Not big orders—larger investors, individual and institutional, are too smart to panic under such circumstances
—but small orders of 100, 200, a few as large as 1,000 shares,
flooded into the Exchange. Most orders were to sell at the
market; the seller was willing to take what he could get.

Orders to buy at the market were conspicuously scarce. To
make matters worse, many buyers who had limit orders to
buy under the previous close withdrew their bids.

I stopped by the Stock Exchange that morning and
watched the floor from the visitor's gallery. It was a deceptive sight. Small groups of men quietly discussed the fairest
opening price for GM, or Steel, or New York Central—none
of the usual torrent of sound that wells up from the floor
and hits the casual visitor. No trace of the frantic shouts
that might have been expected from a market place under
tremendous stress. It was almost somber while the Exchange's most responsible members slowly and deliberately
tried their best to fairly gauge the going value of billions of
dollars' worth of securities.

The volume of trading in round lots that day amounted
to nearly 8,000,000 shares, largest in more than 22 years.
Measured by the Dow Jones average of 30 industrial stocks,
the most popular of all market averages, the market's decline
was the largest since fabulous 1929. Individual declines at
the close of the day ranged from a few cents to a maximum of
$33.25 for one high-priced issue.

For half of the 20 most active issues that day, the volume
of shares in the opening transaction alone was triple or more
the average daily volume in the preceding month.

According to veteran brokers, never before had the openings of so many issues been delayed. There were 1,541 issues listed on the Exchange that day. By eleven o'cock in the morning only 534 had opened. By noon another 283 issues had opened. At three o'clock the total was 1,093, and at the close of the market it was 1,247. Some stocks, of course, do not open on a particular day because no transactions take place in them.

How did the specialists do in the face of this barrage of selling? Pretty handsomely, I should say. They tossed into

TABLE 13

TWENTY MOST ACTIVE STOCKS, SEPTEMBER 26, 1955

	Volume				Opening	Day's
Issue	Opening Trans-action	Total For Day	Daily Avg. Aug. '55	Prev. Close	Net Change	Net Change
U. S. Steel	75,000	202,500	22,887	62⅛	− 7⅛	− 5⅛
Chrysler	70,000	168,300	16,030	99⅜	− 5⅜	− 8¼
Sperry Rand	41,000	128,100	24,773	24¼	− 2¾	− 2
Genl. Motors	55,000	110,800	12,100	143⅞	− 3⅞	− 8⅞
N. Y. Central	30,000	92,900	11,309	48¼	− 4¾	− 4
Penna. R.R.	25,000	88,700	11,674	27¾	− 2¾	− 2¾
Radio Corp.	20,000	78,200	6,296	50¾	− 5¼	− 5
Republic Steel	25,000	74,500	7,983	53⅞	− 4⅞	− 5½
Anaconda	27,000	74,000	13,035	75⅜	− 6⅜	− 8¼
American Air Lines ..	35,000	73,400	10,643	24¾	− 3¼	− 2
Kaiser Alum.	25,000	70,100	5,835	39⅝	− 5⅜	− 4
Alleghany Corp.	25,200	65,900	7,139	9⅝	− 1⅝	− 1⅛
Genl. Electric	25,000	65,600	11,048	51⅞	− 3⅞	− 3¼
Intl. Tel. & Tel.	25,000	58,400	5,626	29⅝	− 2¾	− 2¾
Phillips Petr.	20,000	58,000	8,487	79⅜	− 7⅞	− 5⅜
Royal Dutch Petr.	14,000	57,600	7,587	86	−10	− 6⅝
Bethlehem Steel	25,000	55,600	4,861	164	− 8¼	−14
Colorado Fuel	20,000	53,700	12,939	32⅛	− 3⅝	− 3⅞
Standard Oil (N. J.)..	15,000	52,900	7,496	139⅛	−10⅛	− 8⅝
Avco Mfg.	24,000	52,100	8,413	6⅜	− ⅜	− ⅛

(Excludes General Motors "when issued," first traded 9/26/55.)

the market at the openings of all issues just short of $50,000,-
000. They finished the day owning about $25,000,000 more
stock than they owned at the opening. In retrospect, these
purchases by the specialists have the air of insured investments. But when they were committing fortunes to buying
stock on September 26, 1955, they could not conceivably have
known the future course of the market. They bought—and
hoped for the best. In the process, the investor was given
price protection.

The New York Stock Exchange made a detailed study of
the market that day—actually, an unprecedented study.
Table 13 shows the 20 stocks most actively traded that day.
Table 14 shows the position of all specialists throughout September 26. Table 15 shows the composition of the market
on September 26 as compared with the average of the market
on June 8 and June 15, 1955, two normal days for which
the Exchange analyzed in detail each transaction that took
place.

TABLE 14

POSITION OF ALL SPECIALISTS, SEPTEMBER 26, 1955

	Shares	Estimated Value
Long position before opening [1]	1,750,935	$54,100,000
Short position before opening [1]	99,961	4,200,000
Net long position before opening [1]	1,650,974	49,900,000
Value of position at opening prices 9/26/55		46,400,000
Dollar decline from previous close		3,500,000
Purchases at the opening [2]	1,099,350	49,100,000
Sales at the opening [2]	68,020	2,100,000
On-balance purchases at opening [2]	1,031,330	47,000,000
Total purchases	1,759,360	80,100,000
Total sales	1,163,810	52,500,000
On-balance purchases	595,550	27,600,000
Net position at close	2,246,524	$73,400,000

[1] Based on previous (Friday) closing prices.
[2] Necessarily assuming that all openings occurred simultaneously.

TABLE 15

COMPOSITION OF THE MARKET, SEPTEMBER 26, 1955

Purchases and Sales
(Round lots only)

Source of Business	Shares	Per cent of Volume 9/26/55	6/8 and 6/15/55 PTS
NYSE members:			
Floor trading, own account	322,680	2.1	3.3
Other members, firms' own account[1]	763,149	4.9	5.2
As specialists	2,923,170	18.8	11.8
As odd-lot dealers	356,670	2.3	2.8
Institutions & intermediaries [2]	1,226,000[3]	7.9	15.8
Nonmember broker/dealers	590,000	3.8	3.8
Foreign [4]	574,000	3.7	(3.7)[5]
Total public individuals	8,766,451[3]	56.5	57.3
Total purchases and sales	15,522,120	100.0	100.0
Total round-lot volume (one side).	7,761,060[6]		6,271,000

[1] Originating off the floor.
[2] Excluding nonmember broker/dealers.
[3] Estimated.
[4] Institutions and individuals.
[5] 1.8 per cent foreign institutions, 0.9 foreign individuals, and 1.0 foreign nonmember broker/dealers.
[6] Includes transactions previously unreported; approximate reported volume was 7,720,000 shares.

Lest the specialist be depicted as an unusually pure strain of angel, there are a few things that can be said against him. There is no question that, through the information he carries in his book, he has a more intimate knowledge of the market than you, the casual investor. And it may be claimed with some logic that when the specialists supported the market on September 26, 1955, they did so with the conviction that the public was going hog wild and that prices would eventually recover. Their purchases at lower prices, in other words, were considered by them to be no more than sound investments.

As it turned out, September 26 was a profitable day for the great majority of specialists. But, as a well-known advertisement currently points out, hindsight gives us perfect vision. Most of us are not used to staking $500,000 or $1,-000,000 or more on the course of the market—and, if I were able to, I'd like to have more substantial information than a panicky public's state of mind.

I rode down the elevator at 11 Wall Street that day with a couple of members of the Exchange.

"How did you make out today?" one asked the other.

"Pretty good, I thought. Figured I came out just about even."

"Well, what's wrong with that?"

"Nothing, nothing at all. Turns out, though, that I ended up 3,000 shares long."

It was a rough day.

CHAPTER 12

How to Buy and Sell a Few Shares:

Odd Lots

A GREAT MANY PEOPLE believe that going into a broker's office with less than $5,000 or $10,000 is like going into Tiffany's to buy a cheap alarm clock. That just isn't so.

There are some brokerage firms, of course, that specialize in underwritings or estate management and are not geared to handle small orders. In fact, they do a commission business only as a favor to important customers.

But there are other firms, and a great many of them, that take an active interest in handling the accounts of the so-called small investors. Frequently their operations are highly mechanized, and from an operational viewpoint it does not make any difference to them whether they buy or sell ten shares or ten hundred.

So if you have only a few hundred dollars to invest, don't be dissuaded by any preconceived ideas. The broker may not break open a bottle of champagne at the mere sight of your smiling face coming through the door, but he will give you the courteous consideration to which any customer is entitled.

Any order for 1 through 99 shares is called an odd lot. A round lot is 100 shares or multiples of 100. There's one exception to this rule. Several hundred stocks traded on the Exchange are relatively inactive—they are mostly preferred issues—so the Exchange has designated 10 shares as the unit of trading. In these stocks, an odd lot is 1 through 9 shares.

The method of handling odd lots is wholly different from the way in which round-lot orders are executed. At the same time, the two methods are closely linked. If you want to buy or sell 17 or 34 or 97 shares, why not do it without concerning yourself with something with the improbable name of an odd lot?

The answer goes back almost a hundred years. When the call market was in operation, the president of the Exchange would announce the name of the stock for sale and the number of shares available—79 shares of Erie, perhaps, or 118 shares of Great Northern. When the continuous auction market went into effect, around 1870, bids and offers were still made in any number of shares. Then as the volume of trading increased, and following the introduction of the ticker tape, it became obvious that it would be much more convenient if trading were conducted in a standard multiple; the 100-share unit of stock appeared to be the most satisfactory, and it still is.

For a while the odd lot disappeared from the floor of the Exchange. If a broker had an order to buy or sell less than 100 shares of stock, it was largely a matter of negotiation with another broker; the odd-lot market was, in effect, an over-the-counter market. The next step happened when a few members of the Exchange set themselves up on the floor as odd-lot dealers, but it was still a negotiated market; the odd-lot dealer would try to sell at the highest price he could get and buy at the lowest. This turned out to be a rather cumbersome way of doing business, so another refinement was introduced. The odd-lot dealers eventually decided to buy or sell stock at the current bid and offer for round lots. If the bid was $20 a share, an order to sell was executed at $20; if the offer was $21, an order to buy was executed at $21.

Today's system represents one more refinement, because the price is directly tied to the price in the auction market for round lots. Buying or selling odd lots now is one of the most complicated operations in the securities business—and it is carried out as smoothly as whipping cream.

When you decide to buy 25 shares of U. S. Steel common at the market, here is what happens: Your broker wires your order to New York, where it is immediately relayed to the floor of the Exchange. The floor clerk of your broker's firm writes out the order on a special form for odd lots and transmits it by pneumatic tube to the post where U. S. Steel is traded.

At that post there are at least four odd-lot brokers who are members of the Exchange but work exclusively for the odd-lot firms. Your order is directed to the representative of one of the two odd-lot firms which do more than 99 per cent of all odd-lot business on the Exchange. One is De Coppet & Doremus, the other is Carlisle & Jacquelin.

The odd-lot brokers on the floor are known technically as associate brokers, but they are really dealers, not brokers. A broker in a transaction is your agent; a dealer sells to you something he owns, or buys from you for his own account. However the odd-lot firms themselves use the term odd-lot broker, so we'll go along with them.

Your order is time-stamped and picked up immediately by an odd-lot broker at the U. S. Steel post. The odd-lot broker is, literally, in a somewhat odd position, because he can't refuse to buy the stock you want to sell or refuse to sell the stock you want to buy. Think of that in terms of the 1,100 or so common stocks traded on the Exchange, and you'll see the magnitude of the problem. Of necessity, the odd-lot firms must maintain an inventory of thousands and thousands of shares in order to be able to satisfy the needs of the public.

At one time the market value of the inventories of the two odd-lot firms ran well into the millions. The inventory of one firm in a popular stock like U. S. Steel alone amounted to as much as 5,000 shares or even more. Today it appears to be the policy of the two firms to trim their inventories to a bare minimum. The number of shares of one stock kept on hand by one odd-lot broker might amount to less than 100 shares, of another stock perhaps a maximum of 500 shares.

When your odd-lot order to buy reaches the floor, the odd-lot broker has several choices. If he owns enough U. S. Steel stock—and, in the case of a well-traded stock like Steel, he probably does—he sells your own broker the number of shares you want. If he does not own enough Steel stock, he can go into the auction market and buy, for his own account, 100 shares of Steel, out of which he will fill your order. Or he may sell Steel short to provide the stock you need, borrowing the shares from another broker to make delivery. Eventually, he must cover his short sale—unless, in the meantime, he has bought enough odd lots of U. S. Steel stock from the public.

So each odd-lot broker on the floor has three jobs. First, to execute the orders he receives from commission brokers; second, to buy or sell round lots in the auction market; third, to maintain the size of the inventories he carries in various stocks in line with the policy laid down by the firm that employs him.

Now, who decides the price you pay for your odd lot? It's a matter of a good deal of pride with the odd-lot firms that the odd-lot price is determined normally by the next price in the round-lot auction market. They claim, with a good deal of justification, that the person buying or selling as few as 5 or 10 shares of stock participates in the benefits of the auction market. Your own order to buy 25 shares of U. S. Steel, in effect, is subject to the same market factors—at the time your order is executed—as an order to buy 1,000 shares of Steel. If you were selling 25 shares of Steel, the price you received would reflect the same factors affecting the sale of 1,000 shares of Steel.

The moment the odd-lot broker on the floor receives your order, he steps to the position at the trading post where that particular stock is traded. The next transaction in the round-lot market, called the effective sale, puts your order into effect. The price of execution—the price you pay or receive—is the price of the effective sale plus or minus the so-called differential charged by the odd-lot firm.

Odd-lot brokers, by the way, like to point out that the investor who is buying or selling odd lots never is told that his order was not executed because there was stock ahead. Ten other odd-lot orders to buy U. S. Steel might have reached the trading post at precisely the same time as yours, and all of them would be executed at the same time and same price as yours.

Let's say your order to buy 25 shares of U. S. Steel reaches the post at 2:30 P.M. Five minutes later the odd-lot broker watches 200 shares of Steel change hands at $60 a share. He immediately executes your order at $60.25 a share, time-stamps his report of the transaction, and sends it back by pneumatic tube to your own broker's telephone clerk, who in turn gives the details to his office. The 25 cents a share that the odd-lot firm adds to the market price is his charge for handling your order—and, in view of the services he performs, it seems a fairly reasonable one.

If the price of the stock you bought amounted to less than $40 a share, his charge would be even less—only 12½ cents a share.

If you had sold 25 shares of U. S. Steel, you would have received $59.75 cents a share—that is, the market price minus the odd-lot differential of 25 cents a share. If you had sold 25 shares at $20 a share, you would receive $19.87½ cents a share—that is, the market price minus the odd-lot differential of 12½ cents a share on stock selling at less than $40 a share.

When your broker sends you your statement, it will show only the price of execution, which is the actual price you received or paid after deduction or addition of the odd-lot differential.

The question is frequently raised as to why the odd-lot firms don't eliminate their brokers on the floor and simply execute odd-lot orders on the basis of prices reported on the ticker tape. The answer goes back to the claim of these firms that each odd-lot order is tied directly to the *next* round-lot order following receipt of the odd-lot order. There is a normal lag of one to four minutes between the actual execution of a round-lot order and the appearance on the ticker tape of the details of the transaction; it's a fairly safe statement that more than half of all orders appear on the tape within two minutes of their execution. Still, there is a lag; and, if the tape should be running well behind floor transactions, the lag might be considerable.

During this lag the price of a security may change, so the customer has the protection of having the price of his order geared directly to an actual round-lot transaction. Arguments over the price of execution of an odd-lot order do arise, so the odd-lot firms have meticulous time controls along every step in the complicated route of executing an odd-lot order. As a matter of fact, other member firms of the Exchange frequently consult the odd-lot firms to determine the timing of an order with as much precision as possible—round lots as well as odd lot.

While most odd-lot orders are based on round-lot transactions, there are exceptions. You may want to buy or sell a few shares of a relatively inactive stock, and you don't want to wait hours, or even days, before another round-lot transaction takes place. So you tell your broker to sell on the bid—or to buy on the offer. The current bid and offer on XYZ may be 20–20½, which means the highest bid to buy is $20 a share and the lowest to sell is $20.50 a share. Your order to buy on the offer would be executed at $20.62½ a share, or the offering price of $20.50 plus the odd-lot differential of 12½ cents a share. The selling price to you would be $19.87½, or the bid of $20 a share minus the odd-lot differential of 12½ cents.

Or, again in the case of an inactive stock, you might instruct your broker to execute your order in the basis market. At the end of the trading day, the two odd-lot firms get together and establish basis prices for all stocks customarily traded in round lots of 100 shares (the basis market is not used for stocks in which the round lot is 10 shares). Their list includes only those issues not traded during the day for which the bid and offer are two points or more apart. ABC Corporation common did not sell all day, and the bid and offer at the close was 90–94. So the two odd-lot firms decide on a basis price of, say, 92. All market orders to buy will then be executed at $92.25 a share and orders to sell at $91.75 a share.

The odd-lot investor has the choice of using the same types of orders that are available to the round-lot trader. He may designate his order as a day order, a GTC (good till canceled) order, a limit order, a stop order, or a short sale. In addition, he can use a stop-limited order, an order to be executed at the opening, an order to be executed at the close, an order with or without sale, an immediate or cancel order, or a scale order. Those terms are a little fancy for the average investor, but your broker can give you the details.

You may run into the not unpleasant problem of selling the 160 shares of General Motors Corporation common stock left to you by a deceased and properly lamented maiden aunt. There's just one way of selling the 160 shares if you want to dispose of them all at once. You sell 100 shares as a round lot and 60 shares as an odd lot. Of course there is nothing to prevent you from selling 10 shares a day for 16 trading days if you want to—although, on the other hand, I can't think of any good reason you might want to.

An analysis of odd-lot transactions produces some intriguing facts, facts that are especially interesting if you have the notion that the small investor is a pariah in the market. During 1956 there were some 4,100,000 separate odd-lot transactions on the Stock Exchange, as compared with a total of 4,200,000 in 1955.

Because of the smaller number of shares involved in an odd-lot transaction, the share volume of odd-lot transactions in relation to round-lot share volume is much less.

The number of shares the public bought and sold in odd lots amounted to 117,600,000 in 1956, compared with 122,-800,000 in 1955, 105,566,946 in 1954, and 72,733,728 in 1953.

The average amount of money involved in each odd-lot transaction in 1955 and 1956 was $1450, and the average number of shares bought or sold was 28. In 1954, the figures were $1,325 and 29 shares; and in 1953, $1,176 and 28 shares.

From a price viewpoint, odd-lot traders seem to set their sights a little higher than their round-lot brothers. During 1955 and 1956 the average price per share on all odd-lot trades was $52. In 1954 the figure was $44.23 per share for odd lots, while in 1953 it was $41.24.

Another oddity of the odd-lot business is that the number of shares bought and sold in odd lots on any day is not included in the "reported" volume of business for that day. This does not constitute flagrant discrimination against the odd-lot broker or investor but results from a combination of tradition and the mechanical functioning of the market. Volume on the Exchange is always reported as a total of the number of shares bought—or sold—in round lots. Smith sells 100 shares, which are bought by Jones; the reported volume is 100 shares.

In the odd-lot market, though, each purchase and each sale are really separate transactions. Smith sells 19 shares to the odd-lot broker; that's one transaction. Jones buys 25 shares from the odd-lot broker; that's another transaction.

Each day the two principal odd-lot firms report their volume of business to the Exchange, which makes the data public immediately. The report looks like this:

	Customers' Purchases	Customers' Short Sales	Customers' Other Sales	Customers' Total Sales
Number of Shares...	198,565	1,366	140,710	142,076

The above information covered transactions on February 28, 1957, and was released March 1.

Wall Street is full of adages and has been for decades. Many of them sit comfortably on a solid base of quicksand. Others, sharp and bitter, contain more than a little of cynical truth.

One of the favorites is that the public—i.e., the odd-lot public—is wrong most of the time. According to this theory, net odd-lot sales increase when the market advances and contract when the market declines. Several Wall Street pundits feel so strongly about this that they have concocted theories of market behavior based almost entirely on the ratio of odd-lot sales to odd-lot purchases.

Like most facile interpretations of the market, this theory can be safely ignored. I find it of more significance that over the years odd-lot purchases have consistently outnumbered odd-lot sales—and over the years the course of the market generally has been upward.

CHAPTER 13

Short Selling:

Some Facts and Fancies

IN SOME QUARTERS, the mere mention of short selling can fan the fires of moral indignation to white heat. Short selling does not carry the same stigma as beating your aged mother over the head to finance a trip to the local pub—not quite as much, anyway—but for many people it ranks high among the more exotic of the deadly sins.

Historically, there is some justification for this attitude. In the formative years of the securities markets, the days when not even a license was required for stealing, short selling was truly a scourge that cost innocent people, and some not so innocent, millions and millions of dollars. The short sale has always been a legitimate business operation, but in the past its abuse became a fine art. Today there are so many restrictions governing the short sale that abuse is all but impossible.

The amount of misinformation and the lack of information about short selling are astonishing. For years, whenever the market declined, the financial editor of a major metropolitan newspaper, a man with long experience as a financial reporter and interpreter, consistently reported that short selling was a factor. Time and time again, competent people pointed out to him that it was mechanically impossible for short selling to depress prices. He was a man of firm character, however, and evidently felt that nobody was going to make a fool out of him. He died several years ago, but if he were still alive I am sure he would still be reporting, with undiminished assurance and complete lack of accuracy, "Short selling helped to push prices lower on the Stock Exchange today."

Selling for Profit

When you buy 100 shares of XYZ common, presumably you do so with the belief that the price will advance; or, at the least, that it will not decline. But suppose you decide that XYZ common will not advance, but instead is due for a decline. Instead of buying the stock, you sell it short—that is, sell shares you do not actually own. When you buy stock, you anticipate an advance; when you sell stock short, you anticipate a decline. Why a purchase to make a profit should be considered a true and even lovable expression of the American way of life, while a short sale to make a profit is tinged with obloquy, is not entirely clear. Here is one case in which the profit motive has a split personality.

Let's see what happens when you make a short sale. You have been keeping an eye on XYZ common for months; you have watched it go higher and higher. Finally XYZ gets to $95 a share, a price that you feel is entirely unjustified by the company's earnings, earnings prospects, and dividend record. You are convinced, after a study of the company's position, that a decline in the price of XYZ is inevitable, so you tell your broker to sell short 100 shares of XYZ common.

Your order will be transmitted immediately to the floor of the Stock Exchange—which does not mean, by any manner of means, that your order will be executed immediately. The long arm of the SEC stretches out at this point and flags your order.

The SEC says that you cannot sell any security short at a price below the price of the last transaction. Suppose XYZ sells at $94.75 and, in the next transaction, at $95. You can sell XYZ short at $95.

But suppose XYZ sells at $95 and then at $94.75. You cannot sell short at $94.75. This is why: The SEC also states that you cannot sell short unless the price is *above* the next preceding different price. Suppose XYZ sells at $94.75, then at $95 and again at $95. You can sell short at $95, because the price is higher than the preceding *different* price. But in the case mentioned earlier, where the price fell from $95 to $94.75, the preceding different price was the higher one.

It's easy to see now why short selling cannot depress the market: as soon as a stock declines in price, a short sale immediately becomes forbidden.

Now, let's say your broker has sold short 100 shares of XYZ for your account. You don't own any of the stock, so your broker has to go out and borrow it. He has several sources of supply. He may own 100 shares of XYZ himself and lend it to you. Or he may borrow the stock from the account of another customer who has bought the stock on margin; it is customary practice for the buyer of stock on margin to sign an agreement with his broker authorizing him to lend the stock for such purpose. Or the broker may go to an individual who makes a business of lending stock.

At this point you may wonder why anybody should lend you or your broker 100 shares of XYZ, although you both are undoubtedly very charming people. The answer is that it's profitable. The borrower of the stock deposits with the lender the market value of the stock in cash, and the lender has the use of this money until the loan of stock is repaid. In some cases the lender may have to pay interest for the use of this money, but in most cases such stock is loaned flat— that is, no interest payment is made.

Occasionally, stock is loaned at a premium. The available supply of stock may be limited, and the lender is in a position to demand and get a daily fee for lending the stock. Usually this fee is limited to $1 per 100 shares, although—somewhat rarely—the premium has been far higher. Professor Leffler in his book *The Stock Market,* cites a brief period in 1927 when stock of Wheeling and Lake Erie Railroad was loaned at a premium of $7 per share per day.

The short seller pays any premiums or interest charges—a fact which should be taken into consideration in making a short sale.

Now, what happens after you have sold 100 shares of XYZ short, borrowed the stock in order to make delivery on your sale, and owe somebody 100 shares of XYZ?

Well, you may have been entirely right in your diagnosis of XYZ common. Day by day the price slips a little lower. Eventually it reaches $80 a share or thereabouts, and you decide that's it. The stock may go lower, you figure, but it seems unlikely. And, while you are waiting for a further decline, the price might advance. So you decide to cover your sale.

Covering a short sale means simply that your broker buys 100 shares of XYZ for you in the regular auction market. He takes the stock, repays the lender, and, of course, recovers your deposit. So now you are in the excellent position of having bought 100 shares of stock at $80 a share and having sold it at $95—a profit of $15 a share minus commissions, transfer taxes, and any charges incurred for borrowing the stock in the first place.

That's one side of the picture. The other side is considerably bleaker. Your diagnosis of XYZ common may have been completely correct. It *was* overpriced at $95 a share, the price at which you sold short. Unfortunately, the market did not agree with you. Let us assume that as soon as you sell short, XYZ starts advancing—from $95 a share to $98, to $103, to $108. By the time its gets to $110 a share you become concerned. High time you did, too; if I were in your shoes, I'd be concerned when the price reached $100.

XYZ may continue to advance indefinitely, despite all the statistical evidence in the world to show that it shouldn't. But, sooner or later, you must cover your short sale—and the only way you can get the stock that you must repay is to buy it in the open market. So at $110 you give up, and buy 100 shares of XYZ. You have bought 100 shares of stock at $110 and sold at $95, leaving you with a loss of $15 a share, plus commissions, transfer taxes, and any charges incurred for borrowing the stock in the first place.

When you take a long position in a stock—that is, buy it— your loss cannot exceed the price you paid. If you bought XYZ as an investment at $95 a share, the most you could lose is $95. But if you take a short position, your possible loss is theoretically unlimited.

Of course, as a short seller you can protect yourself to a degree. If you sell XYZ short at $95 and are satisfied with a profit of $5 a share, you put in a stop order to buy at $90, which immediately becomes a market order if the price declines to $90 a share or lower. Or you can limit your possible loss by putting in a stop order to buy at, say, $100 a share. Using a stop order to cover a short sale at a higher price is theoretically good, but it's a little like informing a drowning man that the nearest land is only one mile away, not two. Either way, he loses.

The New York Stock Exchange has several rules designed to prevent abuse of the short selling technique. For instance, the Exchange says that you must put up at least $1,000 in cash when you sell a stock short. The Exchange, too, forbids short sales in any listed stock selling for less than $5 a share. Stock may be sold short on margin just as it may be bought on margin, a subject that is discussed elsewhere in this book. However, the short seller must maintain a slightly higher cash equity in his margin account than a person long of the stock—30 per cent against 25 per cent.

One question frequently raised in connection with a short sale is: Who gets the dividends on stock that is borrowed to sell short? The lender does, and the borrower is responsible for giving to the lender any cash or stock dividends paid while the stock is borrowed.

Who Are the Short Sellers?

It seems quite likely that most short selling is done by brokers in the normal course of their business. I don't mean to imply that "the normal course of their business" means that short selling is undertaken as a result of special information, or that the public is harmed in any way by such sales. Roughly between 3 and 4 per cent of all transactions on the New York Stock Exchange represent short selling—and I suspect that more than half are what we might call professional short selling, as opposed to short selling undertaken to make a profit in a declining market.

The specialist on the floor of the Stock Exchange, for instance, may find that demand for a particular stock far outruns the available supply, and as a result the price may tend to advance too sharply. He may not own enough of the stock to supply the market, so instead he sells short. He may or may not make a profit on the transaction, but the motive behind such a short sale is simply to maintain an orderly market.

Similarly, the odd-lot dealer may have an order on hand to buy 30 shares of Amalgamated Bedspreads, a stock which, it happens, he does not own. Rather than go into the auction market and buy 100 shares of Amalgamated, he will fill the order by going short the 30 shares. As a matter of fact, this particular type of operation by the odd-lot dealer is considered so important that the Securities and Exchange Commission exempts such transactions from the short selling rule.

In other cases, short selling almost invariably revolves around an unusual situation. A particular company may find itself in trouble because of management problems. A group of men may buy control of a company, and the public may interpret the operation as simply a way of milking the company of its assets. Competition may drive a corporation to the wall. The public may anticipate an unfavorable court ruling, perhaps on taxes or an antitrust proceeding, that might have a deleterious effect on the company's earnings. All of these situations and others may well lead to speculative short selling.

The Short Interest

Once a month the New York Stock Exchange issues a record of all listed stocks in which a short interest exists as of the middle of the month. The figures are interesting to a market student for several reasons. A rise in the total short interest is regarded by many market observers as a healthy sign. Let's say there is a total short interest of 2,500,000 shares after a period when the market as a whole has been advancing. Fine, says one school of thought. Those 2,500,000 shares eventually must be covered, so if the market declines there is a tremendous latent buying power. If the short interest contracts, which it usually does when the market declines, you may hear faint whimpers of apprehension because a built-in market cushion is gradually being worn down.

On the other hand, a sudden sharp increase in the short interest in an individual stock may be regarded as a danger signal. If the short interest in XYZ jumps from 50,000 shares on August 15 to 750,000 shares on September 15, obviously something must be going on. Unfortunately, the Exchange's report cannot state just what is going on—quite likely the Exchange itself doesn't even know—but such a jump should cause the wary owner of that stock to look around.

One of the impressive things to me about the Exchange's short interest report—a typical report is shown in Appendix B—is the insignificant amount of stock that is short in relation to the total amount of stock outstanding.

Bear Raids and Corners

The bear raid was an accepted market practice for decades, and it was these raids that hurt the public the most. One man, or more often a group of men, would select a particular stock and start selling short. The short selling was accompanied by a carefully planned propaganda campaign that got the word around that the company selected was in for bad times. If bankruptcy could be predicted, so much the better.

The combination of false rumor and short selling started the price of the stock on its way down. As the price dropped, margined stock would be thrown on the market. Stockholders who couldn't stand the sight of their own stock declining added to the selling. Finally, when the price had dropped far enough, the manipulators would cover their short sales and make a handsome profit—and if a number of people got hurt in the process, well, it was all in a day's business.

The short sale was also part of a manipulative technique known as the corner. The theory of the corner was simplicity itself—you merely bought, or acquired control over, all of the available supply of a stock. People who had borrowed the stock and sold it short found that there was no stock that they could beg, borrow, or steal to cover their short sales. So they covered on the terms laid down by the people controlling the stock—terms that normally were based on the same Christian charity and sense of fair play that, at a later day, characterized the operations of the Gestapo.

Corners, happily, belong to the past. In the securities market today, they are virtually impossible. In fact one of the few corners that I can recall in recent years occurred in the commodities market. An ambitious gentleman tried to corner—of all things—the world supply of pepper. It didn't work.

Selling Against the Box

One of the few effective hedges in the stock market is short selling against the box. A hedge, as you know, is simply a method of protecting a profit or avoiding a loss. For instance, you have bet $10 that the Yankees would win the World Series. Then the score gets to three games even and you start to worry. You decide that the Yankees have a better than even chance of losing, and you can't afford the $10. So you bet another $10 that the Dodgers will win the Series. You have hedged your first bet. Now you can't lose—but you can't win either.

So let's say you own 100 shares of XYZ Corporation on which you have a substantial paper profit. You don't want to jeopardize that profit, but you've heard that the stock may be due for a setback. At the same time, you don't want to sell, perhaps because of tax considerations.

This dilemma can be resolved very neatly. You sell short

100 shares of XYZ by borrowing the stock; you keep your own stock in your safety box. Then one of two things can happen.

The price declines, and you cover your short sale by buying the stock in the open market. Your gain on your short sale is offset exactly—give or take a few dollars—by your loss on the stock you still own. Or you can cover your short sale by delivering the stock you own. Same thing happens—your profit on the short sale is balanced by the decline in the market price of the stock you owned.

Or the price of XYZ advances after you have sold short. Again, you have the choice of covering your short sale by buying the stock in the open market or by delivering the stock you have in your safety box. In either case, your loss on the short sale is balanced by the advance in the price of the stock you owned.

Stock Options

There is nothing either mysterious or difficult to understand about a stock option. European investors, large and small, have been using stock options in security markets for 100 years and longer, ever since such markets were first organized. In this country, however, the rank-and-file investor until recently has avoided the use of put and call contract options, which he regards as a specialized and complicated technique.

Essentially, a stock option is a contract, paid for in advance, in which the holder has the right to buy (in the case of a call contract) or sell (in the case of a put contract) a specified number of shares (generally 100) at a fixed price (normally the market price at the time the contract is made) at any time within the period covered by the contract (usually 60 days, 90 days, or 6 months).

SPECULATIVE CALL OPTION

Consider the speculative possibility first. Let us assume you feel that XYZ is priced low at $70 a share, and that it could advance to $85 a share in three months. To buy 100 shares under current 70 per cent margin rules would require a cash investment of $4,900. Unwilling to tie up this amount of cash and take the market risk that such a commitment involves, you buy for $400 a call option giving you the right to purchase 100 shares at 70 within 90 days.

In that period, suppose XYZ climbs to 82. You could exercise your right to buy 100 shares at 70 from the endorser of the contract (a member firm of the New York Stock Exchange) and immediately sell it in the open market at 82, for a profit of $1200, less the price of the contract ($400) and usual brokerage commissions and taxes. If your judgment is wrong and XYZ drops to 50, your loss is limited to $400 (the price of the call option), whereas an outright owner of the stock would have a paper loss of $2,000 and the possibility of further decline. It is particularly interesting to note that at no time is your possible loss greater than the cost of your option contract.

SPECULATIVE PUT OPTION

To show the use of a put contract for speculation, let us consider the following. You feel that XYZ selling at 70 has a good chance of declining to possibly 50 in the next 90 days. You buy a put option contract at 70, good for 90 days, for $350. If at any time in the 90-day period XYZ should decline to 50, you buy 100 shares in the market at 50 and deliver it to the maker of the put contract at 70, showing a profit of $2,000, less the cost of your option contract ($350) and brokerage commissions and taxes.

CHAPTER 14

Protection in the Market:

Fear Thyself

I HAVEN'T GOT THE FIGURES to back up this theory, but it's my belief that far more money has been lost in the securities market by the rigorous application of pure foolishness than by fraud and deceit. The man or woman who is determined to be a sucker inevitably will be a sucker, all laws and good advice to the contrary.

At one time the investing and speculating public was treated with a lack of candor, to put it mildly, that would not be tolerated today by the securities industry. Then—as now—the public showed an astonishing eagerness to be shorn.

The pool operation was a typical example of skullduggery, now outlawed, that was regarded as a perfectly proper business practice only two or three decades ago.

In essence, the pool was a market maneuver by a small group of men to acquire large amounts of a particular stock at a comparatively low price, raise the price of the stock by a number of artificial devices, and then unload the stock without breaking the market.

150

The public, oddly enough, was aware of the operations of pools. But, rather than rise up and demand that pools be outlawed, the public was much more interested in trying to ride along with the pools—buying when the insiders bought, selling when the insiders sold.

The Securities and Exchange Commission

A federal investigation of the collapse in securities prices in 1929–1933 was as inevitable as a political candidate coming out in favor of motherhood. The investigation, a mammoth operation even as federal investigations go, produced—among other legislation—the Securities Act of 1933 and the Securities Exchange Act of 1934. The 1933 act—the so-called "Truth in Securities" law—had the objective of providing investors with complete information about securities offered for public sale and of prohibiting deceit and fraud in the sale of securities generally. The 1934 act was intended to extend investor protection to securities listed on registered securities exchanges, such as the New York and American Stock Exchanges.

Administration of the two acts was eventually given over to the Securities and Exchange Commission, known familiarly as the S.E.C.—or the SEC. Control of credit in the market is provided for in the 1933 act, but the regulatory authority is the Federal Reserve Board rather than the SEC.

Cornerstone of the SEC's power is its authority to demand full disclosure about a company and its securities—to give the public the facts and let the public make its own decisions. This sounds like unassailable logic, but it doesn't always quite work out, for the well-proved reason that the public is a perverse beast.

Before an issue of securities can be offered for sale to the public, the company must file with the SEC a registration statement, which provides a detailed description of the company and its securities. The SEC does not attempt to pass upon the merits of a security. If you want to sell stock in a company formed for the express purpose of supplying the hen market with dentures, go to it. Just be sure you give all the facts, including your own recompense as an expert on the subject of hen dentures.

Despite a great deal of effective educational work by the SEC, many people persist in believing that registration with the SEC is the equivalent of SEC approval of the merits of a security. This the SEC does not give; nor—and the SEC would be the first to say so—is it desirable that the SEC should act as an investment advisory service.

In addition to the registration statement, the SEC requires that the prospective investor must be given a prospectus that sets forth the salient data contained in the registration statement. In theory, the prospectus provides the investor with the information needed to make an investment decision. If ever there was a document conceived to make life miserable for the investor, the prospectus is it. The purpose of the prospectus is, without question, laudable. But the prospectus itself is a 40- or 50-page document written by lawyers who evidently have spent some years under duress in a broker's office. Jim Caffery, onetime chairman of the SEC, is reputed to have said, "You can lead an investor to a prospectus but you can't make him read it."

Some of these statements have been simplified, but the results have been none too successful. The prospectus is a strong dish of tea, any way you take it. But despite their complexities, the registration statement and the prospectus are invaluable aids to the experienced investor and should be ranked first among sources of information. Still, each is a document that requires more than a little knowledge, and if you are a new investor, I suggest you let your broker do the interpreting.

There are several exemptions to the registration requirements of the SEC, one of which has turned out to be quite a headache for the SEC as well as for investors. Offerings of securities not exceeding $300,000 in amount may be exempt from registration. The issuer is required to register the issue, but the information required is meager in comparison with the voluminous requirements of a larger registration. Regulation A, which covers these exempted issues, was promptly seized upon by some companies to circumvent the intent of the law. In the past few years, many Regulation A filings have been for penny stocks, which have been described in terms liberally larded with the magic word "uranium." Unfortunately, the proceeds of such issues were so frequently used to liberally compensate the issuers for their time and trouble—and possibly to satisfy a penchant for Cadillacs—that very little was left over with which to do any prospecting or mining.

The Ontario Securities Commission has one regulation at its disposal which the SEC has toyed with using, and which seems to have considerable merit.

In the United States, a man selling $250,000 worth of stock in a promotional venture may find that the best he can do is dispose of $200,000 worth of it. It's only natural that he should take, say, $175,000 of the proceeds to compensate himself for his efforts and the risk he has assumed. Being an honest man, he will use the balance of $25,000 to hunt for oil or uranium or whatever he wants to hunt for. If the $25,000 turns out to be inadequate—well, he's done his best.

In Ontario, on the other hand, any money he receives from the sale of stock is placed in escrow until all or most of the stock is sold and there is enough money to be used for prospective purposes. If the issue can't be sold, the money is returned to the buyers of the stock.

The next time you are approached with a proposition to buy stock in a first-class uranium, gold, oil, or iridium company, at least do yourself the favor of looking at the brief registration statement that the company is required to file with the SEC. Keep an eye out for two things: first, the proportion of the proceeds of the issue that will go to the promoters or the underwriters or both; second, the exact status of the venture—whether it's a going company, a company with potentially productive property, or a company that can't start operations until billions of gallons of water have been pumped out of an abandoned mine shaft.

If you discover—and the gentleman who is trying to sell you stock will go to any length to avoid making the admission, up to and including fibbing—that the company is not registered with the SEC, just hang up the phone or throw away the letter.

If the stock is a Canadian issue, you have the help of a list called the "Canadian Restricted List," which includes stocks being offered for sale in the United States in violation of the Securities Act of 1933. You can get the list from SEC headquarters in Washington or any of the nine regional offices of the SEC. The addresses are shown in Appendix C. Inclusion of a company in this list does not mean per se that the security is worthless. But just bear in mind that selling such securities in the United States is a violation of federal law designed to protect the investor.

I must admit that the names of some of these Canadian companies are as entrancing as the salesman's pitch. In July, 1956, for instance, you had the opportunity of buying such issues as Keylode Cobalt Silver Mines, Kabour Mines, Antimony Gold Mining and Smelting, Consolidated Quebec Yellowknife Mines, and Resolute Oil and Gas. I'm particularly fond of the last one—it has an Eagle Scout quality to it that lulls away the slightest suspicion.

Some brokerage firms maintain their own "black" or "gray" lists of securities, which they urge their customers to shy away from. They'll buy these issues for you—if you insist—but only on receipt of a written order and an acknowledgment that this investment requested by the customer is contrary to the firm's recommendation.

I'd like to make it clear that I am not opposed to buying shares in a highly speculative company. Some of them do pay off. If you can afford the high mortality rate of such companies, if you know what you are doing—why, go to it. I don't believe in the attitude, though, of people who say, "Look, Joe, it's only 26 cents a share—how can I go wrong?" Multiply 26 by 1,000 and you've got the answer.

Insiders

In the bad old days, corporate insiders often used their positions to make a fast dollar with a complete and callous disregard for the interest of their own stockholders. The idea that the management and directors operate a corporation as a sort of trusteeship for the stockholders has burgeoned slowly, and only with a sizable assist from the Congress.

The law now requires that any officer or director of a listed company, or any stockholder owning as much as 10 per cent of the stock, must file reports with the SEC and the exchange on which the stock is listed showing any change in the amount of holdings. These reports are known as Form 4's and are available for public inspection. Insiders must also file with the SEC and the exchange the amount of stock owned at the time of initial registration; this information is reported on Form 5's and is also available to the public. (Appendix F shows a Form 4 report as issued by the New York Stock Exchange.)

These requirements sound fine and undoubtedly do act as a deterrent to shady practices. The financial press keeps an eye on the reports and is quick to report on unusual transactions. There are drawbacks, though. One is that Form 4—showing changes in ownership—need not be filed until the tenth day of the month following that in which the transaction was made. If, as president of XYZ Corporation, you buy 1,000 shares on January 5, you have until February 10 to report the transaction. Efforts have been made to shorten the time lag, but thus far they have not been successful.

The second drawback is that insiders are sometimes forgetful. I've heard of several cases in which the insider forgot to file a Form 4 for a couple of years, certainly an interesting example of selective amnesia. I'm not implying that these omissions had any fraudulent intent—but fraud is a possibility. The SEC has never acted when there was a long delay in filing the Form 4, probably because the SEC has no power to take punitive action but must refer the case to the Department of Justice.

Insider reports may be a good clue to the investment worth of a security as interpreted by the company's own management. If the Form 4's show over a period of time that President Smith of a well-known company has been steadily adding to his holdings, that would certainly seem to be good evidence that President Smith believes in the future of his company.

On the other hand, Form 4's may be deceptive as well, especially when a stock option is being exercised. A corporation executive who has the option of buying stock in his company at $20 a share when the market price is $25 may exercise the option merely to sell the stock immediately for a sure profit. On one occasion an executive in one of America's leading motion picture producing companies, in fact it was Loew's Inc., exercised an option to buy 50,000 shares of the company's stock, a purchase amounting to around $1,000,000. The question may be raised whether, in similar situations, the stock is a drag on the market until it is liquidated or whether it is purchased to hold as an investment.

In order to prevent the unfair use of inside information, the 1934 act also provides that any profit realized by a director, officer, or 10 per cent owner of a listed stock from a short-term transaction is recoverable by the company. A short-term transaction is defined as a sale and purchase, or purchase and sale, within six months. The company itself may sue to recover the profit, or a stockholder may sue on behalf of the company.

Insiders are also prohibited from selling short stock of their own company.

Proxies

"Corporate raiders"—"Management wreckers"—"Despoilers of fine companies"—these terms have been much in the news in the past few years, particularly in the cases of such monumental corporate battles as the Montgomery Ward, New Haven, and New York Central proxy contests. Plainly, anybody who is a raider, a wrecker, or a despoiler, or maybe all three at once, is a bad 'un. Actually, the terms are often applied by management to any minority stockholder or stockholder group who has any ideas about running the company that differ from management views.

These dissident stockholders may or may not be right, but they are permitted to express their views and, if possible, induce other stockholders to join them. Their motives may be all wrong—and sometimes they are—but motivation is open to interpretation, and in any case the rights of owner-ship cannot be denied.

The SEC cannot pass on the merits of a proxy contest any more than the Commission can judge the merits of an individual security. But the SEC has laid down a set of rules governing the solicitation of proxies which should make unnecessary the often violent name-calling that has characterized some proxy contests. *If* proxies are solicited, the SEC insists that each person solicited be furnished by the management with adequate and accurate information so that he can cast his vote as an informed person.

In addition, recently adopted measures require that any person who challenges management in a proxy fight must provide stockholders with such information as his principal occupation, home address, business address, participation in any other proxy contest within the past ten years, criminal record if any, and direct or indirect ownership of the company's stock. The intent of these new regulations is clear.

If proxies are not solicited, and there is nothing in the law to require solicitation, the SEC's rules and regulations fall by the wayside. The New York Stock Exchange can take a great deal of pride in a new regulation that requires all companies seeking listing on the Exchange to agree to solicit proxies; about 95 per cent of presently listed companies already make it a practice to do so. This is one more protection given the investor who buys a stock listed on the New York Stock Exchange.

Through the Back Door

SEC rules and regulations relating to disclosure of information, misuse of insider information, and regulation of proxy solicitation apply only to securities listed on a registered securities exchange—with the exceptions of securities subject to the Public Utility Holding Company Act of 1935 and the Investment Company Act of 1940. Some over-the-counter companies do follow pretty much the same standards as listed companies, but most do not. You might remember that when you consider buying an unlisted stock, or an unlisted stock with trading privileges on an exchange.

Many qualified companies—banks, for instance—refuse to list their stocks on a national exchange simply because of the wide range of information they would be obliged to make public. Up to a few years ago, there was only one bank stock listed on the New York Stock Exchange, the Corn Exchange Bank. When that bank merged with the Chemical Bank, the merged company declined to apply for listing—probably on the general grounds that banks are subject to too many regulations anyway.

There has been a great deal of agitation to extend to owners of unlisted securities at least some of the safeguards available to owners of listed securities. The SEC has recommended such action, and so have several of the exchanges. Bills that would do the trick have been offered in Congress, but they have not been adopted—for reasons I'd like to know more about. One proposal, made by the SEC itself, would extend the protection of the 1934 Act to unlisted companies having more than $3,000,000 in assets and more than 300 security holders.

Sooner or later, in my opinion, securities traded over-the-counter will become subject to closer regulation. In the meantime, be careful. I don't mean to imply that you can buy a listed security with the blithe assumption that everything will turn out for the best merely because the stock is listed. Don't buy any stock, listed or unlisted, until you find out what you can about the company—but you'll soon learn that it's a good deal easier to get the facts about a listed company.

Manipulation

The SEC is also charged with the responsibility of preventing manipulative practices that interfere with the free play of supply and demand in an open market. Pools are taboo, along with wash sales and matched orders. In the wash sale you are the buyer of 100 shares of stock—and you are also the seller of 100 shares of the same stock. A matched order is along the same lines, except that you are the seller and a friend of yours is the buyer.

These transactions are effected, of course, to create apparent active trading in a security. Transactions effected to raise or lower the price of a stock in order to induce other people to buy or sell the stock are also prohibited. Spreading rumors, or false or misleading information designed to persuade others to buy or sell a stock, is forbidden.

Enforcement

A news story carried by the Dow Jones news ticker in the summer of 1956 gives a good illustration of the SEC's attitude and method of operation. Here is the story under a Washington, D.C., dateline:

The Securities and Exchange Commission disclosed it is investigating the market activity on the American Stock Exchange of common stock of Northeast Airlines beginning August 3.

On that date Northeast stock jumped from $9\frac{3}{4}$ as the market opened to $12\frac{1}{2}$ after 24,000 shares had changed hands—on Monday August 6 another 12,800 shares were traded and the stock, after rising to $13\frac{3}{8}$ closed at $12\frac{3}{4}$.

An SEC official said that the Commission, as a routine matter in the case of unusual fluctuations of securities, launched its staff investigation "almost immediately" after the jump in the price of Northeast shares on August 3. He said the Commission always investigated unusual fluctuations in the price of a security traded on an exchange to see if parties are "artificially influencing the price of the stock."

The SEC is less interested in seeking out violators of the law and clapping them in jail than in preventing and eliminating violations of the law. If the Commission wants to get tough, it has three avenues open. First, it may apply to a U. S. district court for an order enjoining acts or practices alleged to violate the law. Second, in case of fraud or other willful violations of the law, the SEC may turn the facts over to the Department of Justice with a recommendation for criminal prosecution. Third, the Commission may suspend or expel members from exchanges or the over-the-counter dealers' association. The Commission may also deny registration to, or revoke the registration of, a company that does not comply with the disclosure provisions of the law.

Investment Advisers

The SEC has numerous other powers in the regulation of the securities industry. In Chapter XVII I shall mention the Investment Company Act of 1940, relating to mutual funds and investment companies. But the Investment Advisers Act of 1940 may have some passing interest for investors with sizable portfolios—say $50,000 and up.

Under the Act, persons who advise others about their securities transactions for a fee are obliged to register with the SEC. Considering the sums of money that some investment advisers handle or control, the requirements are on the skimpy side. By and large, you can qualify as an investment adviser if you can write your name in block letters, although that is not expressly required by law. I believe investment advisers are also required to be citizens of the United States.

The Act makes it unlawful for investment advisers to engage in practices that constitute fraud or deceit. It requires that they disclose the nature of their interest in transactions executed for their clients and prohibits profit-sharing arrangements.

The customers of investment advisers—there are not many more than 1,000 registered with the SEC, by the way—are usually institutions, estates, or wealthy individuals. Fees usually range from $\frac{1}{2}$ of 1 per cent of the portfolio down, perhaps as low as $\frac{1}{10}$ of 1 per cent. Obviously an investment adviser must have pretty well-heeled customers if he's going to stay in business.

For the investor with a few thousand, and maybe even a few hundred thousand dollars on his hands, advice is available—at a price—from the investment advisory services.

Other Safeguards

The Securities and Exchange Commission is the dominant regulatory agency in the securities business. For sheer volume and strictness of regulatory activity, the SEC's closest contender is probably the New York Stock Exchange. But there are also other agencies that take an interest—from passing to intense—in the problem of keeping the securities industry as clean and wholesome as a spring day.

You've probably heard the phrase "blue sky law." It is said to have originated in the comment of a judge who gave as his opinion that a certain security had the approximate value of a patch of blue sky. Each of the states has a securities administrator (their names and addresses are listed in Appendix D) whose job it is to administer state securities laws as enacted by the particular state. In some states, the blue sky laws are tough and effectively administered—Ohio comes to mind, for one. In others, there is not much more than token observance of loose statutes. If you have a problem regarding fraud, though, it might be worth your while to get in touch with your state securities administrator.

You can also draw on the help of the attorney general of the state in which you live. Some states have an assistant attorney general who specializes in securities frauds, and these boys can really get rough. New York State has one of the strictest set of laws pertaining to securities frauds.

Backing up these authorities—and sometimes leading them—is the National Association of Better Business Bureaus. There are nearly 300 scattered across the country, and their work, for the most part, is highly effective. The Association of Better Business Bureaus, Inc., located at Room 723, Chrysler Building, New York 17, New York, has a booklet listing all regional bureaus in the 48 states, a copy of which can be obtained by getting in touch with that organization. Usually there is a close degree of cooperation between the Better Business Bureaus, the SEC, and the attorneys general.

You will also find that, if your local newspaper has a financial editor, he will usually be delighted to help you out if you have a problem involving fraud or misrepresentation in the sale of securities.

At the risk of being monotonous, don't wait until you've been taken by a fast-talking phony securities salesman before you start complaining. Consult a reputable broker before you make an investment, or one of the agencies I've mentioned. Most people hate to admit that they've been suckers—which is an important reason that swindlers always have an audience.

And, whether you're dealing with a smooth salesman who says he hails from Saskatchewan or a deacon in your local church who sells securities on the side—remember, it's your money.

CHAPTER 15

You and Your Broker:

A Man's Best Friend

IF YOU FINALLY MAKE the decision that for the first time you'd like to invest, you're faced with problems that have bothered a great many investors. How do you find a broker? What do you do with a broker when you find one? Is he going to try to persuade you to buy General Motors when you really want to buy Chrysler? Can you depend on him to make money for you? Should you have a letter of introduction? How do you know he's honest?

Finding a broker is really no trouble at all. What to do with him when you get him is entirely up to you. You may form a lifelong association that is emotionally and financially rewarding. Or you may drive yourself into a chronic tizzy simply because you won't accept the fact that a broker is neither a tusked ogre intent on binding you into slavery nor a prescient encyclopedia of investment information who can easily make your fortune if he really wants to.

164

First of all, how do you find a broker? Your initial try could be a friend or business associate, someone you know whose judgment you respect. Or take a look at the financial section of your newspaper; many of the brokers in your city or town regularly advertise their services.

You might try the business or financial editor of your local paper. They're experts in their field, and they're more than willing to help out their readers. The yellow pages of your telephone directory are another source of information. Look under the heading "Stock Brokers"—and, if you want to be really careful, the subheading "New York Stock Exchange Members," because there you will find listed only member firms of the Exchange.

You may live in a city, town, or rural community in which there is no broker, but don't let that worry you. Not long ago the New York Stock Exchange had as its guest a young lady who had the distinction of having purchased the millionth share of stock bought through the Monthly Investment Plan (the Plan is described in Chapter 17). Turned out she was living in Moscow—not Moscow, Idaho, but Moscow, U.S.S.R. She had read an advertisement in a magazine about the Monthly Investment Plan and immediately opened an account by mail. Lest I give the impression that advertising in this country is so persuasive that it may convert Russia into a nation of capitalists, I should point out that the young lady was a State Department employee.

Some people never see their broker; all their transactions, including the opening of an account, are handled by mail. If you'd like to have the names of the brokers in your state who are members of the New York Stock Exchange, just drop a note to the Exchange, and they'll promptly mail you the list.

Still another way to put your finger on a good broker is

through your bank. As a matter of fact, all your investment business may be transacted through your bank. Banks themselves are frequently customers of brokerage firms, so they are in a position to recommend a firm with which they do business.

Some banks make no charge for forwarding your orders to buy or sell securities; others make a nominal charge such as $1 a transaction or the actual cost of a telegram or telephone call to the broker.

It should be mentioned that when you go to a banker with the idea of buying stocks, you may be greeted with a certain lack of enthusiasm, particularly if your banker is outside an urban area. Bankers by training are highly cautious and conservative individuals, who have one eye on the law and the other on their customers' deposits. Their idea of a good investment is a first mortgage of $10,000 on property worth $50,000. This is fine—as far as it goes. After all, if you have $200 in the bank on Monday, you want to be reasonably sure that it is still there on Tuesday.

But even banks that operate trust departments and invest funds entrusted to them in stocks and bonds have a blind spot when it comes to individual investments. This is an attitude which, fortunately, is rapidly changing. In the meantime, though, don't be alarmed if your banker implies that you are a hotheaded fool because you want to buy a few shares of American Telephone. He'll still try to help you, but he may need a little nudging.

What Your Broker Can Do for You

Before we even try to draw the pattern of the perfect broker, let's take a look at what you can realistically expect from your broker.

First of all, you should expect unswerving honesty—and

this is exactly what you will get from the vast majority of brokers. There are a handful of shady, unscrupulous, or even outright dishonest brokers, but even a casual check of their references should enable you to judge them for what they are.

If you deal with a member firm of the New York Stock Exchange or any other exchange that exercises rigorous control over the activities of its members, you've already just about eliminated the possibility of dishonesty. Member firms of the Stock Exchange, for instance, have a solvency record that surpasses that of the nation's banks.

You should expect a high degree of professional competence, a thorough knowledge of the securities business. Your broker should have a working knowledge of state and federal legislation relating to the securities business, and a knowledge of the rules and regulations of the stock exchanges. Before he recommends the purchase of a particular security, he should accumulate all the information possible about it, analyze it, and present it to you in an understandable form. He should be familiar with tax considerations affecting your investments.

If your broker is associated with a firm with an extensive and competent research department, so much the better for you. Smaller firms without their own research staff usually depend on the help of one or more professional advisory services, and the benefits of these services are passed along to you.

You can expect your broker to devote a certain amount of time to your individual problems. Bear in mind, though, that the only profit your broker earns from you is his commission. The commission he earns on a transaction involving a few hundred dollars does not warrant his spending the week end trying to figure out the ideal way for you to invest your money. If you have $25,000 to invest, naturally you're entitled to more attention.

You can expect your broker to offer you the best advice he can, but he's not an oracle and he's not infallible.

If you prefer, your broker will do no more than take your order and execute it for you. You can seek his advice and accept or reject it as you see fit. You can also give him a certain amount of discretion in handling your account—say, the exact time to buy or sell—or you can ask him to take complete charge of your account, buying and selling when he thinks best. A small fee, usually arrived at by mutual consent, is charged for this custodial service.

You can expect your broker to keep your securities for you, a procedure I highly recommend. Replacing a lost stock certificate is costly and time-consuming. The company issuing the stock must be notified, so that the stock cannot be illegally sold by somebody else; if it has been sold before you get around to notifying the company, you may have a lawsuit on your hands to establish ownership.

You have to post an indemnity bond, obtainable from an insurance company, to insure the issuing company against loss in case the certificate shows up in the possession of a person who bought it in good faith. That bond will cost you roughly 6 per cent of the market value of the stock, so if you lost $1,000 worth of stock, you'll be minus $60 for the bond.

Just in passing, remember always to use registered mail when you forward stock certificates, and never sign your certificate until you have to.

Don't hesitate to ask your broker to get you a price quotation on a security you may be interested in buying. That's part of his trade, and he'll be glad to accommodate you.

Your broker should *not* recommend that you switch from one stock to another every few weeks. He may offer you compelling reasons behind each recommendation, but I can assure you that he's merely trying to pile up his commissions. When you find that constant switching is recommended, I suggest you simply move your account elsewhere. Switching is a plague in the securities business which reputable firms will not countenance.

What You Can Do for Your Broker

Treat your broker with the same fairness and honesty you expect from him. His advice is tailor-made, and he can't do his best for you unless he has a clear picture of your resources and investment objectives. You can talk to him with the same frankness you would use with your lawyer, and you can be sure he will hold in complete confidence any personal information with which you supply him. Give him some idea of your financial resources—your income, the property you own, your family background, your prospects for the future. Let him know precisely whether you're looking for capital gains, dividend income, a combination of both, or highly speculative situations.

If you rely almost wholly on your broker's advice, don't expect infallibility because you won't get it. Nobody—but nobody—can predict with a degree of perfection the short or intermediate trend of the market as a whole or of a particular stock. If your broker is right six times out of ten, you're doing all right. If he's right seven times out of ten, you've got a veritable paragon; hang on to him. Anything above that ratio is sheer accident.

For long-term recommendations, you can expect a little better batting average; but again, don't expect perfection.

Some investors use their broker strictly as a whipping boy. This is unfair to the broker, but I suppose does have some therapeutic value for the customer's ego. In these cases the investor consistently asks and consistently ignores his broker's advice. When the investor makes the wrong decision, he makes sharp yelping sounds and denounces the broker as a "dirty so-and-so and I oughta turn him in to the SEC." If the customer happens to be right, his broker is dismissed as a "punkin head who couldn't find a giraffe in a flock of sheep."

Too much of this treatment tends to make the broker twitchy, so have a heart. Try to admit your mistakes—and credit your broker with good judgment when he shows it.

Lukens Steel not long ago scored a spectacular price advance for a period of months. I can imagine the anguished complaints that investors showered on their brokers for their failure to recommend buying Lukens at the bottom and selling at the top.

"You call yourself a broker—any dope would know that stock was hot. Why didn't you get me in on it?"

Lukens happened to be a stock I was interested in, and I checked every possible source I could think of, when the stock started to move up, to find out what was going on. The stock kept going up and up and up—and I never did find out why it did.

Brokers don't know everything, and they are the first to admit it.

On one occasion a thoroughly competent broker friend of mine recommended a low-priced stock to a number of his customers. He had learned that an advertising promotion by the company for one of its products had turned out to be inordinately successful. Wholesalers and jobbers from all parts of the country swamped the company with orders. A substantial rise in the company's earnings seemed inevitable—and so did an increase in the price of the stock.

But the public had the last word in this case. They didn't like the product, and they didn't buy it. Orders were canceled and inventories returned to the company. The whole operation resulted in a sizable loss for the company, and the stock declined.

That broker did his best for his customers—but, let me remind you again, brokers are not infallible.

Brokers, like other people, come in all sizes and shapes, all temperaments and personalities. Your first selection, and maybe your second and third selections may not pan out the way you anticipated. But at least give the guy a chance. When you do find a broker you like and respect, a man whose personality is compatible with yours, a man who does a good job for you—hang on to him. You have an asset that will last you through life.

Opening an Account

Don't feel that you have to steel yourself to walk into a broker's office. Brokers like to have people walk into their offices—just remember that brokers are in business to make a living, and they can't stay in business without customers. Maybe you've got a wallet bulging with $1,000 bills, maybe you want to open a Monthly Investment Plan account with payments of $40 every three months, or maybe you just want to talk things over. Whichever it is, you'll be welcome.

Some offices may have a receptionist behind the front door to steer you in the right direction. In others you may wander in and find nobody who seems to be much interested in what you're doing or why you're there. If that happens, look for somebody who appears to be working there and say you're thinking of opening an account. You'll be surprised how glad they are to see you.

On your first visit, you'll probably meet the office manager. In a small office, the manager himself may take care of you; if the office is of any size, more likely you'll be turned over to a registered representative. A registered representative used to be known as a customer's man, but the latter term fell into some disrepute because of the questionable antics of the customer's men of twenty-odd years ago. The customer's man was often somewhat of a dilettante who got his job because of his father's connections and who made a living selling stocks and bonds to his father's friends. Good club connections were regarded as essential.

Today's registered representative is a professional who has had on-the-job training and has qualified for his position by passing an examination administered by the Stock Exchange.

Opening an account with your broker—in this case the registered representative—is roughly the equivalent of opening a charge account with a department store. You'll be asked your name, address, place of employment, where you want your mail sent. You'll be asked for a credit reference —the firm, understandably, wants to be sure you will pay your bill after you've made your purchase.

That's all there is to it.

CHAPTER 16

Why Prices Go Up and Down:

Measuring the Market

THE STANDARD EXPLANATION for fluctuations in the stock market, either in individual stocks or the market generally, is the operation of the law of supply and demand. When more people want to buy than sell, prices advance. When more people want to sell than buy, prices decline. This isn't quite accurate; it is not the number of people who buy or sell but the *amount* of stock bought or sold. Your sale of 1,000 shares of a stock plainly outweighs the purchase of 100 shares of the same stock by each of five other people.

This is a good theory and it has the virtue of impregnability. You can't argue with it—but the theory omits more than it tells.

Many people find it strange that one share of American Telephone & Telegraph Company or Union Carbide & Carbon, or any other company you can think of, may be worth so much at ten o'clock and so much more or less at eleven o'clock. Nothing about either company has changed while the market makes these price evaluations; same management, same product or service, same prospects for the future.

It seems even stranger that the price of a share in these companies may vary quite drastically from week to week or month to month, despite the absence of any significant change in the company or the state of the nation—despite even the lack of prospects for a change.

The answer, of course, is supply and demand. A company has just so many shares of stock outstanding, and each owner may have different ideas regarding the worth of his stock.

But you are interested more in the causes of supply and demand, not merely their effects. For instance, you might be disturbed by the effect of the roof of your house falling in because you were watching your favorite television program when it happened. But—assuming that you don't want to be disturbed again for the same reason—you'll probably take a considerable interest in what caused the roof to collapse in the first place.

The stock market is also affected by purchases or sales that are made without reference to price. Take yourself. You wake up Tuesday morning, open the morning mail, and find a check for $5,000 from the estate of an interred uncle. You decide to invest the money—or, anyway, part of it—in a sound security. You don't know the condition of the market and you don't care. You're just interested in buying a good stock.

Or take yourself again. You wake up Wednesday morning, open the morning mail, and find that you've miscalculated your tax bill by $1,000. There's just one way for you to raise the money, and that's to sell the few shares of American Telephone that you bought in the days when your arithmetic was better—or your tax return wasn't checked so closely. You don't know the condition of the market and you don't care. You're just interested in raising some money in order to keep out of the pokey.

This goes on, believe it or not, all over the country, every day in the week. Still, you point out, these are really random motivations. Most people, you feel sure, buy or sell stocks for reasons other than those inspired by personal considerations. Big reasons, like the state of the nation, or the fear of war, or the interest rate, or the price-earnings ratio, or the business cycle. Maybe so, but the facts are sometimes difficult to reconcile with the market's action.

To complicate any attempt at analyzing market fluctuations, we should try to distinguish between short-term factors and long-term factors—to say nothing of public psychology. Analysis becomes even more intriguing when you realize that prices are affected not only by the people who buy and sell securities but also by the people who do not buy and sell. The purchase or sale of a security may be an expression of price opinion—and, just as surely, an opinion on price may be expressed by the refusal to buy or sell.

Before we even dabble in the murky waters of the causes of market fluctuations, let's see how such changes are measured.

The Averages

If you mention "the Street" to an American broker, or "the City" to a British stock jobber, each knows precisely what you are talking about. There's only one Street, which is Wall Street, and only one City, which is London's financial district.

"How's the market?" is another well-known phrase, but its meaning is not quite so precise. There's only one market, of course, which is the New York Stock Exchange. There are roughly 1,500 common and preferred stocks listed on the Stock Exchange; but the "how," nine times out of ten, refers only to the price fluctuations of 30 out of the 1,500 stocks. Offhand, this would appear to have the same logic as trying to deduce the age of a man from the size of his eyeball, but there is some sense to the system.

The 30 stocks I mentioned are those in the Dow Jones industrial average, which is far and away the most popular measure of the trend of the market. They are listed in Table 16 together with prices and yields on September 3, 1929, and December 31, 1956.

If you're wondering who Dow Jones is, Dow Jones & Company publishes *The Wall Street Journal* and operates the Dow Jones News Ticker, a financial news service that distributes the news to subscribers all over the country on a six-inch-wide strip of paper.

The functions of a market average are to indicate the trend of the market and to measure daily fluctuations. This is an operation that calls for the utmost speed. Most people with an interest in the market want to know what has happened as soon after it has happened as possible; they don't want to read about it in a quarterly review published months after the event. So an average is made up of a small group of representative—at least in theory—stocks, so that the average can be calculated rapidly. The D-J industrial average is computed five times a day, at 11:00 A.M., noon, 1:00 P.M., 2:00 P.M., and 3:30 P.M. Results are published on the D-J news ticker roughly 12 minutes after each hour except for the closing average, which comes out at about 3:42 P.M. in preliminary form and 4:10 P.M. in final form.

Along with the industrial average, Dow Jones publishes at the same time an average of 20 railroad stocks, an average of 15 utility stocks, and a composite of all 65 stocks. The rail average has considerable significance to followers of the Dow Theory, which I will explain later, but the utility average and composite average are usually slighted.

As a historical guide to the market's action, the D-J industrial serves its purpose well. As a measure of daily fluctua-

TABLE 16

THIRTY STOCKS INCLUDED IN DOW JONES INDUSTRIAL AVERAGE

Stock	Price[1] 9/3/29	Price 12/31/56	Price-Earnings Ratio 1929	Price-Earnings Ratio 1956	Yield 1929	Yield 1956
Allied Chemical & Dye ...$	88.62	$ 97.13	28.1	20.5	1.7%	6.0%*
American Can	22.73	41.38	22.7	15.0	2.8	4.8
American Smelt. & Refining	53.80	57.50	12.9	8.6	3.1	6.1
American Tel. & Tel.	303.88	171.38	24.0	15.9	3.0	5.3
American Tobacco	101.87	73.38	17.7	9.8	4.9	6.8
Bethlehem Steel	46.79	49.63	12.7	13.0	4.3	4.3
Chrysler Corporation	36.50	70.00	14.8	30.6	4.1	4.3
Corn Products Refining ...	38.13	29.63	19.9	12.6	3.5	5.1
E. I. du Pont de Nemours.	54.37	192.75	31.1	23.5	2.5	3.4
Eastman Kodak	30.96	87.75	22.6	17.1	3.7	3.0
General Electric	33.02	60.25	44.2	24.5	1.5	3.3
General Foods	36.50	43.50	19.8	12.1	4.1	4.1
General Motors	12.10	44.00	13.4	14.6	4.1	4.5
Goodyear Tire & Rubber..	27.03	83.38	12.5	13.8	4.3	4.7*
International Harvester ...	47.30	38.50	20.0	12.2	1.8	5.2
International Nickel	55.38	105.75	37.7	16.3	1.8	3.5
International Paper	23.00	105.00	—	14.9	3.4	5.1*
Johns-Manville	34.50	49.00	25.6	12.9	1.5	4.6
National Distillers	6.04	26.75	24.2	12.7	—	5.8*
National Steel	18.18	77.75	10.6	11.0	3.3	5.1
Procter & Gamble	31.67	50.75	32.0	16.6	2.3	3.7
Sears Roebuck	13.76	28.63	26.4	13.0	1.4	5.1*
Standard Oil of Calif.	19.47	49.25	21.4	11.6	3.2	3.3
Standard Oil of N. J.	11.19	58.75	15.1	14.3	2.6	3.6
Texas Company	17.59	59.88	14.3	10.9	4.3	3.9
Union Carbide & Carbon..	45.83	115.75	34.9	23.8	1.9	2.7
United Aircraft	75.83	89.75	30.3	12.7	—	3.3
U. S. Steel	43.62	73.50	12.4	12.2	2.7	3.5
Westinghouse Electric	72.47	57.50	28.6	57.5	1.7	3.5
Woolworth	100.50	43.63	27.4	12.2	2.4	5.7
Average [2] ....$	50.08	$ 71.06	22.66	33.80	2.9%	4.4%

[1] Adjusted for stock split and stock dividends.

[2] Average price times earnings does not include International Paper, while the average yield figures do not include National Distillers or United Aircraft.

* Includes stock dividend.

tions, the average leaves much to be desired unless you know exactly what the figures represent. Incidentally, the D-J industrial gives pretty much the same picture of the market as other averages using a much larger number of stocks, or stock indices that are based on complicated calculations.

I suppose it's a fair statement to say that there's nothing wrong with the average itself; the trouble lies with the stocks that make up the average. If you have the patience to put up with a little arithmetic, I believe I can make myself clear.

Here is an average made up of three issues:

		Price
Stock A	....	100
Stock B	....	150
Stock C	....	200
	3)	450 (150

With the three issues closing at those prices, the market's average is 150. Next day, the closing prices of the three issues are the same, but stock B has thrown a wrench into the works by splitting three for one. Theoretically, stock B drops from 150 to 50, on the ground that if one share was worth 150, the same share split into three parts is worth 50 for each part. So the average is figured like this:

Stock A	....	100
Stock B	....	50
Stock C	....	200
	3)	350 (116.67

However, it wouldn't make much sense to report that the market had declined from 150 to 116.67 when there had been no change in the prices of the three issues except for the purely mechanical change in the price of Stock B.

So the experts who make up the averages have several solutions. One is substitution. If stock B, selling at 150, splits three for one, throw it out and substitute another stock selling for about 150. This may be a little difficult because there may not be another stock selling even close to 150 that would qualify for inclusion in the average.

Another solution is the constant divisor. 450 divided by 3 gives 150. What we need, then, is a figure that, when divided into 350, will also give 150. In this case the figure is 2.33.

Here's how the average would be figured with the new divisor of 2.33:

```
Stock A  .......  100
Stock B  .......   50
Stock C  .......  200
           2.33)  350   (150.21—which is close enough.
```

This is what has happened to the D-J industrial time and again, and the result is that the average does give a distorted picture of the market. In the early days of simplicity and short skirts, the total of the 30 stocks was divided by 30. To-day, as a result of stock splits and stock dividends, the total of the 30 stocks is divided by *4.566*. The divisor, of course, changes whenever there is a stock split or stock dividend in any of the issues included in the average.

Thus today a one-point change in the D-J industrial is equivalent to a change of 21.9 cents in the arithmetical aver-age of the 30 stocks.

For accuracy's sake, it might be noted that the D-J in-dustrial average was first computed in 1896 on the basis of 12 stocks. In 1916 the number was increased to 20, and in 1928 to the present 30.

In the famous "heart" market of September 26, 1955, the market dropped 31.89 points according to the D-J industrial average. However, the maximum decline of any of the 30 stocks in the average was $15.87½ a share, and the strict arithmetical decline was only $5.87½ a share.

No question that the decline on September 26 was an un-

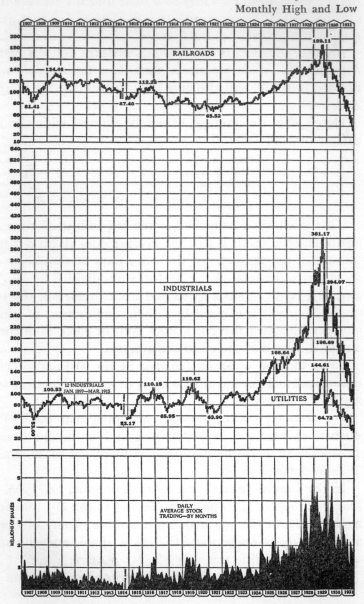

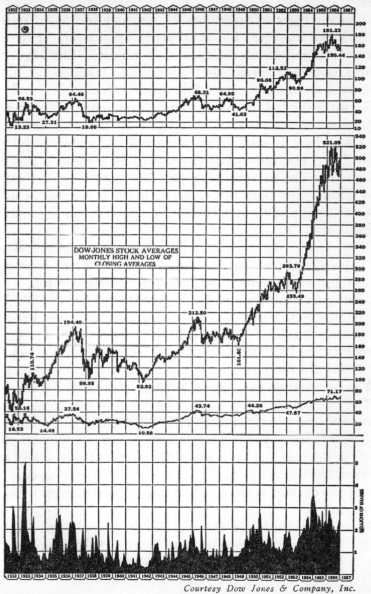

DOW-JONES STOCK AVERAGES
MONTHLY HIGH AND LOW OF
CLOSING AVERAGES

Courtesy Dow Jones & Company, Inc.

usually severe one, but the average did give a distorted picture.

If on the night of September 26, someone had asked you, "How's the market?" the appropriate answer would have been, "The industrials dropped 31.89 points." The answer would have been correct—but misleading. Inflation has hit us from a lot of angles, including the averages.

To make the D-J industrial average even more misleading, it is often expressed—even by brokers—in terms of dollars. You may hear it said, "The industrials advanced $2.40 a share," or "The industrials dropped $1.50 a share." Don't believe it. The average advanced 2.40 points or declined 1.50 points. Any resemblance between dollar changes in individual stocks and point changes in the averages is purely coincidental.

The course of the market from 1907 through 1956 is shown in Table 17. If nothing else, the chart proves that the long-term trend of the market has been consistently upward.

Averages or indices are also prepared by *The New York Times,* the New York *Herald Tribune,* the Associated Press, the Moody Service, Standard & Poor's Corporation, and the Securities and Exchange Commission. Standard & Poor's and the SEC's are computed more scientifically than the others, but in my opinion they are all subject to misinterpretation.

The averages can be helpful to the investor if he approaches them with the proper caution. A glance at the chart in Table 17 shows pretty clearly that there were a number of times in the past fifty years when the market clearly was in a pronounced slump or a pronounced rise. The wary investor, at any one of those periods, would take those trends into consideration.

Even daily changes in the averages may be of some mild help if the investor realizes that market fluctuations are highly magnified by the averages. These changes do affect public sentiment, and public sentiment in the market is a potent factor.

Standard & Poor's quite recently has come out with an average of 500 issues listed on the New York Stock Exchange which is calculated hourly, a few minutes after the hour, by a specially designed electronic computer. This is undoubtedly the fastest and most comprehensive average ever prepared. It will be interesting to note from experience how it diverges, if at all, from the D-J average.

News and the Market

Newspapers—and newspaper readers—like zesty headlines. It's more fun to learn that "market soars on election results" than "market up, volume small." Each headline describes the same market, but you've got to admit the first one has more reader appeal. Like the averages, though, the headlines can be misleading.

Frequently specific news events do have a decisive effect on the market, to the extent that they influence the decisions of a large number of people to buy or sell. But to state that the market declined on a given day because of a rise in the rediscount rate, or advanced another day because of a flood of excellent earnings reports, is merely rationalization. Joseph Mindell, an acute student of the market, used flossier language when he called this rationalization "the fallacy of single cause thinking."

There have been some rare exceptions, notably the market's reaction to President Eisenhower's heart attack. There seems to be little question that an overwhelming proportion of selling on that day was influenced solely by the President's illness. And, significantly, the selling was stimulated not so much by what *had* happened but what might happen in the future because of the President's heart attack.

Another clear-cut case of market reaction to a single news event occurred September 5, 1939, after the United States had declared its neutrality. Heavy demand was generated by the belief that the United States could stay out of the war and that our economy would be stimulated by European demand for goods and material.

It goes without saying that these observations do not apply to an individual stock but only to the market as a whole. The price of a particular stock is often influenced by a single news development. An unexpectedly favorable earnings report, discovery of a new oil field, omission of a dividend, a merger proposal—any of these and many more may cause a decisive price move.

The Exchange Magazine, the official publication of the New York Stock Exchange, published an extremely illuminating study on the subject of news and the market in the May, 1956, issue. Conclusions of the study, which covered the period of 1935–1955, should be helpful to any investor or speculator.

First, the study said, the market, *on a day-to-day basis,* seems to have gradually become more stable over the past two decades. There is some evidence, too, that the market's *annual* price movements have become less pronounced.

Second, the study pointed out, there appears to be little question that the market during the 21-year period studied was more sensitive to news inherently or potentially unfavorable to the market than to favorable developments. To put it another way, the market found it easier to decline suddenly than to advance.

"In some cases," *The Exchange* noted, "the sensitivity of the stock market seemed to be a form of defense against a sudden development which defied immediate interpretation or analysis."

Third, the study found little correlation between pronounced or even violent brief fluctuations and the market's long-term trend.

The study's interpretation of the September 26, 1955, market soundly stresses the importance of psychological factors in price movements.

"Prior to September 26, 1955," the magazine said, "the market's trend had dramatically reflected investor appraisal of a number of economic considerations, among them business conditions, earnings and dividends, prospects for the future—and a federal administration widely regarded as sympathetic to the problems of business and industry.

"These factors all added up to market confidence, and confidence was shocked by the President's illness."

The market break on September 26 was one of the largest on record; but, as an appropriate postscript, it should be pointed out that the ground lost was quickly recovered, and the market—as measured by the averages—again moved ahead to new record high levels.

The moral of these facts and observations seems pretty clear: Don't be stampeded by the headlines into buying or selling. Money is probably the scariest commodity on earth. A big boo from a big banker, a colonic irritation in high places, a mumbled curse against the Western imperialists by an obscure sultan who happens to control billions of gallons of oil—these are solemn happenings. Still, don't make the mistake of the unfortunate lady who rushed from the elevator of a burning building and jumped out the window. She beat the other passengers to the ground floor by a heady margin, but the elevator was still in operation.

The Stock Exchange's study emphasizes this point.

"Despite the market's reflex action to shock treatment," the article said, "it seems reasonable to conclude that the underlying trend is influenced more by deep-seated economic factors—plus the intangible but weighty factor of confidence."

Appendix E tabulates some of the changes of 2 per cent or more in the market since 1935, as measured by the D-J industrial average, and the news factors causing the changes as reported by the financial press.

Discounting the News

Discounting the news in the stock market is somewhat like a young couple anticipating pregnancy. You can't always be sure.

For many years the stock market was regarded as a reliable barometer of the nation's economic health, and the record endorses this theory—up to a point. But the record has been so bad in, say, the past thirty years that the theory must be applied with extreme caution.

Discounting the news is another way of saying that the market anticipates the future. In the past, surges of prosperity were frequently preluded by strong advances in the general level of stock prices. Businessmen, noting the upward trend in the market, were encouraged to make future commitments that tended to stimulate business expansion. These commitments—such as increased production, more aggressive sales promotion, introduction of new products, higher wages—in turn encouraged demand for stocks. This was back-scratching on a very high level.

But look at the market's behavior in 1929–1932. For five or six years, with numerous interruptions, the market had sailed ahead to the record high reached in 1929. There had been warning signs, such as the fantastic amount of credit in use in the securities markets, the spread between stock prices and per share earnings, the warnings of such sober journals as *The New York Times.* The ultimate collapse of the whole United States economy, surely an event of some importance, was no more anticipated by the market than the exact date of the first trip to the moon. In this case, as a matter of fact, the market had less to do with anticipating the future than *causing* the future.

Or take a later period. Toward the end of World War II it was generally accepted by the initiated that a postwar slump was inevitable. Production did slacken in 1945, a development that the market not only did not anticipate but ignored by surging ahead to the peak reached in 1946. Then, with an almost Russian distaste for logic, the market anticipated the most prosperous years in the nation's history by falling flat on its face.

The Dow Theory

I mention the Dow Theory more in sorrow than in anger, to illustrate what shouldn't happen logically in the market, but does. The theory, in essence, is an interpretation of the market's action that falls just short of attempting to forecast the market. I say even that much with some trepidation, because there is no precise body of dogma at which one can point with the confident assertion: *"That* is the Dow Theory."

The theory is based upon the Dow Jones industrial and rail averages. If one of these averages advances beyond a previous high point and this advance is confirmed by a similar advance in the other average—to use the language of the theorists—this is taken as evidence that the basic trend of the market is upward. If one of these averages declines below a previous important low point and the decline is confirmed by a drop in the other average, the market is in a basic downward trend.

"Who cares?" should be the normal reaction to this explanation. The market *has been* in a basic upward move or *has been* in a basic downward trend. So what? Either of those facts is of little importance to the investor or speculator, who is more interested in the future of the market than its past. *The catch* is that when a bull or bear market *has been* signaled by the averages, the upward or downward trend is likely to be continued, according to interpreters of the theory. The trend may continue for a day or a year after one average has confirmed the action of the other—the theory is silent on that point—or it may never get under way, which has also happened.

September 3, 1946, was a bad day for the market. It was so bad that the Securities and Exchange Commission undertook the most detailed analysis of the market's action on a single day ever attempted. The trouble was that the market was close to a resistance point of 186.02 points, according to the Dow Theory. The market had closed on August 30, the last day of trading before September 3, at 189.19. If the market broke through 186.02, it might be faced with muddy grounds. There were sellers on hand early that day. The market started to decline. Tension mounted in brokerage offices throughout the country. When the 11:00 A.M. average was printed on the Dow Jones news ticker, the resistance point had not quite been reached, but almost. Selling increased. At 11:38 the news ticker said that at 11:30 the industrial average was near its February low, which was also the resistance level. Prices continued to drop.

At 12:12 the news ticker printed the noon average; it was 184.24, below the resistance level. The Dow Theory had signaled a bear market.

The SEC study brought forth the information that a little

more than 25 per cent of all shares sold had been sold because of the fact that the Dow Theory had signaled, or was about to signal, a bear market.

The market continued to decline after September 3 and then leveled off in one of the longest periods of inaction on record—during a period when the United States economy had never been healthier.

Don't believe too strongly in theories, even when they work. Q.E.D.

CHAPTER 17

Some Approaches to the Market:

Do-It-Yourself Investing

OVER THE YEARS a fascinating array of formulas and techniques has been developed to reduce the element of risk in the stock market to as near zero as possible. Many of these theories, perhaps most, are based upon painstaking and scientific analyses of past records; analyses undertaken in the perennial and somewhat wistful belief that the past is a sure guide to the future. Other theories have more airy bases, but at times have showed results as impressive as their respectable competitors.

One of my favorites, from the viewpoint of ingenuity, was based on a popular comic strip. The captions in the strips were interpreted by a man of many talents who had a side line as a market counselor. The interpretations were surprisingly good, but the authorities decided that this method of market analysis did not wholly contribute to the public weal.

190

Another theory, with even more dubious claim to success, is founded on the belief that the public is always wrong. The public tends to buy stocks at the peak of an advancing market, according to this view, and tends to sell toward the bottom of a declining market. A refinement of this theory is based on odd-lot transactions; when odd-lot purchases outnumber sales, that's the time to sell, and when odd-lot sales outnumber purchases, that's the time to buy.

Some of my best friends are chartists, and I also know one or two astrologers. A chartist is a man who plots the action of the market on a graph and interprets his findings with the same air of final authority as a political pollster. If you should ever find yourself in the company of a respectable gentleman who, with the passion of the true believer, starts telling you about double bottoms, triple bottoms, broadening bottoms, or dormant bottoms, don't write him off as a student of steatopygous contours—just leave the room.

One of the many areas of human knowledge in which I have a profound ignorance is sun spots. There have been strong efforts to link the action of the stock market with sun spots, but I can't help feeling—and I say this almost apologetically—that the link must be a tenuous one. I have a little more sympathy with theories that attempt to connect the market with the business cycle, but even here I believe the theorists have a long way to go.

The trouble with theories and the stock market is that people are involved, and the art of predicting human behavior is still an art. Thomas Carlyle, who noted that economics is the dismal science, was only half-right.

Market theories, by and large, attempt to remove or minimize the element of decision. Some theories attempt to take the problem of timing out of the hands of the investor, others try to solve the problem of diversification. Some do both. None of the theories I know of is infallible, and a few of them may get you into real trouble.

Dollar Averaging

Perhaps the best of all the various methods of planned investing is dollar averaging. Dollar averaging is simple and frequently works. To apply the plan you need a steady income, an iron will, and faith in the future.

If you can afford to invest $25 a month, month after month, for five years or ten years, dollar averaging may be the solution to your investment problem. The managers of institutional investment funds, such as college endowments or labor pension funds, often follow the principle of dollar averaging—which is a pretty good recommendation.

Dollar averaging ignores fluctuations in the market, and that is the theory's major source of strength. You buy stock by the dollar's worth, just as you might buy gasoline for your car. If the price of the stock declines, your fixed dollar investment will buy more shares; if the price advances, you buy fewer shares. Curiously, you can make a profit by dollar averaging even if you sell your stock at a price below the price of your first purchase. You can make money, in other words, even in a declining market—*if* the market does not decline too much.

Dollar averaging—also known as dollar cost averaging—means simply that a person invests a fixed amount of money in a given stock at regular intervals. For example, he may decide to invest $100 per month in a certain stock. He will then receive four shares in January when this stock is at $25 a share, and five in February when the stock has dropped to $20. The average *price* of these nine shares was $22.50, but because he bought more shares at $20, the average *cost to him* per share was only $22.22.

In Table 18 the person using the dollar cost averaging system had an average cost of $9.375 per share, since 128 shares were accumulated. Had the person used a share averaging system he would have bought 120 shares for the same dollar amount, resulting in an average cost of $10 per share.

TABLE 18

RESULTS OF DOLLAR AVERAGING

	Price	Equal Dollars Invested		Equal Number Shares Bought	
		Investment	Shares Bought	Investment	Shares Bought
1st Month	$ 7.00	$ 100	14.3 Shares	$ 70	10 Shares
2nd "	6.00	100	16.7 "	60	10 "
3rd "	8.00	100	12.5 "	80	10 "
4th "	10.00	100	10.0 "	100	10 "
5th "	11.00	100	9.1 "	110	10 "
6th "	13.00	100	7.7 "	130	10 "
7th "	15.00	100	6.7 "	150	10 "
8th "	12.00	100	8.3 "	120	10 "
9th "	11.00	100	9.1 "	110	10 "
10th "	9.00	100	11.1 "	90	10 "
11th "	8.00	100	12.5 "	80	10 "
12th "	10.00	100	10.0 "	100	10 "
Total		$1200	128.0 Shares	$1200	120 Shares

Average Cost per Share .... $9.375 .... $10.00

The question of when to sell remains, of course, with the individual. If the person sells his stock at a price above his average cost per share, he will have made money through dollar averaging, and stocks in well-managed companies in growing fields can be expected to increase in value over the long run, although they may fluctuate from day to day.

But of course it is possible to select a stock that moves in just one direction—downward. Dollar averaging won't do the trick for you in a case like that, nor will any other investment plan. This is an important point about dollar averaging. The plan will take care of timing for you—it won't take care of selection. But when you have the option of selecting stocks like General Motors, or General Electric, or General Dynamics, or any one of hundreds of other companies that will fail to grow with the country only if management is intent on bankruptcy, it calls for a special kind of genius to hit on an issue that can't find its own bottom.

One of the most convincing documents favoring the theory of dollar averaging that I have ever seen is a study by the Bureau of Business Research of the University of Michigan, published in 1953.

The study covers the period 1937 to 1950. It assumed that $92,000 was invested each year, at a specific time, in 92 common stocks listed on the New York Stock Exchange—$1,000 each year in each stock. In order to eliminate intentional or accidental bias, decisions as to timing and selection were made at random; or, as the study points out, "The present study has been deliberately and consistently designed to make the poorest showing possible whenever alternative choices were available."

Stocks selected included all industrial common stocks listed on the Exchange with trading volume of one million shares or more in the calendar year 1936. The selection was adhered to even when it became obvious that a particular stock should be eliminated for sound investment reasons. The portfolio is shown in Table 19.

The date of each annual investment, January 15, was selected at random. The Dow Jones average of 30 industrial stocks was just about the same at the start of the period cov-

TABLE 19

ALL INDUSTRIAL COMMON STOCKS LISTED ON THE NEW YORK STOCK EXCHANGE
WITH TRADING VOLUME OF ONE MILLION SHARES OR MORE DURING 1936

Allied Stores
Allis Chalmers
American Radiator
Armco
Anaconda
Armour
Avco
Baldwin Locomotive
Barnsdall Oil (Sunray)
Bendix Aviation
Bethlehem Steel
Boeing
Budd Manufacturing
Calumet & Hecla
Canada Dry
Celanese
Chrysler
Commercial Solvents
Consolidated Oil
Consolidated Textile
General Baking
Continental Motors
Continental Oil
Curtiss-Wright
Curtiss-Wright A
Distillers Corp.—Seagrams
Douglas Aircraft
Electric Auto-Lite
Electric Boat
General Electric
General Motors
Gimbel Brothers
Goodrich
Goodyear
Graham-Paige
Houston Oil
Hudson Motor
Hupp Motor
Interlake Iron
International Nickel of Canada
Kennecott Copper
Loew's
McKesson & Robbins
Minneapolis-Moline
Montgomery Ward
Murray Corporation of America

Nash-Kelvinator
National Biscuit
National Dairy Products
National Distillers
Newport Industries
North American Aviation
Ohio Oil
Otis Steel
Packard Motor
Paramount Pictures
Phillips Petroleum
Pure Oil
RCA
RKO
Remington Rand
Reo Motor
Republic Steel
Schenley Distillers
Sears Roebuck
Servel
Shell Oil
Simmons Company
Socony Vacuum
Sparks-Withington
Sperry Corporation
Standard Brands
Standard Oil of California
Standard Oil of Indiana
Standard Oil of New Jersey
Studebaker
Superior Oil
Texas Company
Texas Pacific Coal & Oil
Tide Water Association Oil
Timken-Detroit Axle
United Aircraft
United Air Lines
U. S. Rubber
U. S. Steel
Walworth
Warner Brothers
White Motor
Wilson & Company
Woolworth
Yellow Truck & Coach
Youngstown Sheet & Tube

ered as at the end; if the study had been extended through 1956, the results would be even more impressive.

Cash dividends and cash received from the sale of stock dividends were reinvested. Stock rights were exercised at the earliest possible date. Table 20 shows the results.

TABLE 20

INVESTOR-CONTRIBUTION AND MARKET VALUE OF TEST PORTFOLIO
OF COMMON STOCKS

	Investor-Contribution	Market Value of Portfolio	Ratio of Market Value to Contribution
1937	$ 92,000	$ 92,000	100%
1938	184,000	149,514	81
1939	276,000	255,589	93
1940	368,000	326,386	89
1941	460,000	412,083	90
1942	552,000	486,074	88
1943	644,000	690,273	107
1944	736,000	1,074,540	146
1945	828,000	1,580,878	191
1946	920,000	2,724,886	296
1947	1,012,000	2,169,708	214
1948	1,104,000	2,363,253	214
1949	1,196,000	2,525,266	211
1950	1,288,000	3,028,855	235

"The January 15, 1950, market value of the portfolio," the study noted, "is equivalent to the accumulation that the investor would have had if he had invested $92,000 each year on January 15 for fourteen years at a compound interest rate of 12.2 per cent."

If dollar averaging can show such results based on a random selection of stocks, dollar averaging plus intelligent selection should certainly be given a good deal of thought by the investor who is not out to make a killing but is interested in capital appreciation over an extended period.

The Monthly Investment Plan

The Monthly Investment Plan is a pay-as-you-go investment technique developed by member firms of the New York Stock Exchange. MIP, as it is usually called, is an excellent investment method for two reasons: it leans heavily on dollar cost averaging and it provides an easy yet sound way for the low- to medium-income investor to purchase stocks.

Ruddick C. Lawrence, the Exchange's Vice President in charge of Public Relations and Market Development, has played a key role in encouraging public acceptance of MIP. I asked him if he'd like to comment on the growth of the Plan and he wrote me early in 1957:

Until the Monthly Investment Plan was first introduced to the public in January, 1954, member firms of the New York Stock Exchange did not know how people throughout the country would respond to such a plan for investing out of income on a periodic basis. After three years of experience with the Monthly Investment Plan, the answer is clear—and heartening.

Throughout the nation investors have started to buy their own shares of American business for as little as $40 a month, or even $40 a quarter. A few brief statistics illuminate the exciting growth of this investment technique: Over 93,500 plans have been started; more than $52,000,000 has been invested in well over a million shares of common stock listed on the New York Stock Exchange. In addition, some 160 additional new plans are being opened each day. Without any doubt, the Monthly Investment Plan has become a meaningful force in the old securities market place.

Even so, these figures cannot suggest the impact that MIP has had on countless individuals everywhere. They dramatize for the public the fact that member firms welcome people who are considering only modest stock purchases. The great bulk of MIP investors look on the Plan as a simple and sensible way to buy shares in America by the dollar's worth. They seek both dividend and profit possibilities. They have tended overwhelmingly to concentrate on blue chip securities and to reinvest their dividends. They appreciate that MIP is for the long term and is not a get-rich-quick vehicle.

These factors, more than anything else, are among MIP's greatest assets. The Monthly Investment Plan has helped to bring share-ownership within easy reach of America's middle-income millions.

I agree with Mr. Lawrence. MIP is a real contribution to the needs of investors.

MIP has been criticized on the ground that it is a relatively high-cost operation, a criticism which seems to me to be somewhat on the captious side in view of the plan's basic merits. The commission on each investment of less than $100 is a flat 6 per cent. When the investment is $100 or more, the commission is $3 plus 1 per cent, with a minimum of $6. Thus it would be a good deal less expensive for you to save up your $40 each month and invest a total of $480 a year. It's a good theory but I shudder to think what would happen if it were carried over to the automobile business. Too many people find it virtually impossible to establish a fund for any purpose—to buy a car, to buy a share of stock, to buy a house. It's a lot easier to make payments at regular intervals.

I've heard the suggestion made that one way to get around the high cost of small investments is to borrow from the bank and repay the loan in monthly installments. Actually the cost of investing via a bank loan is higher, assuming a 6 per cent effective interest rate on an unsecured personal loan, than through MIP. Let's say you borrow enough to net you $1,200, which would cost you in interest charges about $75. The commission on your $1,200 investment would amount to $15, a total cost of $90. If you invested $100 a month through the Monthly Investment Plan, though, commissions would amount to $72, so in this case you would actually save a few dollars investing through MIP.

Or let's say you borrow a net of $480. The commission on your $480 investment would be $7.80, plus interest on the loan of $28.80, a total of $36.60. But the commissions on 12 investments of $40 each would be $27.00.

MIP is noncontractual and does not involve dues, penalties, management charges, or any other kind of fee, hidden or otherwise. You can cancel your plan whenever you want to and you may even skip two or three payments.

Under MIP you buy stock by the dollar's worth, which, of course, is a keystone of dollar averaging. If your monthly payment is $40 and the stock you are buying sells at $30 a share, your account is credited with 1.280 shares; $38.40 is used to purchase your stock while $1.60 represents the commission. You can arrange to have your dividends sent to you directly or automatically reinvested; the great majority of plans call for automatic reinvestment.

You own the stock you buy, of course, the minute your order is executed. However, you normally do not receive your certificate until your plan is completed or until you have accumulated 50 shares. If you want your certificate earlier, a nominal charge is made.

You can vote your stock just as any other stockholder and sell it whenever you wish.

Surprisingly, some MIP investors pay in as much as the maximum of $999 a month, so evidently wealthier investors also find some merit in the plan. The average payment, though, is less than $100.

On the assumption that the great majority of MIP investors are newcomers to the market, they are either getting excellent advice from their brokers or putting a great deal of time and thought into making their selections. Table 21 shows the 50 issues most popular with MIP investors and it is a choice selection indeed. I am particularly impressed by the fact that the list includes two closed-end investment trusts, which are discussed later in this chapter.

TABLE 21

FIFTY MOST POPULAR STOCKS

Monthly Investment Plan

(based on number of plans as of December 28, 1956)

Name of Stock	Number of Plans	Name of Stock	Number of Plans
General Electric	3,256	General Dynamics	420
General Motors	2,693	United Fruit	411
Dow Chemical	2,230	Standard Oil of California	398
Standard Oil (N. J.)	1,924	Columbia Gas System	392
Sperry Rand	1,821	Safeway Stores	384
Radio Corporation	1,739	Pacific Gas & Electric	372
American Tel. & Tel.	1,364	American Cyanamid	371
Tri-Continental Corp.	1,215	National Biscuit	365
American Airlines	807	Int'l Business Machines	319
E. I. du Pont de Nemours	792	Carrier Corp.	318
Phillips Petroleum	750	Consolidated Edison	317
Lehman Corporation	679	Minnesota Mining	317
Union Carbide & Carbon	661	Texas Company	314
Gulf Oil Corporation	637	Long Island Lighting	286
Olin Mathieson Chemical	595	Standard Oil of Indiana	285
Monsanto Chemical	590	Sunray Mid-Continent Oil	277
Sears, Roebuck	587	Commonwealth Edison	274
Westinghouse Electric	586	Aluminum Ltd.	268
U. S. Steel	582	Sinclair Oil	264
Kaiser Aluminum & Chemical.	487	Socony Mobil Oil	256
United Gas	482	Canadian Pacific Ry.	254
American Can	476	Detroit Edison	250
Reynolds Metals	459	Southern Company	250
Aluminum Co. of America	431	Pfizer (Chas.) & Company	247
Eastman Kodak	428	Greyhound Corporation	232

At the end of MIP's first three years of operation, well over 1,000,000 shares of stock had been bought through the plan and about 93,500 individual plans started. A total of

$51,700,000 had been invested. These figures admittedly are not very impressive when measured against a single day's volume on the exchange of 2,000,000 shares or more. The answer is that the great majority of Exchange members find it more profitable to sell mutual funds than MIP plans, irrespective of their relative merits.

Despite this cavalier treatment, I believe the Monthly Investment Plan is solidly entrenched with the investing public as a sound method of accumulating common stocks.

Mutual Funds

There are two kinds of investment companies. One, better known as the mutual fund, is the open-end investment trust; the other is the closed-end investment trust. The basic difference between a mutual fund and a closed-end investment trust is that the mutual buys and sells its own shares. Shares in a closed-end trust are bought and sold in the open market.

The mutual fund is a pool of money formed by purchasing shares in the fund. For instance, you and nine friends might each contribute $10,000 to form a mutual fund with assets of $100,000. The assets are used to purchase the securities of other companies. A mutual fund is willing—I might even say eager—to sell additional shares to other people. But there is no public market in the shares of a mutual fund; the fund itself sells the shares, and the fund buys back its own shares when people want to sell. The price is based on the fund's net asset value per share, which is figured by dividing the market value of the fund's assets by the total number of shares outstanding. Mutuals usually calculate the market value of their assets twice a day.

The price paid by the buyer of shares in a mutual fund is based on the net asset value per share plus a so-called loading charge—really a commission—which averages around 8 or 9 per cent of the net asset value. In a few special cases *no* loading charge is made, or it amounts to only 1 or 2 per cent. In addition to the loading charge, the owner of shares in a mutual fund is tagged with an annual management fee amounting to around one-half of 1 per cent of the value of his investment.

Mutual funds will buy back their own shares, usually at no charge, or at most a nominal one.

The investment objectives of mutual funds range from the highly conservative to the frankly speculative. Some funds invest their resources only in bonds. Self-styled balanced funds spread their capital over bonds, preferred and common stocks, and cash. Some specialize in high-grade common stocks, others in growth stocks, others in stocks with a record of high dividend payments. Some stick to one or a handful of industries, others seek for a high degree of diversification.

In the past few years a new group of funds has sprung up, funds specializing in atomic energy stocks, Canadian stocks, television stock, uranium stocks. One fund, now defunct, was formed to finance Broadway shows.

The growth of mutual funds in recent years is one of the phenomena of the securities industry. In 1940 there were 68 open-end investment companies with fewer than 300,000 shareholder accounts. At the end of 1956 there were 135 mutuals, members of the National Association of Investment Companies (plus some 15 nonmembers). These 135 embrace 2,518,000 shareholder accounts. The year-end market value of open-end funds increased from $770 millions in 1944 to $9,046 millions at the end of 1956.

In 1956 the funds redeemed $433,000,000 in shares but sold $1,347,000,000 in new shares, leaving a net gain of $914,-000,000.

Probably the main reason for the growth of mutuals has

been aggressive selling, selling so aggressive that in 1950 the Securities and Exchange Commission published a code that was designed to prevent the public from getting extravagant ideas about the investment potentials of mutuals. Late in 1956 the SEC had under study a program to tighten up still further on what could be said about a mutual fund and what couldn't.

If you have never been approached by a mutual fund salesman, it's probably because you live in a lighthouse off the coast of Maine. When the salesman does get to you, though, he will emphasize these points about a mutual:

1. Diversification. You're not putting all your eggs in one basket. Maybe, if the worst comes to the worst, one or two stocks in a fund may turn out to be flea-carriers—but look at the protection you get from the other issues in the fund, which have been selected with uncanny foresight.

2. Expert management. Mutual funds are administered by skilled professionals, securities analysts who probe deep into every factor that might affect the value of a stock.

3. Ready marketability. You can always sell your shares in a mutual fund when you want to.

4. Federal regulation. Mutual funds operate under the Investment Company Act of 1940, which is administered by the Securities and Exchange Commission.

The best of these arguments is diversification. No question about it that a man who owns just one or two stocks is more vulnerable to the vicissitudes of the market than the man who owns a share in 50 or 100 issues. At the same time, the diversification offered by a mutual does have the effect of holding down the performance of the entire portfolio. Out of 50 or 100 or even more stocks in a fund, some will inevitably pull down the others. You may find it far more profitable—and I certainly believe this to be true—to concentrate on one or two or three individual stocks, depending of course on the soundness of your selection.

The claim of expert management may be a dubious one. Some funds are extremely well managed; others are not. The best way to find out is to look at the record of the individual fund.

Funds are readily marketable, but so is any security listed on a stock exchange. Under some conditions, as a matter of fact, a mutual does not have to buy back its stock on demand.

Federal regulation of investment companies is fine but—as in other areas of the securities business under the eye of the SEC—full disclosure is the key. The SEC does not tell any investment company what or when to buy or sell.

Before you decide to buy a mutual, look at the prospectus.

Closed-End Investment Companies

The closed-end trust, unlike the mutual fund, has a fixed number of shares outstanding, and the price of these shares is determined by supply and demand. The larger trusts are listed on the New York Stock Exchange, and the market price may be above or below the net asset value per share of the stock.

The cost of buying diversification through a closed-end investment company is considerably less than through a mutual fund. This advantage, though, may be offset for some investors by the wider range of the portfolios held by some mutuals as compared with closed-end companies.

On the other hand, I don't know of any mutual fund that offers the profit possibilities of the special situation as exploited by several closed-end companies, notably Atlas Corporation. In a typical special situation, the investment company may acquire operating control of a corporation, put in new management if necessary, perhaps modify the company's policy, and in short convert a sluggish operation into a highly profitable enterprise.

Another advantage cited in favor of the closed-end companies is that their managements are not influenced to any degree by the necessity for buying and selling the company's own shares. A mutual, for instance, must keep part of its assets in cash in order to be in a position to redeem its own stock. A closed-end company has no such obligation.

Investment companies got a well-deserved black eye as the result of the excesses of the 1920's, when the general attitude in Wall Street was, "Anything goes, fellows." There were only a handful of open-end companies then, while literally hundreds of closed-end companies flourished, if that's the word, and most were guilty of practices that are remembered today with regret and sorrow. The investment company then was not so much an investment technique as a method of paying off some investment banker's mortgage, peddling securities that would raise the eyebrows of a Montreal stock swindler, and providing fancy salaries for consultants, special advisers, and other insiders.

Even then, though, there were men and firms who were thoroughly aware of their responsibilities to the public and who cherished their good name. For instance, I recently ran across the annual report of the Lehman Corporation, a closed-end investment trust that was established, of all times, on September 24, 1929. The report, in a sense, is a saga of financial integrity.

"A stockholder who paid $104 for one share of capital stock of the Lehman Corporation when it was originally issued September 24, 1929, and kept his investment continuously since then," the report stated, "held on June 30, 1956, six shares of capital stock with a total net asset value of $314.40 and a market value of $278.91.

"During this period, he received in dividends, including those declared June 27, 1956, a total of $111.79 paid from the corporation's net ordinary income and a total of $116.83 from profit realized on investments."

That's pretty good going.

To sum up, open-end and closed-end investment companies relieve the investor, at least in part, of the burden of diversification and timing. In addition, some of them provide the investor with intriguing choices as to the degree of risk he is willing to assume and the opportunity to exploit special situations. But investment companies, like any other securities, should not be bought blindfolded; some are good, some mediocre, and some lousy. It's up to the investor to find out which is which.

The bible of the investment company business is Arthur Wiesenberger's *Investment Companies,* published annually. What Mr. Wiesenberger does not know about investment companies, nobody knows. The work is comparatively expensive—$25 a copy—but you may find one in your public library or at your local broker. The book is really a masterpiece of intelligent presentation of a vast amount of statistical data.

Less ambitious but highly informative is a booklet, "Investment Trust and Funds from the Investor's Point of View," published by the American Institute for Economic Research, Great Barrington, Massachusetts.

Formula Investing

Formula plans for investment are designed to take the problem of timing purchases and sales out of the hands of the investor. These plans do not tell you *what* to buy or sell; they do tell you *when* to buy or sell. The plans are keyed to the magnificently simple dictum: buy stocks when they are low, sell when they are high.

Formula investing is not for the run-of-the-mill investor because the plans demand a fairly substantial original investment. However, a bank administering a common trust fund might use a formula plan, and if you're considering establishing a trust fund for as little as $5,000 or $10,000, you might want to have at least an idea of what formula investing is. A common trust fund, by the way, is simply a collection of relatively small individual trust funds that are lumped together and administered as a unit.

Formula investing was given a great deal of prestige when several colleges—notably Yale, Oberlin, and Vassar—announced they were using formulas to invest part of their endowments. The most successful methods seem to veer away from rigid adherence to mathematical formulas, and instead allow a certain amount of flexibility and use of good judgment.

CONSTANT DOLLAR PLAN

This is probably the simplest type of formula plan. Let's say the investor starts out with $50,000. He decides that half will be employed to purchase common stocks, while half will be used to buy bonds or retained as cash. He also decides that the dollar value of his common stock investment will be allowed to vary only within predetermined limits. The value of his common stocks declines, say, $5,000 to $20,-000; so he sells $5,000 worth of bonds and invests the proceeds in common stocks, bringing the value of his common stock investment back to $25,000. Or if the value of his stocks increases by $5,000, he sells stocks and uses the profit to buy bonds or to place in his cash account.

CONSTANT RATIO PLAN

This is based on maintaining a predetermined percentage of the market value of the assets of the fund in common stocks and a specific percentage in bonds or cash. Thus if the investor had decided upon a ratio of 60 per cent stocks and 40 per cent bonds or cash, any percentage variation from the norm of, say, 5 or 10 percentage points would call for a shift in holdings to restore the portfolio to the proper ratios.

VARIABLE RATIO PLAN

The third type of formula investing is probably the most frequently used. This type of plan is tied directly to an arbitrarily selected median or norm. The norm might be, for example, 250 on the Dow Jones industrial average. At that level of the average, half of the fund's assets will be invested in bonds or kept in reserve as cash, half in stocks. Changes in the portfolio will be made whenever the average advances or declines a predetermined number of percentage points. If the average declines to 200, for instance, the percentage of the value of stocks held might be increased to 60 per cent; at 150, stock holdings would be boosted to 70 per cent; at 100, they would be boosted to 80 per cent. Similarly, in a rising market stock holdings would be cut to 40 per cent when the average reached 300, to 30 per cent at 350, to 20 per cent at 400, and to 10 per cent at 450. Under this plan, obviously, the selection of the median is of prime importance —whether the median is the D-J industrial average, the Department of Commerce's cost of living index, or the Federal Reserve Board's index of industrial production.

Formula plans have paid off. There's little question that they work—but there is a question whether they are the ultimate solution to the requirements of the investor who is willing to put some thought into timing and selection.

The constant dollar plan seems to be the most vulnerable to criticism. For instance, if the plan were started at the top of a price cycle, the investor would inevitably run into substantial losses. This plan, too, allows little room for growth and makes little provision for the long-term upward trend of the market. The constant ratio plan is more elastic and does afford some room for growth. The variable ratio plan would seem to be the best of all—although, as I mentioned, its success hinges almost entirely upon the selection of the norm. All plans appear to have the drawback of assuming that bonds—the defensive section of the portfolio—will show little variation in price. Bonds, even the best, can putter along for years without decisive price swings: they can also show surprising agility—which portfolio managers have discovered to their sorrow—when the cost of borrowing money sharply advances or declines.

Formula plans, in general, can be ignored except for investors with substantial assets who will be content with a limited return on their investment.

Pyramiding

Pyramiding is the stock market equivalent of Russian Roulette. It's speculation at its worst—fast, tricky, dangerous and sometimes profitable. In the bad old days, in the 1920's, pyramiding was a favorite trading device. After all, it's pretty exciting to build up a paper profit running into thousands of dollars on a cash investment of a few hundreds. Fortunately, the high margin requirements of today virtually eliminate pyramiding as a speculative device.

Pyramiding is the fine art of taking a little whipped cream, adding a liberal portion of hot air, spicing with essence of cloud, and producing a fortune. Here's how it used to work.

You started out with $1,000 in cash. You bought on margin of, for the purposes of this fairy tale, 10 per cent. A 10 per cent margin sounds almost fantastic now, but in 1929 a customer with a good credit rating could get away with no margin at all. Today the margin requirement is 70 per cent —which means that you put up 70 per cent of the value of your purchase in cash—and the chances of a reduction to any-where near 10 per cent are roughly equal to those of William McChesney Martin walking up Fifth Avenue stark naked.

Your $1,000, based on a 10 per cent margin, buys $10,000 worth of stock—or, figuring the stock costs $10 a share, you buy 1,000 shares. At this point, incidentally, you owe your broker $9,000.

Lo and behold, the price of your stock advanced to $20 a share, a net gain of $10 a share. You had a paper profit now of $10,000, or a total equity in your account of $11,000—that is, your original investment of $1,000 plus your profit of $10,000.

Now you started pyramiding. With your buying power of $110,000 you could buy 5,000 shares of stock at $20 a share— again assuming the purchase was made on a margin of 10 per cent. 5,500 shares at $20 each cost $110,000; 10 per cent of that sum was $11,000. At this stage you owed your broker $99,000.

The price of your stock advanced another 10 points to $30 a share. (The mathematics of this are hard to believe, but it happened time and again.) Your profit on the 5,500 shares bought at $20 each amounted to $55,000. Add to that your original investment of $1,000, and the profit you made on your first purchase of $10,000. Total: $66,000. Now your buying power had jumped to $660,000, with which you bought 22,000 shares at $30 each. If you were the worrying type, you might have been interested in knowing that you owed your broker $594,000.

Incredible? Sure, but keep on going. The price of your

stock got up to $60 a share. Then you have an equity of $3,003,000—and buying power of $30,030,000. Your 1,000 shares had grown to 500,500. Not bad for an original investment of $1,000.

It just happened that $10 stocks did not always go to $60. It also happened that an account with a 10 per cent margin could be wiped out faster than you'd like to say "scat" to the income tax collector. Mathematically, though, pyramiding was fascinating—even if you went broke applying the theory.

Pyramiding on a 70 per cent margin, by the way, produces miserable results in contrast with those achieved on a 10 per cent down payment. In the case of a $10 stock that advances to $60 a share, your equity increases to $10,724.60 and your buying power to $15,321.20. Instead of holding 500,500 shares, the best you can do is 255.4 shares.

Figures are certainly entertaining.

Follow the Experts

The ultimate question that faces every investor is how to select a stock. Right this moment, if you have $1,000 clutched in your clammy little fist and you want to invest your money in a good common stock, how do you pick your stock? There are all sorts of methods available to you, ranging from consulting a broker to making your own painstaking analysis of stocks that appeal to you for one reason or another.

One intriguing approach is to base your selection on what the experts in the field have done. By experts, I mean the professional money managers who guide the investment decisions for the huge sums of money accumulated by college endowment funds, insurance companies, banks, and the like. You can very easily find out what they have bought and how much. The decisions of these funds have not been lightly reached and should not be ignored, but I would suggest a certain amount of caution in using this type of information.

First, you can't find out *when* an institutional investor has bought 10,000 shares of XYZ or sold 10,000 shares of ABC common. By the time the report has reached you, the fund managers may have completely reversed their thinking about a particular stock. The report, as of the year end, may show a substantial acquisition of U. S. Steel. Six months later, when you receive the report, you don't know if U. S. Steel is still favored or not.

Second, it's a little disquieting to discover that one fund, widely respected for its good judgment, has sold 10,000 shares of General Electric, while another fund, equally well respected, has bought 10,000 shares of GE.

Two valuable guides, though, may be obtained from studying the portfolios of the experts. If Yale University's endowment fund buys 1,000 shares of XYZ in one year, 2,000 shares the next year, 5,000 shares the following year, and 5,000 shares the year after that—well, obviously, it would seem worth while to give a little closer study to XYZ.

Also, if a particular stock shows up in the portfolios of scores of funds, I'd be inclined to think that such popularity must be deserved.

"Dividends Over the Years," a pamphlet published by member firms of the New York Stock Exchange and available from any one of them, includes a table of stocks most favored by institutional investors. The list is based on a survey of the security holdings of more than 1,400 funds, including fire, casuality, and life insurance companies, investment trusts, endowment funds, and common trust funds. The survey was made by Data Digests Inc. Table 22 shows the favorites on the basis of the most recently available information.

TABLE 22

STOCKS LISTED ON THE NYSE MOST FAVORED BY INSTITUTIONAL INVESTORS [1]

Number of Institutions	Company	Number of Institutions	Company
729	Standard Oil (N. J.)	275	Pacific Gas & Elec.
590	General Electric	274	American Cyanamid
588	American Tel. & Tel.	272	Southern Cal. Edison
563	General Motors	270	Texas Utilities
546	Union Carbide	269	Consumers Power
528	E. I. du Pont de Nemours	264	American Can
503	Phillips Petroleum	264	Niagara Mohawk Power
483	Texas Company	263	International Harvester
430	Socony Mobil Oil	248	National Lead
413	Gulf Oil	247	Intl. Business Machines
412	Westinghouse Electric	246	National Dairy Prod.
384	Kennecott Copper	240	U. S. Steel
376	Commonwealth Edison	233	General Foods
367	Sears Roebuck	233	Johns Manville
364	Standard Oil of Calif.	232	Ohio Edison
342	American Gas & Electric	231	Central & South West.
334	Standard Oil of Indiana	226	Union Pacific RR
317	Allied Chem. & Dye	220	Shell Oil
313	Monsanto Chemical	219	Cleveland Elec. Ill.
300	Eastman Kodak	216	Middle South Util.
391	Dow Chemical	210	Atch. Topeka & San. Fe
290	Continental Oil (Del.)	209	Con. Edison N. Y.
286	Penney, J. C.	209	Continental Can
283	United Gas Corp.	209	Virginia Elec. & Pr.
280	International Paper	200	Philadelphia Elec.

[1] Unlisted bank stocks favored by institutions are not included.

TABLE 23

MOST POPULAR ISSUES AMONG INVESTMENT FUNDS

1.	Standard Oil (N. J.)	14.	General Electric
2.	International Paper	15.	Goodyear
3.	Amerada Petroleum	16.	Goodrich
4.	Texas Company	17.	Union Carbide
5.	General Motors	18.	Phillips Petroleum
6.	U. S. Steel	19.	Aluminum Co. of Amer.
7.	Standard Oil of Calif.	20.	National Lead
8.	Aluminum Ltd.	21.	American Tel. & Tel.
9.	Continental Oil	22.	Sinclair Oil
10.	Bethlehem Steel	23.	Socony Mobil Oil
11.	Gulf Oil	24.	Kennecott Copper
12.	Du Pont	25.	Armco Steel
13.	Intl. Business Machines		

Tabulating these issues is not intended to recommend any one of them, but rather to allow for comparison with other professionally managed portfolios.

Another published list of issues most favored by investors is prepared by Vickers Brothers and published semiannually. Table 23 shows the 25 top favorites among mutual funds and investment trusts.

TABLE 24

TWENTY-FIVE MOST VALUABLE BLOCKS OF COMMON STOCKS LISTED ON THE
NEW YORK STOCK EXCHANGE OWNED JOINTLY BY 66 NEW YORK STATE
MUTUAL SAVINGS BANKS IN 1956

Shares	Common Stock	Market Value
3,400..........	Aluminum Co.	$407,150
12,225..........	American Gas & Elec.	487,472
6,000..........	Climax Molybdenum	428,250
11,600..........	Commercial Credit	580,000
10,150..........	Commonwealth Edison	411,075
4,000..........	Continental Oil	495,000
2,200..........	Du Pont	464,200
6,100..........	Eastman Kodak	558,913
7,500..........	Firestone Tire	637,500
9,500..........	General Amer. Transportation	646,000
8,500..........	General Foods	396,313
10,500..........	General Motors	472,500
5,800..........	B. F Goodrich	475,600
9,000..........	Hercules Powder	434,250
4,000..........	Kennecott Copper	498,000
9,500..........	McKesson & Robbins	451,250
17,500..........	Merck & Co.	586,250
9,500..........	Natl. Dairy Products	377,625
11,000..........	National Tea	448,250
4,500..........	Phillips Petroleum	444,937
8,400..........	Pillsbury Mills	384,300
7,625..........	Socony Mobil Oil	441,297
7,000..........	Sterling Drug	369,250
6,000..........	Union Oil of Calif.	369,750
8,000..........	United Carbon	482,000

Table 24 is still another list of issues selected by the experts. The "expert" in this case is a fund jointly owned by 66 New York State mutual savings banks, a fund that has the primary objective of dividend income.

Here's still another glimpse of the decisions of experts, this time the stocks most popular with common trust funds. (See page 207.) The following, based on a survey of 205 common trust funds administered by 168 banks in 36 states, the District of Columbia, and Hawaii, was made by the magazine *Trusts and Estates*.

TABLE 25

FIFTEEN ISSUES LISTED ON THE NYSE MOST POPULAR WITH
COMMON TRUST FUNDS

Number of Funds	*Common Stock*
157	Standard Oil Co. (N. J.)
151	Union Carbide
151	General Motors
150	American Tel. & Tel.
145	General Electric
138	Texas Company
127	Du Pont
126	Phillips Petroleum
114	Sears Roebuck
110	Socony Mobil Oil
107	Westinghouse Elec.
106	Natl. Dairy Products
100	J. C. Penney
95	Kennecott Copper
92	General Foods

Notice the number of companies that appear almost monotonously in each list? Evidently the experts think pretty well of such issues, as Standard Oil (New Jersey), Du Pont, Union Carbide, General Motors, Phillips Petroleum, Socony Mobil Oil, and Kennecott Copper.

Investment Clubs

The investment club is one answer to the all-important questions of what to buy and when that has caught on with amazing speed in recent years. According to one estimate, there are more than 10,000 clubs with more than 100,000 members.

An investment club is simply a small group of people—a ceiling of 20 on the membership is considered desirable—the members of which contribute a small amount of money each month toward a group investment. Monthly contributions range from $10 to around $25, in a few cases more. The club meets once or twice each month to discuss investment possibilities or the status of an investment already made. Occasionally the club's broker will be invited to sit in on the discussion, but by and large this is strictly do-it-yourself investing.

Clubs may be formed by people working in the same office or living in the same neighborhood—the clubs are not wholly business ventures nor are they wholly social, but a pleasant combination of both.

A great majority of the people who form or join investment clubs are innocents in the field of finance, but I have been told that it doesn't take too many meetings before they are talking fluently about price-earnings ratios, dividend records, managerial competence, and industry prospects.

There exists a National Association of Investment Clubs, at 2224 National Bank Building, Detroit 26, Michigan. Membership in the Association costs only one dollar per year per club member, in return for which you get help on setting up a club, record forms, a monthly newsletter, and other literature. The Association also sponsors investment clinics and forums.

If the idea of an investment club appeals to you, I suggest you talk over forming one with your local broker. Because of widely differing state regulations, there are important legal questions to consider before forming a club.

CHAPTER 18

A New Approach:

Put All Your Eggs in One Basket

SOME STOCKBROKERS, I'm tempted to believe, seem to have taken some sort of Hippocratic Oath at an early stage in their careers, somewhat along these lines:

"I shall advise my clients at regular intervals—monthly, or weekly if they'll stand for it—not to put all their eggs in one basket. I shall advise my clients to diversify their investments because diversification will lead them to riches and happiness."

Maybe that is good advice, maybe not. I personally believe that it is not. My own conviction is that three or four carefully selected stocks—perhaps as many as five—can be a lot more profitable for the careful investor than a hodgepodge of securities chosen mainly because they represent different industries. Diversification is dandy, but not when it's simply for the sake of diversification.

My principal reasons against carrying diversification to an extreme are that one man cannot possibly have an intimate

218

working knowledge of more than a bare handful of companies; and second, that it's a lot easier to select three or four good securities than twenty or thirty. Maybe twenty or thirty issues will give you diversification, but the law of averages tells me that there are bound to be one or two issues in that group that will also give you a headache.

Not to labor the point, I can bolster this argument with the record of several successful investors.

John D. Rockefeller, Sr., managed to amass a tidy number of millions in spite of the fact that he certainly put the lion's share of his savings into Standard Oil stock.

And I've never heard that Henry Ford was a great guy to invest a few thousands in every new security offering.

Every now and then the "insider" reports of the Securities and Exchange Commission show that Alfred P. Sloan, Jr., has a great many eggs indeed in one basket—a basket labeled "General Motors common stock"—with a market value running into many millions of dollars.

Let's look a little more closely at diversification versus nondiversification.

Assume that a well-heeled investor decided—about a decade ago—to buy 100 shares each of 10 common stocks—Stocks A, B, C, D, E, F, G, H, K, and L—all of them selling at $50 a share. Disregarding commissions and taxes, these 1,000 shares would have cost him $50,000.

It seems reasonable to assume further—in view of the performance of the stock market in the past ten years—that some of these 10 stocks chalked up a brisk advance in price; a few moved in exactly the opposite direction; and a few others showed little change.

Consequently, it wouldn't be stretching the laws of probability too much to figure that Stocks A, B, and C were selling in the market at the end of 10 years exactly the same price—$50 a share—as they did a decade earlier.

On the other hand, the market value of the 100 shares of Stock D had risen by the end of the 10 years from $5,000 to $9,000. Stock E hadn't done quite so well—100 shares being worth only $8,500—but Stock F had advanced enough so that 100 shares were worth $10,000. Stock G had performed even better, the 100 shares of that issue having a market value of $12,500.

Unfortunately, however, Stock H had fallen to the point where 100 shares were worth only $4,000 instead of $5,000. Stock K had dipped to a market value of $3,500 per 100 shares, and the market value of 100 shares of Stock L amounted to $4,500.

All in all—and it would be no trick to cite actual issues listed on the New York Stock Exchange that have recorded market performances exactly like the 10 stocks in the alphabetical portfolio—the total market value of the 1,000 shares amounted to $67,000 at the end of 10 years. This represented a net capital gain of $17,000, or 34 per cent—not bad, perhaps, but nothing to shout about when viewed in the light of the market's over-all performance during the last ten years.

Suppose that, instead of buying 100 shares of each of 10 different stocks, our hypothetical investor had bought 300 shares each of Stock D, Stock E, and Stock F? In that case, his total investment would have been slightly less—$45,000; and the current market quotations of his 900-share portfolio would have been $82,500, an increase of more than 83 per cent on a slightly smaller initial investment.

If he had purchased 300 shares each of Stocks D, F, and G, his capital gain on his original $45,000 investment would have been even more impressive—well over 100 per cent. Of course, if he had selected and stuck with Stocks H, K, and L, he would have suffered a loss instead of a gain.

My viewpoint is based on the belief that careful selection

would have by-passed stocks H, K, and L—if not at the out-set, then certainly somewhere along the way.

While I'm establishing my position as a nondiversifier, I am not trying to qualify for admittance to the buy-them-and-leave-them-alone school of thought. Concentrate on a few stocks by all means, but don't consign them to a bank vault as soon as you buy them.

Early in the present century one of the most highly re-garded common stocks of that era—or any other—was New Haven Railroad. The stock sold at about $250 per share, paid generous dividends. Earnings were good, prospects bright. Indeed, so highly did many hardheaded, wealthy New England industrialists regard New Haven stock that they left bundles of it to their heirs, specifically providing in their wills that the beneficiaries might live on the dividends but could not sell the shares for any reason whatsoever. That was fine when New Haven paid generous dividends regularly.

But the time came, and came all too quickly, when New Haven stock didn't pay generous dividends—or any dividends at all, for that matter. Any of the beneficiaries who were farsighted enough to see the railroad's financial troubles coming were powerless to avert their own personal financial disasters, since the terms of the wills wouldn't permit the New Haven stock to be sold.

Getting back to the question of diversification, and to put it bluntly: not one businessman in a thousand, busy trying to get ahead in his own line of endeavor, has the time, pa-tience, or ability to manage a personal portfolio containing 15, 20, or more stocks. The largest number of stocks that can be supervised effectively and intelligently is probably five. If you want to scale that down to three, I won't object.

Time and Trouble

You won't like this advice, but skim over it at least long enough to disagree. Selecting your first stock admittedly is no easy job, but I would like to emphasize that there is never—and let's repeat that—*never* any need to hurry about making an investment. If you doubt it, try this: The next time someone tells you—and someone certainly will, unless you're in solitary confinement—that XYZ shares will run up 16 points in the next 10 days, just make a mental short sale of the stock recommended—and do nothing else. Nine times out of ten, the shares will be *lower* 10 days later—and 30 days later, and 60 days later—than they were the day you got the "tip."

But suppose they're not? Suppose the stock runs up, not 16, but 61 points, in the next days?

Forget it!

If you had purchased the stock on someone else's say-so, you would have been lucky, it's true, but you certainly wouldn't be entitled to take any credit for your investment judgment. And it probably would have encouraged you to keep on taking "tips" until you lost all your quick profits and your capital as well. For all you knew personally about the stock, it could have been issued by some company whose management had invested a large amount of funds in machines to turn out buggy whips in the confident belief that the motor car was merely a passing fad.

Most of the time, though, you will be glad that you ignored the "tip"—no matter who gave it to you.

The only stocks for you to buy are ones that you have selected personally—with the advice and counsel of a good broker, if you like, but certainly not on a "tip" given you by someone who may be considerably less qualified than you to make an intelligent investment decision.

And don't let it bother you if you learn that some stock like Reynolds Metals soared several thousand per cent in market price in a matter of months. Most of the traders on the floor of the Stock Exchange—men who do nothing else but buy and sell shares—didn't make a dime on that stock, so why should you think you should have?

If you are inclined to agree with me that the average businessman will be well advised to confine his portfolio to a maximum of four or five stocks, does this mean that the investor should buy all of them immediately?

Not at all!

First, select one—and again, don't be in a hurry—and then take an equal amount of time, possibly even more, to choose the second one. Then repeat the process with the third, and so on. Unless, of course, you come to the conclusion that two will do you very nicely.

How should you select the first stock? Well, like a businessman, you must know—by reputation, if nothing else—something about companies like General Motors, Standard Oil (New Jersey), Du Pont, or many others of like stature.

Maybe you have other ideas, though. Good—but that may involve hard work. If you have your eye on a particular company, study it—its earnings, dividend record, business history, prospects, market price of its shares in relation to historic highs and lows, everything and anything you can get your hands on. Maybe this will convince you that this particular stock is not for you. If so, fine, keep on looking.

This is not meant to suggest that you can, if you're shrewd enough, call the turn on the short-term course of a company's stock. You can't. But you can decide that, for your individual purposes, the stock of your choice is one you'd like to own for the next five or ten years, regardless of its market price fluctuations in the next six months or a year.

The same procedure is recommended for the second

stock—and the third—and the fourth and fifth if you buy that many.

Even If It Hurts

Now let's assume that you have acquired a three-stock portfolio. In the meantime, the first issue you selected has been a big disappointment to you. It has paid smaller dividends than you expected. Its earnings have fallen below your estimates. And your current appraisal of the management's ability is less enthusiastic than it was 36 months ago.

What then?

There's only one answer:

Sell! It may hurt your pocketbook and it may hurt your vanity; but sell!

There's another possibility that you shouldn't overlook. What should you do if one of the three stocks in your portfolio, which met and continues to meet all your personal investment requirements and standards, fails to advance or even declines?

If you're sure you're right—if earnings are good, dividends reasonable, and management first class—there's only one course for you to pursue:

The longer the stock of your choice continues in the doldrums, the more shares you can add to your portfolio. And more important, the greater will be your eventual profit—if you've selected a good, sound stock and don't lose your nerve when the time comes that you can buy another 100 shares for only $2,500 even though the first 100 you purchased cost you $5,500.

You've got to have the courage to hold on to a stock when you have complete confidence in its future—even boosting your holdings periodically—despite the fact that the market price plainly shows that many another investor has a poorer opinion of the issue than you have.

Perhaps more important, you've also got to have the strength of will to admit you've made a bad investment decision, and sell any stock that doesn't deserve your highest investment rating.

You'll find that managing a three-stock portfolio or a four-stock portfolio will take all the time and thought you can give to it.

But, if you do your job right, you'll find also that this same small portfolio can be surprisingly rewarding.

The following section lists several types of portfolios based on age, income, and investment preferences. Some exceed my limit of three or four issues as the ideal size for a personally administered portfolio but that is done merely to give the reader a wider choice.

I should like to stress that these sample portfolios do not, in any sense of the word, represent a recommendation for any particular stock or group of stocks. They are intended solely to illustrate the possible employment of funds. The comments on each individual issue are typical of those you might get from your own broker—*if* he agrees with the comments.

Tables 26 A, B, C list growth portfolios for age 25 with investments of $7,500, $10,000, and $15,000.

Tables 27 A, B, C list income portfolios for the same age and investment range.

Tables 28 A, B, C list growth portfolios for age 40 for the same investment range.

Tables 29 A, B, C list income portfolios for the same age and investment range.

Tables 30 A, B, C list growth portfolios for age 55 for the same investment range.

Tables 31 A, B, C list income portfolios for the same age and investment range.

TABLE 26

GROWTH PORTFOLIOS

AGE 25

A

$7,500 INVESTMENT

No. of Shares	Company	Approx. Price	Market Value	12 Months Dividends	Income
	Drugs				
50	Schering Corporation .... An important producer of antibiotics and other drugs. Spends large sums for research and development of new drugs. A reasonably priced issue in terms of current and anticipated earnings.	48	$2400	$1.50	$ 75
	Electronics				
70	Consolidated Electrodynamics.. A smaller but rapidly growing producer of advanced equipment in the promising fields of instrumentation and electronics. Devotes unusually large sums to the development of new products.	32	2240	.40	28
	Petroleum				
50	Louisiana Land & Exploration Holds over 700,000 acres of land in southern Louisiana, an area that has become the country's most promising oil province. The company is expected to continue to show outstanding growth in earnings.	56	2800	1.20[1, 2]	60
	Total Portfolio		$7440		$163
	Yield 2.2%				

[1] Indicated annual dividend rate.
[2] Adjusted for 3 for 1 split on May 21, 1956.

B
$10,000 Investment

No. of Shares	Company	Approx. Price	Market Value	12 Months Dividends	Income
	Air Conditioning				
40	Carrier Corporation .... Leading producer of all types of air conditioning equipment, the demand for which is expected to increase manyfold over the next decade. Company has an established record of earning power which should continue to improve in the years ahead.	58	$2320	$2.40	$ 96
	Drugs				
50	Schering Corporation	48	2400	1.50	75
	Electronics				
75	Consolidated Electrodynamics..	32	2400	.40	30
	Petroleum				
50	Louisiana Land & Exploration.	56	2800	1.20[1, 2]	60
	Total Portfolio .... Yield 2.6%		$9920		$261

[1] Indicated annual dividend rate.
[2] Adjusted for 3 for 1 split on May 21, 1956.

C
$15,000 INVESTMENT

No. of Shares	Company	Approx. Price	Market Value	12 Months Dividends	Income
	Air Conditioning				
40	Carrier Corporation	58	$2320	$2.40	$ 96
	Drugs				
50	Schering Corporation	48	2400	1.50	75
	Electronics				
70	Consolidated Electrodynamics..	32	2240	.40	28
	Glass				
30	Owens-Corning Fiberglas .... The leading and most dynamic company in the rapidly expanding glass fiber industry. This exciting new material is expected to enjoy increasing utilization in many phases of the building industry. The company recently announced plans for a major 3-year expansion program.	75	2250	.80[1, 3]	24
	Paper				
50	Kimberly-Clark .... The largest producer of both sanitary wadding products (Kotex sanitary napkins, Kleenex cleansing tissues, Delsey toilet tissue) and publication-type coated printing papers. The company's research laboratories recently announced the development of a paper garment fabric which should have interesting and far-reaching applications.	53	2650	2.00[1]	100
	Petroleum				
50	Louisiana Land & Exploration.	56	2800	1.20[1, 2]	60
	Total Portfolio		$14,660		$383
	Yield 2.6%				

[1] Indicated annual dividend rate.
[2] Adjusted for 3 for 1 split on May 21, 1956.
[3] Adjusted for 2 for 1 split on May 18, 1956.

TABLE 27

INCOME
PORTFOLIOS
AGE 25

A

$7,500 INVESTMENT

No. of Shares	Company	Approx. Price	Market Value	12 Months Dividends	Income
	Railroad				
40	Chesapeake & Ohio	62	$2480	$3.50	$140
	The largest carrier of soft coal, the demand for which is expected to benefit from the growing importance of foreign markets and domestic public utility usage. The company's dividends are well covered by current earning power, and increasing disbursements to stockholders may be expected over the years.				
	Retail Trade				
60	May Department Stores........	40	2400	2.20	132
	A leading department store chain with a good record of earnings growth and a generally strong capital structure. Long-term prospects for improved earning power and dividend pay-out are good.				
	Utilities—Electric				
80	Columbus & Ohio	32	2560	1.60	128
	An important electric power generating utility in central and southern Ohio. Sales and earnings are showing a satisfactory upward trend as a result of this region's growth in population levels and industrial activity.				
	Total Portfolio		$7440		$400
	Yield 5.4%				

B
$10,000 Investment

No. of Shares	Company	Approx. Price	Market Value	12 Months Dividends	Income
	Bank				
150	Marine Midland	17	$2550	$0.85	$128
	A bank holding company that owns twelve banks and operates 148 banking offices in 73 communities in New York State. The company's growth prospects are impressive, and the longer-term outlook is for increased dividend disbursements.				
	Railroad				
40	Chesapeake & Ohio	62	2480	3.50	140
	Retail Trade				
60	May Department Stores	40	2400	2.20	132
	Utilities—Electric				
80	Columbus & South Ohio	32	2560	1.60	128
	Total Portfolio		$9990		$528
	Yield 5.3%				

C
$15,000 INVESTMENT

No. of Shares	Company	Approx. Price	Market Value	12 Months Dividends	Income
150	**Bank** Marine Midland	17	$2550	$0.85	$128
120	**Finance** Beneficial Finance .... A leader in the small loan industry with over 1000 branch offices. This expanding company has an excellent record of earnings growth, and the shares are attractive for secure income and moderate growth.	21	2520	1.00	120
40	**Railroad** Chesapeake & Ohio	62	2480	3.50	140
60	**Retail Trade** May Department Stores	40	2400	2.20	132
75	**Utilities Communications** International Tel. & Tel. ..... This company is primarily a producer of electronic and communication equipment. Aside from a relatively generous yield, these shares also have merit for long-term capital growth.	32	2400	1.80[1]	135
80	**Utilities—Electric** Columbus & Southern Ohio...	32	2560	1.60	128
	Total Portfolio		$14,910		$783

Yield 5.3%

[1] Indicated annual dividend rate.

TABLE 28

GROWTH PORTFOLIOS

AGE 40

A

$7,500 INVESTMENT

No. of Shares	Company	Approx. Price	Market Value	12 Months Dividends	Income
	Drugs				
50	Schering Corporation	48	$2400	$1.50	$ 75
	Electronics				
60	Radio Corporation of America. An established company with a long record of demonstrated earning power in the rapidly growing field of electronics. The company is an acknowledged leader in the development of significant new products and techniques. The emergence of color television should be a major factor in the company's growth.	42	2520	1.50	90
	Petroleum				
20	Shell Oil .... A leading domestic integrated oil company with activities concentrated for the most part in North America. The company has shown outstanding growth in terms of reserves, and its present holdings, particularly in offshore Louisiana and Canada, augur well for continued growth.	118	2360	2.50[4]	50
	Total Portfolio		$7280		$215
	Yield 3.0%				

[4] Plus 4% stock dividend on December 5, 1955.

B
$10,000 INVESTMENT

No. of Shares	Company	Approx. Price	Market Value	12 Months Dividends	Income
	Air Conditioning				
40	Carrier Corporation	58	$2320	$2.40	$ 96
	Drugs				
50	Schering Corporation	48	2400	1.50	75
	Electronics				
60	Radio Corporation of America.	42	2520	1.50	90
	Petroleum				
20	Shell Oil	118	2360	2.50[2]	50
	Total Portfolio		$9600		$311

Yield 3.2%

[2] Adjusted for 3 for 1 split on May 21, 1956.

C
$15,000 INVESTMENT

No. of Shares	Company	Approx. Price	Market Value	12 Months Dividends	Income
	Air Conditioning				
40	Carrier Corporation	58	$2320	$2.40	$ 96
	Drugs				
50	Schering Corporation	48	2400	1.50	75
	Electronics				
60	Radio Corporation of America.	42	2520	1.50	90
	Paper				
50	Kimberly Clark	53	2650	2.00[1]	100
	Petroleum				
20	Shell Oil	118	2360	2.50[2]	50
	Retail Trade				
70	Federated Department Stores..	34	2380	1.60[1]	112

70 Federated Department Stores.. The nation's second largest department store chain, operating such stores as Abraham & Straus in Brooklyn, Bloomingdale's in New York, and Filene's in Boston. The company has an outstanding record of continued growth in terms of both sales and earning power and should continue to benefit from the growing importance of suburban shopping centers and increasing population and national income levels.

Total Portfolio $14,630 $523

Yield 3.6%

[1] Indicated annual dividend rate.
[2] Adjusted for 3 for 1 split on May 21, 1956.

TABLE 29

INCOME PORTFOLIOS

AGE 40

A

$7,500 INVESTMENT

No. of Shares	Company	Approx. Price	Market Value	12 Months Dividends	Income
	Railroad				
40	Chesapeake & Ohio	62	$2480	$3.50	$140
	Retail Trade				
60	May Department Stores	40	2400	2.20	132
	Utilities—Electric				
80	Columbus & Southern Ohio ...	32	2560	1.60	128
	Total Portfolio		$7440		$400
	Yield 5.4%				

B

$10,000 INVESTMENT

No. of Shares	Company	Approx. Price	Market Value	12 Months Dividends	Income
	Finance				
150	American Investment Co. of Ill. One of the largest personal finance companies, operating about 400 offices. Since 1945 the company has shown satisfactory growth in volume of loans and earning power, and the current dividend is regarded as relatively secure.	16	$2400	$1.00[1]	$150
	Railroad				
40	Chesapeake & Ohio	62	2480	3.50	140
	Retail Trade				
60	May Department Stores	40	2400	2.20	132
	Utilities—Electric				
80	Columbus & Southern Ohio ...	32	2560	1.60	128
	Total Portfolio		$9840		$550
	Yield 5.6%				

[1] Indicated Annual Dividend Rate.

C
$15,000 INVESTMENT

No. of Shares	Company	Approx. Price	Market Value	12 Months Dividends	Income
	Building Supplies				
125	Ruberoid	20	$2500	$1.40	$175
	A leading producer of building materials with an established record of earning power and an unusually strong financial condition. The dividend is considered secure and should continue to improve over the years.				
	Finance				
150	American Investment Co. of Ill.	16	2400	1.00[1]	150
	Railroad				
40	Chesapeake & Ohio	62	2480	3.50	140
	Retail Trade				
60	May Department Stores	40	2400	2.20	132
	Utilities—Electric				
80	Columbus & Southern Ohio ...	32	2560	1.60	128
80	Minnesota Power & Light	28	2520	1.40	126
	A public utility with a satisfactory record of earnings improvement. The dividend is considered secure, and long-term prospects for growth in the region served are promising.				
	Total Portfolio		$14,860		$851

Yield 5.7%

1 Indicated annual dividend rate.

TABLE 30
GROWTH PORTFOLIOS
AGE 55

A
$7500 INVESTMENT

No. of Shares	Company	Approx. Price	Market Value	12 Months Dividends	Income
	Chemical				
20	Union Carbide & Carbon	119	$2380	$3.00	$ 60
	Electronics				
60	Radio Corporation of America.	42	2520	1.50	90
	Petroleum				
20	Shell Oil	118	2360	2.504	50
	Total Portfolio		$7260		$200
	Yield 2.8%				

B
$10,000 INVESTMENT

No. of Shares	Company	Approx. Price	Market Value	12 Months Dividends	Income
	Air Conditioning				
40	Carrier Corporation	58	$2320	$2.40	$ 96
	Chemical				
20	Union Carbide & Carbon	119	2380	3.00	60
	Electronics				
60	Radio Corporation of America.	42	2520	1.50	90
	Petroleum				
20	Shell Oil	118	2360	2.504	50
	Total Portfolio		$9580		$296
	Yield 3.1%				

4 Plus 4% stock dividend on December 5, 1955.

C
$15,000 Investment

No. of Shares	Company	Approx. Price	Market Value	12 Months Dividends	Income
	Air Conditioning				
40	Carrier Corporation 58		$2320	$2.40	$ 96
	Chemical				
20	Union Carbide & Carbon 119		2380	3.00	60
	Electronics				
60	Radio Corporation of America 42		2520	1.50	90
	Paper				
20	Kimberly Clark 125		2500	3.00[5]	60
	Petroleum				
20	Shell Oil 118		2360	2.50[4]	50
	Retail Trade				
70	Federated Department Stores.. 34		2380	1.60[1]	112
	Total Portfolio		$14,460		$468
	Yield 3.2%				

[1] Indicated annual dividend rate.
[4] Plus 4% stock dividend on December 5, 1955.
[5] Plus 5% stock dividend on December 19, 1955.

TABLE 31

INCOME PORTFOLIOS

AGE 55

A

$7,500 INVESTMENT

No. of Shares	Company	Approx. Price	Market Value	12 Months Dividends	Income
	Railroad				
60	Great Northern .... A major U. S. railway which has shown exceptionally stable earning power and slow growth throughout the past few years. The company is in good financial condition and excellent physical condition, and the recently increased dividend rate affords a generous yield.	40	$2400	$2.50	$150
	Retail Trade				
50	Allied Stores .... The nation's largest chain of retail department stores. The company has a long history of sound earning power and good prospects for moderate long-term growth.	50	2500	3.00	150
	Utilities—Electric				
150	New England Electric System.. Supplies electricity to the New England area. This area is benefiting from the growth in the large number of electronics companies situated there.	17	2550	1.00[1]	150
	Total Portfolio		$7450		$450

Yield 6.0%

[1] Indicated annual dividend rate.

B
$10,000 INVESTMENT

No. of Shares	Company	Approx. Price	Market Value	12 Months Dividends	Income
	Finance				
150	American Investment Co. of Ill.	16	$2400	$1.00[1]	$150
	Railroad				
60	Great Northern	40	2400	2.50	150
	Retail Trade				
50	Allied Stores	50	2500	3.00	150
	Utilities—Electric				
150	New England Electric System..	17	2500	1.00[1]	150
	Total Portfolio		$9850		$600
	Yield 6.1%				

C
$15,000 INVESTMENT

No. of Shares	Company	Approx. Price	Market Value	12 Months Dividends	Income
	Building Supplies				
125	Ruberoid	20	$2500	$1.40	$175
	Finance				
150	American Investment Co. of Ill.	16	2400	1.00[1]	150
	Railroad				
60	Great Northern	40	2400	2.50	150
	Retail Trade				
50	Allied Stores	50	2500	3.00	150
	Utilities—Electric				
90	Minnesota Power & Light	28	2520	1.40	126
150	New England Electric System..	17	2550	1.00[1]	150
	Total Portfolio		$14,870		$901
	Yield 6.1%				

[1] Indicated annual dividend rate.

NOTE: The above portfolios were compiled by the Research Department of Bache & Co. Prices are as of August 30, 1956.

CHAPTER 19

Information:

Where to Get It and How to Use It

ONCE YOU'VE DECIDED that you would like to own securities, the next step, of course, is to get the necessary information upon which to make intelligent investment decisions. Is there any scarcity of printed material available to the new investor who wants to increase his general investment knowledge?

Far from it! In fact, there's so much available that the inexperienced investor is more likely to be snowed under by a bewildering mass of reports, studies, analyses, opinions, statistics, and recommendations than he is to wonder where he can find something to read about securities.

The New York Stock Exchange recently made a survey of the type of material distributed to customers and prospective customers by its member firms. This research disclosed that, on an annual basis, 296 "Big Board" member firms issue an estimated 30,700 market letters, running to 46,800 pages, not to mention 15,500 pieces of sales literature aggregating

37,300 pages. If you put all this material in a single pile, it would rise about 35 feet in height and would weigh more than 900 pounds. But the members don't stop there: they also distribute 1,800 special reports, totaling 7,000 pages.

It goes without saying, of course, that no one would try to read all the market letters, reports, studies, comments, and opinions distributed by nearly 300 stock brokers. But this doesn't mean to imply that it is a waste of time to read brokers' letters. That isn't the case. A good market letter can prove invaluable to the intelligent investor; a poor one might much better be left unread.

How does the investor decide which market letter is the one for him?

There's only one correct answer to that question: trial and error. Get hold of as many different letters as you can (and you can get a great many with practically no effort; just ask the broker to put you on his mailing list). Read them carefully; decide for yourself which ones ring true and which contain little material of value.

When you come across a market commentator who seems to be saying that the market will certainly rise if prices improve, cross him off your list.

However, we're getting ahead of ourselves. Let's put first things first.

To begin with, the well-informed investor must be at least reasonably well informed on practically every subject. To achieve such a status, he must read the daily newspapers steadily, avidly, intelligently. Stocks don't just rise and fall because "they"—those mysterious, never-identified powerful interests in Wall Street—want them to move in one direction or the other. They rise or fall in strict conformance to the law of supply and demand, and this law, in turn, depends on the hopes, fears, ambitions, prejudices, knowledge, misinformation, and convictions of thousands of people everywhere. When a majority of people believe that the outlook for security prices is good, the market tends to rise. When a majority is convinced that the outlook is dreary, prices are likely to decline.

When one man reads in the early evening edition of his favorite newspaper that the situation in the Near East is worsening, he may sell his stocks because of his conviction that war, which almost always exerts a depressing influence on securities, is imminent. Fortunately, perhaps, the majority of investors—convinced that the latest crisis won't necessarily bring on World War III—aren't panicked into dumping their shares.

But newspapers don't confine their news articles to items that can be interpreted in more than one way. They also serve up a great variety of facts that are unswervingly true: facts about business, about government, about politics, about specific industries, and about particular companies within those industrial groupings.

Opinions and facts aren't necessarily the same thing. You may, if you desire, choose to believe that a certain automobile manufacturer will run away with the popularity sweepstakes in 1957. That's fine. But, if your morning newspaper tells you that your pet motor maker's share of the auto industry's first quarter sales to car buyers slumped to 11 per cent from 18 per cent in the same three months of last year, you'll be a pretty stubborn individual if you don't revise your estimates of the company you favor.

Good as they are, the regular daily newspapers aren't sufficient for the investor who hopes to be well informed on factors that may influence the trend of security prices. Most people who devote their lives to the securities business make it a practice to read *The Wall Street Journal* every day that it publishes, and the same practice is recommended without hesitation for every individual who now owns, or ever hopes.

to own, securities. *The Wall Street Journal* is the nation's largest and most authoritative business and financial publication. It employs a large staff of experienced, competent, trained news gatherers and editors. They know the facts of business and financial life, and they present those facts to the public intelligently. This business paper has bureaus in a number of the nation's largest cities, as well as correspondents in most other big cities. It is honest, fearless, forthright.

A companion publication—*Barron's Weekly*—is less comprehensive in its coverage of business and financial developments, but it is just as honest and forthright.

The Exchange Magazine—published monthly by the New York Stock Exchange, and available to the public at the bargain rate of only $1 per year—contains a surprisingly large amount of valuable factual material. Few publications make a better presentation of dividend payments on listed common stocks, sample portfolios of important institutional investors, growth stock performances, and similar studies.

Forbes Magazine has many devoted readers in the financial community.

The Federal Reserve Board in Washington publishes a monthly bulletin containing a vast amount of statistical material, particularly on fiscal subjects, which is available nowhere else to the same extent. And the various regional Federal Reserve Banks—New York, Boston, Chicago, and others—issue monthly publications that frequently contain articles of real value to investors.

Some of the nation's largest commercial banks publish monthly bulletins or summaries. Of such publications, most Wall Street experts and certainly a majority of working financial writers rate the publication of the First National City Bank of New York in the top spot. The unusually high batting average of the National City's "Letter" in calling the turn, insofar as the general business trend is concerned, has few equals. The Cleveland Trust Company's monthly review has many avid readers, as do the publications of banks in Chicago, Boston, San Francisco, Los Angeles, and other big cities.

So now you know how and where to get the facts—and opinions—on which investment decisions are based: from brokers' letters, reports, and studies; from daily newspapers; from special publications of various types.

The rest is up to you. It's your money; and, regardless of how much help and guidance you may get from your broker—and such help is yours for the asking—the final decision must be yours.

If you have the ability to read, digest, interpret, and evaluate the thousands upon thousands of words and figures you've studied, you should be able to buy sound stocks, for sound reasons.

The stock market may—and almost certainly will—rise and fall from time to time. Some of its fluctuations may seem to you to be completely capricious, and you'll probably be right. But, if you do your homework diligently and intelligently, there's no reason why investing can't be a rewarding experience for you, just as it has been for many thousands of people in the past and will be for many thousands more in the future.

CHAPTER 20

Taxes

THE INVESTOR is directly concerned with a number of taxes that apply to securities transactions. Ignorance of how these taxes are calculated can be costly when you're faced with the melancholy task of filling out your income tax return.

Capital Gains Tax

Any gain realized from the sale of securities is subject to federal tax. The deciding factor as to the size of the tax is the length of time you have owned the security before selling it at a profit. If you have owned the security for six months or less, your profit is regarded as a short-term gain; if you have held the security for more than six months, your profit is regarded as a long-term gain.

In selling a security you may incur a loss which also is classified as either a short-term or a long-term loss. The government, in its wisdom, does not tax your loss—as a matter of fact, you may apply all or part of your loss to reduce any capital gain you may have established. You may apply a short-term gain against a short-term loss to arrive at a

246

net short-term gain or loss. You may also apply a long-term gain against a long-term loss to arrive at a net long-term gain or loss. Here are some of the possibilities:

1. Net short-term gain only.	100 per cent of the gain is taxable at the same rate as your ordinary income.
2. Net long-term gain only.	All of the gain is taxable at an effective rate of 25 per cent *or* your ordinary income rate, whichever is lower. If your income bracket subjects you to a personal income tax rate of 20 per cent, your net long-term gain should be taxed at that rate. If you're in the 30 per cent tax bracket, you'll select the 25 per cent rate.
3. Net short-term gain exceeds net long-term loss.	All of the excess is taxable at the same rate as your ordinary income.
4. Net long-term loss exceeds net short-term gain.	All of such loss up to $1,000 is deductible from ordinary income. Any sum over $1,000 may be carried forward and used as a short-term capital loss, up to a maximum of $1,000 annually for the next five years.
5. Net short-term loss exceeds net long-term gain.	Same as Number 4 above.

The capital gains tax is a subject on which large segments of the securities industry can become violent. One bad feature of the tax is that it is really self-imposed; it's up to the individual to decide whether or not he wants to accept the tax. In other words, if you have a substantial profit on a security you purchased three years ago, you may decide not to sell because you don't want to pay a capital gains tax.

The arbitrary distinction between a short-term and long-term gain is also subject to criticism, on the ground that it tends to make tax considerations replace good business judgment. For instance, you may have a substantial profit on a security you have owned for only three months. If you sell, that gain is subject to taxation at your full ordinary income rate. So, instead of selling as good judgment may dictate, you decide to hang on for another three months to take advantage of the capital gains tax rate. In the interval, your profit may be wiped out.

G. Keith Funston has been a particularly sharp critic of the capital gains tax and recently came up with a substitute proposal that should merit study. He proposed a tax-deferred treatment of capital gains, on the theory that the individual who sells one stock and fully reinvests the proceeds of that sale in another stock has not realized a real gain. Congress has recognized the validity of this argument in another field. Suppose you sell today for $25,000 the house you bought ten years ago for $15,000. That profit is not taxable—*if* you use the proceeds to buy another house for $25,000 within a year after the sale of the first house.

Double Taxation of Dividends

This is a tax with all the earmarks of real injustice. A corporation that makes a net profit pays a tax on it at the corporate rate of 52 per cent. When the corporation distributes to its stockholders in the form of dividends all or part of the profit left over after the corporate tax bite, the stockholder is walloped by having his dividends taxed at the individual income tax rate. Hence the phrase "double taxation of dividends." Interest on corporate bonds, incidentally, is not subject to the corporate tax, although the individual who receives the interest does pay a tax as if the interest were ordinary income.

In 1954 Congress gave at least token recognition to the fact that double taxation of dividends is not completely equitable. As a share owner you are now allowed to exclude from your gross income the first $50 in dividends you receive each year. If you file a joint return, you and your wife can deduct $100 in dividend income.

In addition, you are allowed a credit of 4 per cent of taxable dividends against the income tax otherwise payable. This is the same as taxing dividends (after the first $50) at 4 percentage points lower than they would otherwise be taxed. If your individual income rate is 20 per cent, the tax rate on dividends received after the first $50 is really 16 per cent.

Corporations, you may be interested to know, do a little better. A corporation receiving dividends from a domestic corporation gets a special deduction of 85 per cent of dividends received.

Transfer Taxes

The federal government, New York State, and a handful of other states impose a tax when a security is sold or transferred from one person to another. Both the state and federal taxes are paid by the seller only—except in the case of odd-lot transactions, when both buyer and seller pay the federal tax.

The New York State tax is collected on all transactions executed in the state, no matter where the seller lives. The tax ranges from 1 cent a share on stock selling below $5 a share to 4 cents a share on stock selling at $20 or more. Federal transfer taxes are based on par value of the security. In the case of no-par issues, they are considered to have a par value of $100.

Tax-Free Securities

For the taxpayer in the higher income brackets, municipal bonds can be very attractive indeed. Municipals exempt from federal tax can be bought to yield from 3½ to 4 per cent as this is written. To get equivalent income from common stocks would require a considerably higher yield—and, of course, a greater degree of risk.

The accompanying Table 32 shows the dividend yield (with 4 per cent credit) necessary to net the same amount after taxes in the form of tax-exempt bond interest. Note that the higher the tax bracket you're in, the higher the dividend yield required to equal tax-exempt bond interest at the various rates.

In order to get the equivalent of a 4 per cent tax-exempt bond yield, a taxpayer in the 22 per cent bracket must get a 4.88 per cent yield, while a taxpayer in the 75 per cent bracket must get a yield of 13.79 per cent.

TABLE 32

DIVIDEND YIELD EQUIVALENTS IN TAX-EXEMPT BONDS

Tax-exempt Bond Yield

Taxable Income (For Joint Return Double These Amounts)	Top Rate Tax	1.5%	2.0%	2.25%	2.5%	2.75%	3.0%	3.25%	3.5%	4.0%
		Dividend Yield (with 4% Credit) Necessary to Net Same Amount after Tax								
Under $ 2,000	20%	1.79%	2.38%	2.69%	2.98%	3.27%	3.57%	3.87%	4.17%	4.76%
$ 2,000 4,000	22	1.83	2.44	2.74	3.05	3.35	3.66	3.96	4.27	4.88
4,000 6,000	26	1.92	2.56	2.88	3.21	3.53	3.85	4.17	4.49	5.13
6,000 8,000	30	2.03	2.70	3.04	3.38	3.72	4.05	4.39	4.73	5.41
8,000 10,000	34	2.14	2.86	3.21	3.57	3.93	4.29	4.64	5.00	5.71
10,000 12,000	38	2.27	3.03	3.41	3.79	4.17	4.55	4.92	5.30	6.06
12,000 14,000	43	2.46	3.28	3.69	4.10	4.51	4.92	5.33	5.74	6.56
14,000 16,000	47	2.63	3.51	3.95	4.39	4.82	5.26	5.70	6.14	7.02
16,000 18,000	50	2.78	3.70	4.17	4.63	5.09	5.56	6.02	6.48	7.41
18,000 20,000	53	2.94	3.92	4.41	4.90	5.39	5.88	6.37	6.86	7.84
20,000 22,000	56	3.12	4.17	4.69	5.21	5.73	6.25	6.77	7.29	8.33
22,000 26,000	59	3.33	4.44	5.00	5.56	6.11	6.67	7.22	7.78	8.89
26,000 32,000	62	3.57	4.76	5.36	5.95	6.55	7.14	7.74	8.33	9.52
32,000 38,000	65	3.85	5.13	5.77	6.41	7.05	7.69	8.33	8.97	10.26
38,000 44,000	69	4.29	5.71	6.43	7.14	7.86	8.57	9.29	10.00	11.43
44,000 50,000	72	4.69	6.25	7.03	7.81	8.59	9.38	10.16	10.94	12.50
50,000 60,000	75	5.17	6.90	7.76	8.62	9.48	10.34	11.21	12.07	13.79
60,000 70,000	78	5.77	7.69	8.65	9.62	10.58	11.54	12.50	13.46	15.38
70,000 80,000	81	6.52	8.70	9.78	10.87	11.96	13.04	14.13	15.22	17.39
80,000 90,000	84	7.50	10.00	11.25	12.50	13.75	15.00	16.25	17.50	20.00
90,000 100,000	87	8.82	11.76	13.24	14.71	16.18	17.65	19.12	20.59	23.53
100,000 150,000	89	10.00	13.33	15.00	16.67	18.33	20.00	21.67	23.33	26.67
150,000 200,000	90	10.71	14.29	16.07	17.86	19.64	21.43	23.21	25.00	28.57
200,000 over	91	11.54	15.38	17.31	19.23	21.15	23.08	25.00	26.92	30.77

APPENDIX A

Ticker Tape Symbols of the 200 Most Active Stocks on the NYSE in 1956

Stock	*Symbol*
Air Reduction Co., Inc.	AN
Alleghany Corp.	Y
Allegheny Ludlum Steel Corp.	AG
Allis-Chalmers Manufacturing Co.	AH
Aluminum Co. of America	AA
Aluminum Limited	ALI
Amerada Petrolcum Corp.	ARC
American Airlines, Inc.	AMR
American Bosch Arma Corp.	BOS
American Broadcasting—Paramount Theatres, Inc.	ABP
American Can Co.	AC
American Cyanamid Co.	ACY
American Export Lincs, Inc.	AEX
American & Foreign Power Co., Inc.	FP
American Machine & Foundry Co.	AMF
American Motors Corp.	AMO
American Radiator & Standard Sanitary Corp.	DT
American Smelting & Refining Co.	AR
American Telephone & Telegraph Co.	T
American Viscose Corp.	VIS
Anaconda Company (The)	A
Anderson-Prichard Oil Corp.	ANP
Armco Steel Corp.	AS
Armour & Co.	AM
Ashland Oil & Refining Co.	ASH
Atchison, Topeka & Santa Fe Ry. Co.	SF
Atlantic Refining Co.	AFI
Atlas Corporation	AZ
Avco Manufacturing Corp.	AV
Baldwin-Lima-Hamilton Corp.	B
Baltimore & Ohio R.R. Co.	BO
Beaunit Mills, Inc.	BEM
Bendix Aviation Corp.	BX
Benguet Consolidated, Inc.	BE
Bethlehem Steel Corp. (Delaware)	BS

Stock	*Symbol*
Boeing Airplane Co.	BA
Borg-Warner Corp.	BOR
Budd Co. (The)	BF
Burlington Industries, Inc.	BUR
Burroughs Corp.	BGH
Callahan Zinc-Lead Co.	ZM
Canadian Pacific Ry. Co.	CP
Case (J. I.) Co.	JI
Celanese Corp. of America	CZ
Chance Vought Aircraft, Inc.	CVA
Chesapeake & Ohio Ry. Co.	CO
Chicago Corp. (The)	CHI
Chicago, Milwaukee, St. Paul & Pacific R.R.	ST
Chicago, Rock Island & Pacific R.R. Co.	RI
Chrysler Corp.	C
Cities Service Co.	CS
Colorado Fuel & Iron Corp. (The)	CF
Columbia Broadcasting System, Inc.	CBS
Columbia Gas System, Inc.	CG
Continental Can Co., Inc.	CH
Continental Copper & Steel Indus., Inc.	CCX
Continental Motors Corp.	CMR
Corn Products Refining Co.	CFG
Cosden Petroleum Corp.	CPM
Crucible Steel Co. of America	XA
Cudahy Packing Co. (The)	CUD
Curtis Publishing Co. (The)	CPC
Curtiss-Wright Corp.	CW
Dan River Mills, Inc.	DML
Deere & Co.	DE
Detroit Edison Co.	DTE
Detroit Steel Corp.	DES
Douglas Aircraft Co., Inc.	D
Dow Chemical Co. (The)	DOW
du Pont de Nemours (E. I.) & Co.	DD
Eastern Air Lines, Inc.	EAL
Electric & Musical Industries, Ltd.	EMI
El Paso Natural Gas Co.	ELG
Evans Products Co.	EVY
Fairchild Engine & Airplane Corp.	FEN
Fedders-Quigan Corp.	FJQ
Ford Motor Company	F
Foremost Dairies, Inc.	FOR
Fruehauf Trailer Co.	FTR
General Dynamics Corp.	GD
General Electric Co	GE
General Motors Corp.	GM

Stock	*Symbol*
General Public Service Corp.	GPV
General Telephone Corp.	GEN
Georgia-Pacific Corp.	GXP
Getty Oil Co.	GET
Goodyear Tire & Rubber Co.	GT
Grace (W. R.) & Co.	GRA
Graham-Paige Corp.	GP
Granite City Steel Co.	GRC
Greyhound Corp. (The)	G
Gulf Oil Corp.	GO
Howe Sound Co.	HW
Hupp Corp.	H
International Harvester Co.	HR
International Nickel Co. of Canada, Ltd.	N
International Telephone & Telegraph Corp.	IT
Johns-Manville Corp.	JM
Jones & Laughlin Steel Corp.	JL
Kaiser Aluminum & Chemical Corp.	KLU
Kennecott Copper Corp.	KN
Libby McNeill & Libby	LJ
List Industries Corp.	RKO
Lockheed Aircraft Corp.	LK
Loew's Inc.	LW
Mack Trucks, Inc.	MQ
Martin (Glenn L.) Co.	ML
Merck & Co., Inc.	MRK
Merritt-Chapman & Scott Corp.	MCS
Mohasco Industries, Inc.	MOH
Monsanto Chemical Co.	MTC
Monterey Oil Co.	MTO
Montgomery Ward & Co., Inc.	M
National Cash Register Co.	NC
National Distillers Products Corp.	DR
National Gypsum Co.	NG
National Theatres, Inc.	NTR
New England Electric System	NES
New York Central R.R. Co.	CN
New York, Chicago & St. Louis R.R. Co.	NKP
Niagara Mohawk Power Corp.	NMK
North American Aviation, Inc.	NV
Northern Pacific Railway Co.	NP
Northrop Aircraft, Inc.	NOC
Ohio Oil Co. (The)	OHO
Olin Mathieson Chemical Corp.	OLM
Oliver Corporation (The)	OF
Pan American World Airways, Inc.	PN
Parke, Davis & Co.	PDG

Stock	Symbol
Penn-Dixie Cement Corp.	DXC
Pennroad Corporation (The)	PNO
Pennsylvania R.R. Co.	PA
Penn-Texas Corporation	PTX
Pepsi-Cola Co.	PEP
Pfizer (Chas.) & Co., Inc. (Delaware)	PFE
Phelps Dodge Corp.	PD
Philadelphia & Reading Corp.	PRG
Philco Corp.	PHL
Phillips Petroleum Co.	P
Pittsburgh Steel Co.	PSC
Pure Oil Co. (The)	PY
Radio Corporation of America	RCA
Rayonier Inc.	RNR
Raytheon Manufacturing Co.	RTN
Republic Steel Corp.	RS
Reynolds Metals Co.	RLM
Reynolds (R. J.) Tobacco Co.	RJ
Rhodesian Selection Trust Limited	RHO
Rockwell Spring & Axle Co.	RKS
Royal Dutch Petroleum Co.	RD
Safeway Stores, Inc.	SA
St. Regis Paper Co.	SRT
Schenley Industries, Inc.	SH
Schering Corporation	SRG
Seaboard Air Line R.R. Co.	SBD
Sears, Roebuck & Co.	S
Sinclair Oil Corp.	L
Socony Mobil Oil Co., Inc.	SOM
Southern Company (The)	SO
Southern Pacific Co. (Delaware)	SX
Sperry Rand Corporation	SY
Standard Oil Co. of California (Delaware)	SD
Standard Oil Co. (Indiana)	SN
Standard Oil Co. (New Jersey)	J
Studebaker-Packard Corp.	SK
Sunray Mid-Continent Oil Co.	SDX
Texas Company (The)	TX
Texas Gulf Producing Co.	TR
Texas Gulf Sulphur Co.	TG
Texas Pacific Coal & Oil Co.	TS
Textron Inc.	TXT
Transamerica Corporation	TA
Tri-Continental Corp.	TY
Twentieth Century-Fox Film Corp. (Delaware)	TF
TXL Oil Corporation (The)	TXL
Union Carbide & Carbon Corp.	UK

Stock	Symbol
Union Electric Co.	UEP
Union Oil Co. of California	UCL
Union Pacific R.R. Co.	UP
United Aircraft Corp.	UR
United Air Lines, Inc.	AL
United Corporation (The)	U
United Dye & Chemical Corp.	UDY
United Fruit Co.	UF
United Gas Corp.	UGC
United Merchants & Manufacturers, Inc.	UDM
U. S. Hoffman Machinery Corp.	HMY
U. S. Industries Inc.	USI
U. S. Pipe & Foundry Co.	CJ
U. S. Plywood Corp.	PLY
U. S. Rubber Co.	R
U. S. Steel Corp.	X
Walworth Co.	WW
Warner Bros. Pictures, Inc.	WB
Western Union Telegraph Co. (The)	WU
Westinghouse Air Brake Co.	WK
Westinghouse Electric Corp.	WX
Wilson & Co., Inc.	WIL
Woolworth (F. W.) Co.	Z
Youngstown Sheet & Tube Co.	YB

APPENDIX B

Typical Short Interest Report

FROM THE NEW YORK STOCK EXCHANGE

FOR 3:30 P.M. RELEASE   FRIDAY, JANUARY 18, 1957

The short interest as of the close of business on January 15, 1957, settlement date, as compiled from information obtained by the New York Stock Exchange from its members and member firms was 2,238,-573 shares. This compared with 2,450,761 shares on December 14, 1956, settlement date, and was the lowest since October 15, 1956, when the short position was 2,205,649 shares. The January 15, 1957, short interest was one-tenth of one per cent of total shares listed. In May, 1931, when the short interest was first reported (5,589,700 shares), the comparable percentage was four-tenths of one per cent, the record high. The totals exclude odd-lot dealers' short positions. As of the January 15, 1957, settlement date, the total short interest in odd-lot dealers' accounts was 108,935 shares, compared with 95,429 shares on December 14, 1956.

The number of issues in which a short position was reported as of January 15, 1957, exclusive of odd-lot dealers' short positions was 852 compared with 877 on December 14, 1956.

Of the 1,501 individual stock issues listed on the Exchange on January 15, 1957, there were 144 issues in which a short position of 5,000 or more shares existed or in which a change in the short position of 2,000 or more shares occurred during the month. A list of these issues showing their short positions, excluding odd-lot dealers' positions, is attached:

	Short Interest		Shares
	1/15/57	12/14/56	Listed
Alleghany Corp	4,525	17,325	3,766,820
Allegheny Ludlum Stl	9,490	9,868	3,781,637
Aluminum Co America	11,747	12,556	20,553,206
Aluminum Limited	5,634	5,505	10,013,847

258

	Short Interest		Shares
	1/15/57	*12/14/56*	*Listed*
Amer Airlines	13,582	14,811	7,886,295
Amer Can Pr	2,700		1,649,332
Amer Cyanamid Co	7,495	9,020	10,302,448
Amer Distilling	5,148	5,203	440,000
Amer & Foreign Power	6,100	4,000	7,268,206
Amer Machine & Fdry	4,006	17,542	2,871,889
Amer Telephone & Tel	1,513	11,532	62,893,561
Amer Viscose	830	3,662	5,144,140
Anaconda Co	14,159	11,705	8,919,086
Armco Steel Co	16,006	8,146	10,882,276
Armour & Co	2,105	4,640	4,156,163
Atlas Corp	7,250	18,773	10,114,590
Babcock & Wilcox Co	6,157	7,835	5,145,654
Baldwin Lima Hamilton ,........	5,841	6,435	4,782,778
Baltimore & Ohio RR	17,317	22,682	2,563,021
Bethlehem Steel	15,942	20,217	10,102,232
Boeing Airplane	17,870	18,940	6,666,690
Boston & Maine RR	5,085	4,608	547,608
Brooklyn Union Gas	11,095	13,200	1,863,410
Callahan Zinc Lead	24,495	17,000	1,802,346
Capital Airlines	7,593	6,345	909,559
Case J I	12,906	8,930	2,262,766
Celanese Corp Amer	9,150	11,825	5,844,954
Chance Vought Arcrft	6,229	3,369	1,084,490
Chi & East Ill RR A	11,000	11,100	75,382
Chi Mil St P & Pac	1,170	3,475	2,123,214
Chi & Northwest Ry	35,850	34,375	815,544
Chrysler Corp	22,373	25,215	8,977,190
Cities Service Co	5,936	4,930	10,110,347
Columbia Gas System	5,142	726	20,643,776
Cons Foods	5,479	8,379	2,229,305
Cons Retail Stores	800	4,429	370,361
Consumers Power Co	2,005		8,239,861
Cont Copper & Steel	8,651	200	1,694,258
Continental Motors	200	2,200	3,300,000
Cooper Bessemer	2,125	4,990	651,800
Copper Range Co	3,157	7,465	1,875,420
Crown Zellerbach	10,315	9,706	13,798,575
Crucible Steel	9,324	7,024	1,818,228
Curtiss Wright Corp	11,600	16,315	7,634,148
Douglas Aircraft	4,955	2,780	3,705,690
Dow Chemical	21,207	18,424	24,787,970

	Short Interest		Shares
	1/15/57	12/14/56	Listed
Dresser Industries	17,331 new	8,100 old	4,344,650
du Pont de Nemours	7,743	7,977	45,604,345
Duquesne Light Co	51,025	35,690	6,600,000
El Paso Natural Gas	56,247	44,547	5,389,389
Fairbanks Morse	9,039	4,919	1,372,170
Fairchild Eng & Air	7,285	7,749	3,038,347
Fedders Quigan Corp	7,570	7,078	1,764,027
Fibreboard Paper	3,731	7,095	1,521,421
Fifth Ave Coach Lns	9,970	2,020	882,575
Firestone Tire & Rubber	7,583	10,217	8,112,721
Ford Motor Co	7,935	23,525	11,405,756
Fruehauf Trailer	41,073	42,949	6,327,957
Gardner Denver	200	5,300	1,797,384
General Dynamics	14,229	12,122	7,722,979
General Electric	57,478	59,120	87,143,662
General Motors	80,310	78,045	279,821,123
Gen Tire & Rubber	6,244	2,402	1,388,354
Georgia Pacific Corp	12,474	13,867	3,113,108
Goodrich B F	10,090	11,721	8,933,184
Goodyear Tire Rubber	19,230	20,242	10,371,661
Grace W R & Co	8,330	7,844	4,493,615
Gulf Oil Corp	5,259	8,681	33,100,682
Hercules Powder	5,407	5,223	8,261,899
Hertz Corp	1,436	3,576	1,815,853
Heyden Newport Chem	8,460	8,360	1,291,031
Hilton Hotels Corp	4,700	8,600	4,115,450
Hupp Corporation	3,905	10,050	3,598,116
Jacobs F L	300	3,700	882,607
Jones & Laughlin Stl	13,592	8,682	6,592,072
Kaiser Alum & Chem	21,475	26,491	14,695,044
Kennecott Copper	6,796	9,256	10,821,653
Lehman Corp	12,563	11,462	9,253,712
Libby McNeill & Libby	600	7,150	4,274,649
Lockheed Aircraft	6,492	5,766	2,952,704
Lukens Steel	19,387	9,522	317,976
McGraw Electric	9,285	12,050	2,285,000
Merritt Chapmn Scott	13,802	4,790	5,733,251
Mpls Honeywell Regul	9,570	9,250	6,613,519
Minneapolis Moline	8,257	11,557	910,019
Minnesota Min	17,007	20,597	16,715,722
Mo Kans Texas RR	52,330	48,505	808,971
Mo Kan Tex RR Pr A	20,045	21,747	667,005

	Short Interest		Shares
	1/15/57	12/14/56	Listed
Mo Pacific RR A	6,268	7,165	1,917,558
Nat Cash Register	31,409	28,983	7,042,610
National Gypsum	2,276	5,379	3,753,227
National Lead	6,938	7,411	11,389,811
National Theatres	600	2,800	2,769,486
New England Elec Sys	5,508	13,732	10,854,683
New York Central RR	12,138	22,775	6,449,479
N Y N H & Hart RR	9,675	13,075	566,788
North Amer Aviation	7,455	9,870	8,015,077
Northern Pacific Ry	8,995	11,799	4,966,952
Northrop Aircraft	37,672	30,510	1,523,878
Northwest Airlines	1,400	9,100	1,271,875
Owens Corning Fbrgls	6,690	5,520	6,261,278
Pan Amer World Airwy	1,850	4,300	6,197,331
Peabody Coal Co	5,812	5,752	7,635,797
Pennsylvania R R	7,465	11,135	13,167,754
Pepsi Cola	1,710	4,090	5,918,655
Phillips Petroleum	2,403	5,403	34,343,286
Pittsburgh Cons Coal	6,020	16,479	9,072,202
Pittston Co	3,490	6,442	973,544
Proctor & Gamble	12,036	9,184	19,499,983
Radio Corp of Amer	8,959	21,510	14,008,656
Republic Aviation	6,882	7,614	1,470,669
Republic Steel	11,698	12,030	15,574,974
Reynolds Metals	19,554	24,836	9,623,361
Royal Dutch Petr Co	6,822 new	4,552 old	10,638,563
St Lou San Francisco	1,570	5,120	1,819,315
St Regis Paper	7,576	8,595	6,953,990
Sears Roebuck	5,299	5,560	74,877,081
Socony Mobil Oil	24,532	9,966	44,390,253
Southrn Calif Edison	23,911	11,740	8,057,333
Southern Natural Gas	300	4,000	4,363,810
Southern Pacific	12,855	15,220	9,047,122
Southern Railway	10,114	9,509	6,491,000
Southwestern Pub Ser	6,000	650	4,087,546
Sperry Rand Corp	3,201	8,227	28,279,304
Standard Oil Calif	2,618	4,618	63,224,386
Standard Oil N J	30,810	28,968	196,761,778
Studebaker Packard	28,932	34,262	6,542,187
Sylvania Elec Prod	9,476	8,308	3,300,206
Textron Inc	5,556	5,953	3,530,248
Thompson Products	5,030	4,035	2,748,489

| | Short Interest | | Shares |
	1/15/57	12/14/56	Listed
Tri Continental Corp	6,496	7,296	5,575,786
Txl Oil Corp	2,240	5,310	5,574,356
Union Carbide Carbon	9,395	17,665	30,498,457
United Dye & Chem Corp	4,650	7,318	887,368
U S & Foreign Secur	5,039	6,079	3,310,815
U S Hoffman Mach	11,570	16,965	2,215,056
U S Industries Inc	12,650	11,050	2,302,512
U S Steel	60,384	76,830	53,699,442
United Wallpaper	5,891	7,941	3,130,126
Va Carolina Chemical	7,515	10,620	501,872
Western Air Lines	4,881	1,523	777,596
Western Union Tel	6,825	11,125	6,231,432
Westinghouse Elec	9,284	12,649	16,744,713
Youngstwn Sheet & Tube	2,005	5,708	3,422,073

APPENDIX C

Securities and Exchange Commission

Regional Offices

Room 334
Appraisers Building
821 Market Street
San Francisco 11, California

Room 573
New Customs House
19th & Stout Streets
Denver 2, Colorado

Washington 25, D.C.

Room 350
Peachtree–Seventh Building
Atlanta 23, Georgia

Room 630
Bankers Building
105 West Adams Street
Chicago 3, Illinois

U. S. Post Office & Court House
Post Office Square
Boston 9, Massachusetts

225 Broadway
New York 7, New York

301 United States Court House
10th & Lamar Streets
Fort Worth 2, Texas

Room 304
905 Second Avenue Building
Seattle 4, Washington

Subregional Offices

312 North Spring Street
Los Angeles 12, California

Room 1074
Federal Building
Detroit 26, Michigan

180 East Kellogg Boulevard
St. Paul 1, Minnesota

1370 Ontario Street
Cleveland 13, Ohio

Room 201
Boston Building
Salt Lake City, Utah

APPENDIX D

State Securities Administrators [1]

ALABAMA
Securities Commission
JOHN PATTERSON, Securities Commissioner
Judicial Building
Montgomery 5, Alabama

ARIZONA
Corporation Commission
ARTHUR TOLL, Director of Securities
Arizona Corporation Commission
Securities Division
205 State Office Building
Phoenix, Arizona

ARKANSAS
State Bank Department
JOHN L. CARTER, Assistant Bank Commissioner
267–272 State Capitol Building
Little Rock, Arkansas

CALIFORNIA
Division of Corporations
W. H. STEPHENSON, Commissioner of Corporations
Principal Office
110 State Office Building
Sacramento 14, California
Branch Offices
243 State Building
San Francisco, California
800 Mirror Building
Los Angeles, California

[1] Source of information is *Blue Sky Law Reporter,* published by Commerce Clearing House, Inc., 1956.

COLORADO
Division of Securities
ROBERT S. DAVIES, Securities Commissioner
Department of Law
Division of Securities
325 State Office Building
Denver 2, Colorado

CONNECTICUT
Bank Commissioner
MELVIN O. HALL, Director of Securities
Securities Division
Department of Banking
State Office Building
Hartford 15, Connecticut

DELAWARE
Attorney General
J. DONALD CRAVEN, Attorney General
Public Building
Wilmington, Delaware

FLORIDA
Securities Commission
JERRY THOMAS, Director
State Capitol Building
Tallahassee, Florida

GEORGIA
Securities Division
BEN W. FORTSON, JR., Secretary of State
MRS. R. W. UTTERBERG, Chief Examiner
Securities Division
214 State Capitol Building
Atlanta 3, Georgia

HAWAII

Treasury Department
KAM TAI LEE, Commissioner of Securities
Treasury Department
Territory of Hawaii
Honolulu, Hawaii

IDAHO

Department of Finance
R. U. SPAULDING, Commissioner of Finance
State Capitol Building
Boise, Idaho

ILLINOIS

Secretary of State
CHARLES F. CARPENTIER, Secretary of State
ROBERT G. CRONSON, Securities Commissioner
Office of the Secretary of State
State Capitol Building
Springfield, Illinois

INDIANA

Secretary of State
CRAWFORD F. PARKER, Secretary of State
F. H. FOUST, JR., Securities Commissioner
203 State House
Indianapolis 9, Indiana

IOWA

Commissioner of Insurance
OLIVER P. BENNETT, Commissioner of Insurance
Securities Department
Insurance Department of Iowa
State Office Building
Des Moines 19, Iowa

KANSAS
Corporation Commission
ROBERT R. LAMMY, Securities Commissioner
Securities Division
State Corporation Commission
New England Building
Topeka, Kansas

KENTUCKY
Division of Securities
J. M. ALVERSON, JR., Director
729 State Office Building
Frankfort, Kentucky

LOUISIANA
State Bank Commissioner
J. W. JEANSONNE, Commissioner of Securities
CHARLES M. WARD, Executive Assistant
651 National Bank of Commerce Building
New Orleans 16, Louisiana

MAINE
Banking Department
HAL G. HOYT, Director
Securities Division
State Banking Department
State Capitol Building
Augusta, Maine

MARYLAND
State Law Department
C. FERDINAND SYBERT, Attorney General
1201 Mathieson Building
Baltimore 2, Maryland

MASSACHUSETTS
Department of Public Utilities
HAROLD C. WHITE, Chief Accountant
FRANK J. DALEY, Senior Accountant
Division of Investigation of Securities
15 Ashburton Place
Boston 8, Massachusetts

MICHIGAN
Corporation and Securities Commission
LAWRENCE GUBOW, Commissioner
Bank of Lansing Building
Lansing 4, Michigan
Detroit Branch
Cadillac Square Building
Detroit, Michigan

MINNESOTA
Department of Commerce
CHARLES L. HAYES, Commissioner of Securities
208 State Office Building
St. Paul 1, Minnesota

MISSISSIPPI
Blue Sky Division
HEBER LADNER, Secretary of State
New Capitol
Jackson, Mississippi

MISSOURI
Secretary of State
WALTER H. TOBERMAN, Secretary of State
JOSEPH W. MOSBY, Commissioner of Securities
Securities Division
Office of Secretary of State
State Capitol Building
Jefferson City, Missouri

MONTANA
State Auditor
JOHN J. HOLMES, Investment Commissioner
Capitol Building
Helena, Montana

NEBRASKA
Department of Banking
HAROLD JOHNSON, Assistant Director and Counsel
Department of Banking
Bureau of Securities
1310 State House
Lincoln 9, Nebraska

NEVADA
Banking Department
GRANT L. ROBISON, Superintendent of Banks
Carson City, Nevada

NEW HAMPSHIRE
Insurance Department
DONALD KNOWLTON, Insurance Commissioner
State House Annex
Concord, New Hampshire

NEW JERSEY
Division of Securities
DAVID F. CONROY, Chief
Bureau of Securities
Attorney General's Office
State House Annex
Trenton, New Jersey

NEW MEXICO
State Bank Examiner
F. GORDON SHERMACK, Securities Commissioner
P. O. Box 416
Santa Fe, New Mexico

NEW YORK
Department of Law
SAMUEL A. HIRSHOWITZ, Special Assistant Attorney General
80 Centre Street
New York 13, New York

NORTH CAROLINA
Secretary of State
THAD EURE, Secretary of State
State Capitol Building
Raleigh, North Carolina

NORTH DAKOTA
State Examiner
G. H. RUSS, JR., Commissioner of Securities
1301 State Capitol
Bismarck, North Dakota

OHIO
Division of Securities
EDMUND H. SAVORD, Chief
Division of Securities
614 Ohio Departments of State Building
Columbus 15, Ohio

OKLAHOMA
Securities Commission
HERSCHAL K. ROSS, Securities Commissioner
State Capitol Building
Oklahoma City, Oklahoma

OREGON
Corporation Department
FRANK J. HEALY, Corporation Commissioner
518 State Office Building
Salem, Oregon
401 Lewis Building
Portland, Oregon

PENNSYLVANIA
Securities Commission
FRANK N. HAPP, Chairman
J. WARREN MICKLE, Commissioner
MRS. ELIZABETH G. ZEIDMAN, Commissioner
Pennsylvania Securities Commission
215 North 2nd Street
Harrisburg, Pennsylvania

RHODE ISLAND
Department of Business Regulation
THOMAS J. MEEHAN, Director of Business Regulation
LOUIS J. BARRY, Securities Commissioner
49 Westminster Street
Providence 3, Rhode Island

SOUTH CAROLINA
Insurance Department
R. LEE KELLY, Deputy Commissioner
405 John C. Calhoun State Office Building
Columbia, South Carolina

SOUTH DAKOTA
Securities Commission
GEORGE O. BURT, Secretary
State Securities Commission
Department of Insurance
State Capitol Building
Pierre, South Dakota

TENNESSEE
Commissioner of Insurance and Banking
ROBERT F. MILLER, Manager
Blue Sky Division
Department of Insurance and Banking
114 State Office Building
Nashville 3, Tennessee

TEXAS

Secretary of State
TOM REAVLEY, Secretary of State
BRADLEY BOURLAND, Securities Commissioner
Office of the Secretary of State
Austin 11, Texas

UTAH

Department of Business Regulation
M. H. LOVE, Director, Securities Commission
307 State Capitol
Salt Lake City 1, Utah

VERMONT

Commissioner of Banking and Insurance
ALEXANDER H. MILLER, Commissioner
Montpelier, Vermont

VIRGINIA

Corporation Commission
H. E. DINWIDDIE, JR., Director
Securities Division
823 State Office Building
Richmond 19, Virginia

WASHINGTON

Department of Licenses
MRS. DELLA URQUHART, Director of Licenses
JERALD C. BAILLIE, Securities Administrator
Securities Division
Department of Licenses
General Administration Building
Olympia, Washington
550 Mercer Street
Seattle 9, Washington

WEST VIRGINIA
State Auditor
Harold J. Powell, Securities Commissioner
Securities Department
State Capitol
Charleston 5, West Virginia

WISCONSIN
Department of Securities
Edward J. Samp, Director
325 State Office Building
Madison 2, Wisconsin

WYOMING
Department of State
Everett T. Copenhaver, Secretary of State
State Capitol Building
Cheyenne, Wyoming

APPENDIX E

Market Changes Related to News Events 1935–1955

Date	D-J Ind.	% Change	Volume	News Developments
1935				
2/18	+ 2.63	+ 2.5	1,911,000	Supreme Ct. gold clause decision
5/28	— 2.98	— 2.6	2,308,000	NRA ended, deflation fears
10/2	— 3.45	— 2.6	2,190,000	Italy invades Ethiopia
1936				
3/9	— 4.36	— 2.8	2,752,000	Germany threatens France
13/14	+ 3.65	+ 2.4	1,426,000	League of Nations invites Germany
11/4	+ 3.99	+ 2.3	3,294,000	Roosevelt sweeps nation
1937				
4/28	— 4.39	— 2.5	2,526,000	FDR warns against cost of living boost
9/27	+ 4.56	+ 3.1	2,209,000	FRB eases credit restriction
10/28	+ 2.96	+ 2.2	2,458,000	Margins lowered
111/6	— 3.67	— 2.9	766,000	Cut in steel production
11/26	+ 4.62	+ 4.1	1,188,000	FDR backs expanded housing
12/13	— 4.00	— 3.2	1,017,000	Japs sink gunboat *Panay*
1938				
1/4	+ 4.04	+ 3.4	942,000	FDR emphasizes rearmament need
3/16	— 4.37	— 3.4	1,023,000	Mussolini & Hitler reaffirm Axis pact
3/29	— 5.33	— 5.0	1,722,000	Silver price cut
14/9	+ 5.75	+ 5.3	1,414,000	Govt. reorganization bill defeated
4/28	— 3.27	— 2.8	537,000	US Steel pays pref. dividends deficit smaller than expected
7/12	+ 2.93	+ 2.2	1,620,000	Steel scrap production up
8/12	— 2.81	— 2.0	1,480,000	Reich mobilizes
9/26	— 3.11	— 2.3	1,226,000	Hitler attacks Benes

1 Saturday

274

Date	D-J Ind.	% Change	Volume	News Developments
9/30	+ 4.29	+ 3.1	1,898,000	"Peace with Honor"
11/9	+ 3.17	+ 2.1	3,099,000	Surprise Rep. election strength
1939				
14/8	— 4.88	— 3.9	1,640,000	Italy invades Albania
8/23	— 3.25	— 2.4	793,000	War risk insurance tripled
19/2	+ 2.84	+ 2.1	1,791,000	England declares war
9/5	+10.03	+ 7.3	5,932,000	U. S. neutrality proclaimed. War stocks up
1940				
5/13	— 7.22	— 5.0	2,558,000	Invasion Lowlands
6/10	— 3.52	— 3.1	971,000	France in retreat
6/11	+ 4.13	+ 3.7	770,000	War stocks up
8/13	— 4.28	— 3.4	641,000	England blitzed
11/6	— 3.23	— 2.4	1,209,000	FDR wins; Reaction pre-election strength
11/7	+ 5.77	+ 4.4	2,083,000	Rise sought in Fed. debt limit; inflation
1941				
12/8	— 4.08	— 3.5	2,028,000	U. S. declares war
1942				
3/6	— 2.45	— 2.3	641,000	War tax proposals
1943	..	..	..	....
1944	..	..	..	....
1945				
7/17	— 3.39	— 2.0	1,556,000	Jap peace rumors
1946				
1/28	+ 4.77	+ 2.4	3,490,000	Ford and Chrysler settle with union
7/23	— 5.32	— 2.7	1,685,000	House passes new price legislation
9/3	—10.51	— 5.6	2,905,000	War boom believed over
10/15	+ 6.08	+ 3.6	2,374,000	Meat controls off; hope all are discontinued
12/9	+ 4.75	+ 2.8	2,841,000	Coal production resumed
1947				
6/11	+ 3.58	+ 2.1	1,349,000	Hope Truman signs tax cut bill

1 Saturday

Date	D-J Ind.	% Change	Volume	News Developments
1948				
5/14	+ 3.78	+ 2.1	3,837,000	D-J industrial gives bull market signal
7/19	— 4.70	— 2.5	2,567,000	Berlin blockade
11/3	— 7.30	— 3.9	3,237,000	Truman beats Dewey
1949	..	..	..	....
1950				
6/26	—10.44	— 4.7	3,949,000	Korean War outbreak
7/12	— 5.51	— 2.7	3,197,000	Korean peace talk
7/18	+ 4.25	+ 2.2	1,823,000	Truman will ask Congress for Korean war funds
12/4	— 5.22	— 2.3	2,501,000	1,000,000 Chinese in Korea
1951	..	..	..	....
1952	..	..	..	....
1953				
4/6	— 5.93	— 2.1	3,047,000	Korean peace talk
1954				
11/3	+ 7.54	+ 2.1	2,699,000	No Democratic landslide
1955				
1/5	— 8.93	— 2.2	4,635,000	Margins up
1/17	— 8.34	— 2.1	3,355,000	Firmer money market anticipated; Fulbright inquiry
3/15	+ 7.92	+ 2.0	3,154,000	Rebound Fulbright
9/26	—31.89	— 6.5	7,720,000	President's illness
9/27	+10.37	+ 2.3	5,504,000	Rebound 9/26
10/3	—10.92	— 2.3	2,720,000	President's mild physical setback

APPENDIX F

Officers' and Directors' Report of Stock Ownership

FROM NEW YORK STOCK EXCHANGE   THURSDAY, FEB. 28, 1957

The following reports of ownership and changes in ownership of equity securities listed on the New York Stock Exchange, filed by officers, directors and large stockholders pursuant to the Securities Exchange Act of 1934 are available for public inspection:

	Date	Bought	Sold	Ownership	Balance Held
CHILDS COMPANY (HOTEL CORP. OF AMERICA)					
Reuben B. Gryzmish, Director					
Common stock	2/9/57	5,000			5,500

This represents a part of the participation of the undersigned in the Joint Venture agreement covering 50,000 shares of common stock reported by A. M. Sonnabend in July 1954

EL PASO NATURAL GAS COMPANY (ORIGINAL REPORT)					
Stuart F. Silloway, Director					
Class B common stock	2/16/57			Direct	57,150

EL PASO NATURAL GAS COMPANY (ORIGINAL REPORT)					
Leon M. Payne, Director					
Common stock Class B	2/22/57			Direct	26,324

FREEPORT SULPHUR COMPANY					
John Hay Whitney, Chairman of Board					
Common stock	1/31/57	5,000		Beneficial *	33,500
				Direct	71,000

GENERAL DYNAMICS CORPORATION					
Robert C. Tait, Director and Sr. Vice President Stromberg-Carlson					
Common stock	1/7/57	7,500		Direct	16,425

WALTER E. HELLER & COMPANY					
C. F. Cunningham, Director					
Common stock	2/18/57			2,128 † Direct	30,025

* Through Greentree Stud, Inc. of which I am a majority stockholder
† Gifts

	Date	Bought	Sold	Ownership	Balance Held
MONON RAILROAD (ORIGINAL REPORT)					
Walter D. Floersheimer, Director and Chairman of Board					
Class A common stock	3/21/57			Direct	20,100
" "				*	11,359
MONON RAILROAD					
Esther Buchman, owner of 10% of common B stock					
Common stock Class A	1/15/57	64,333		Direct	
" " " A	2/20/57		13,500	"	68,298
" " " B				"	19,234
MONON RAILROAD					
Ernest Gallo, Director					
Class A common stock	1/57		1,000		None
" B " "	1/8/57		300		800
NATIONAL AUTOMOTIVE FIBRES INC. (ORIGINAL REPORT)					
George L. Coleman, Director					
Common stock	2/19/57			†	64,486
SUN CHEMICAL CORPORATION (ORIGINAL REPORT)					
Norman E. Alexander, President and Director					
Common stock	2/13/57			‡	27,650
" "				**	5,300
VAN NORMAN INDUSTRIES, INC.					
Samuel J. Spector, direct owner of more than 10% of common stock					
Common stock	1/57		3,000		72,584

* Through Sutro Bros. & Co. partnership
† Holdings of Nafco Inc., a corporation in which I have an interest
‡ 50 Broad Street Inc. and 50 New Street Inc., corporation in which the undersigned owns all the capital stock
** Ansbacher-Siegle Corporation, in which corporation the undersigned owns all the common stock and a majority of preferred stock

APPENDIX G

Common Stock Market Abbreviations
Used in the Press

z	Unit of trading ten shares or sales in full. Rates of dividend in the foregoing table are annual disbursements based on the last quarterly or semiannual declaration. Unless otherwise noted, special or extra dividends are not included.
a	Also extra or extras.
b	Annual rate plus stock dividend.
d	Declared or paid this year, plus stock dividend.
e	Paid preceding year.
f	Payable in stock during this year; estimated cash value on ex-dividend or ex-distribution date.
g	Declared or paid so far this year.
h	Declared or paid after stock dividends or split-up.
k	Declared or paid this year, an accumulated issue with dividends in arrears.
p	Paid this year, dividend omitted, deferred or no action taken at last dividend meeting.
r	Declared or paid in preceding year, plus stock dividend.
t	Payable in stock during preceding year, estimated cash value on ex-dividend or ex-distribution date.
y	Liquidating dividend.
cld	Called.
xd	Ex dividend.
xdis	Ex distribution.
xr	Ex rights.
xw	Ex warrants.
ww	With warrants.
wd	When distributed.
wi	When Issued.
nd	Next day delivery.
q	In bankruptcy or receivership or being reorganized under the Bankruptcy Act, or securities assumed by such companies.

When stock dividend or split amounting to more than 2 per cent has been paid, the year's high-low range and dividend are shown in the new stock only.

Glossary [1]

Accrued Interest: Interest accumulated on a bond since the last interest payment was made.

Annual Report: The formal financial statement issued yearly by a corporation to its share owners.

Arbitrage: A technique employed to take advantage of differences in price. If, for example, XYZ stock can be bought in New York for $10 a share and sold in London at $10.50, an arbitrageur may simultaneously purchase XYZ stock here and sell the same amount in London, making a profit of 50 cents a share, less expenses.

Assets: Everything a corporation owns or is owed: cash, investments, money due it, materials and inventories, buildings and machinery, patents, and good will.

At the Market: An order to buy or sell a security "at the market" calls for its execution at the best possible price when the order reaches the trading floor.

Averages: Various ways of measuring the trend of securities prices on the New York Stock Exchange, the most popular of which is the Dow-Jones average of 30 industrial stocks.

Balance Sheet: A condensed statement showing the nature and amount of a company's assets, liabilities and capital on a given date.

Bear: Someone who believes the market will decline.

Bear Market: A declining market.

Bearer Bond: A bond that does not have the owner's name registered on the books of the issuing company or on the bond and that is payable to the holder.

Bid and Asked: The bid is the highest price anyone has declared that he wants to pay for a security at a given time; the asked is the lowest price anyone will take at the same time.

Big Board: A popular term for the New York Stock Exchange.

---

[1] Adapted by permission from *The Language of Investing*, prepared and published by Members of the New York Stock Exchange.

Blue Chip: Common stock in a company known nationally for the quality and wide acceptance of its products or services, and for its ability to make money and pay dividends in good times and bad.

Blue Sky Laws: A popular name for laws various states have enacted to protect the public against securities frauds.

Board Room: A room for customers in a broker's office where opening, high, low, and last prices of leading stocks are posted on a board throughout the day.

Boiler Room: High-pressure peddling over the telephone of stocks of dubious value.

Bond: Basically, an IOU or promissory note of a corporation. A bond is evidence of a debt on which the issuing company usually promises to pay the bondholders a specified amount of interest for a specified length of time, and to repay the loan on the expiration date.

Book: A notebook the specialist in a stock uses to keep a record of the buy and sell orders left with him by other brokers.

Book Value: The value of a stock as determined from a company's records, by adding all assets (generally excluding such intangibles as good will), then deducting all debts and other liabilities plus the liquidation price of any preferred issues. The sum arrived at is divided by the number of common shares outstanding, and the result is book value per common share.

Broker: An agent, often a member of a Stock Exchange firm or an Exchange member himself, who handles the public's orders to buy and sell securities or commodities.

Brokers' Loans: Money borrowed by brokers from banks for a variety of uses.

Bucket Shop: An illegal operation, now almost extinct, in which the operator accepted a client's money without ever actually buying or selling securities as the client ordered.

Bull: One who believes the market will rise. (*See:* BEAR)

Bull Market: An advancing market. (*See:* BEAR MARKET)

Call: (*See:* PUTS AND CALLS)

Call Loan: A loan that may be terminated or "called" at any time by the lender or borrower.

Callable: A bond issue all or part of which may be redeemed by the issuing corporation under definite conditions before maturity.

The term also applies to preferred shares that may be retired by the issuing corporation.

Capital Stock: All shares representing ownership of a business, including preferred and common.

Capital Gain or Capital Loss: Profit or loss from the sale of a capital asset.

Capitalization: Total amount of the various securities issued by a corporation; may include bonds, debentures, preferred and common stock.

Carrying Charge: The fee charged by a broker for carrying a customer's securities on margin. (*See:* MARGIN)

Cash Sale: A transaction on the floor of the Stock Exchange that calls for delivery of the securities the same day.

Certificate: The actual piece of paper which is evidence of ownership of stock in a corporation.

Collateral: Securities or other property pledged by a borrower to secure repayment of a loan.

Collateral Trust Bond: A bond secured by collateral deposited with a trustee.

Commission: The broker's fee for purchasing or selling securities or property for a client.

Commission Broker: An agent who executes the public's orders for the purchase or sale of securities or commodities. (*See:* DEALER)

Common Stock: Securities that represent an ownership interest in a corporation. If the company has also issued preferred stock, both common and preferred have ownership rights, but the preferred normally has prior claim on dividends and, in the event of liquidation, assets. The terms "common stock" and "capital stock" are often used interchangeably when the company has no preferred stock. (*See:* CAPITAL STOCK, PREFERRED STOCK)

Consolidated Balance Sheet: A balance sheet showing the financial condition of a corporation and its subsidiaries. (*See:* BALANCE SHEET)

Convertible: A bond, debenture, or preferred share that may be exchanged by the owner for common stock or another security, usually of the same company, in accordance with the terms of the issue.

Corner: Buying of a stock or commodity on a scale large enough to give the buyer, or buying group, control over the price.

Coupon Bonds: Bonds with interest coupons attached.

Cover: The act of buying a security previously sold short. (*See:* SHORT)

Cumulative Preferred: A stock having a provision that if one or more dividends are omitted, the omitted dividends must be paid before dividends may be paid on the company's common stock.

Cumulative Voting: A method of voting for corporate directors that enables the share holder to multiply the number of his shares by the number of directorships being voted on and cast the total for one director or a selected group of directors. Cumulative voting is required under the corporate laws of some states, is permissive in most others.

Curb Exchange: Former name of the American Stock Exchange, second largest exchange in the country.

Current Assets: Those assets of a company that are reasonably expected to be realized in cash, or sold, or consumed during the normal operating cycle of the business. These include cash, U. S. Government bonds, receivables and money due usually within one year, and inventories.

Current Liabilities: Money owed and payable by a company, usually within one year.

Current Return: (*See:* YIELD)

Customers' Net Debit Balances: Credit of New York Stock Exchange member firms made available to help finance customers' purchase of stocks, bonds and commodities.

Customers' Man: (*See:* REGISTERED REPRESENTATIVE)

Day Order: An order to buy or sell stock at a specified price which expires on the day the order is given unless executed.

Dealer: An individual or firm in the securities business acting as a principal rather than as an agent. The same individual or firm may function, at different times, either as broker or dealer.

Debenture: A promissory note backed solely by the general credit of a company and not secured by a mortgage or lien on any specific property.

Delivery: The certificate representing shares bought "regular way" on the New York Stock Exchange normally is delivered to the purchaser's broker on the fourth business day after the transaction. If a seller wants to delay delivery of the certificates, he may have his broker offer the stock "seller's option," instead of "regular way," and he may specify the number of days, from 5 up to 60, for delivery.

Depreciation: The amount of money charged against earnings by a company to offset the decline in value of a plant or machine due to age, wear and tear, and obsolescence during its useful life.

Director: Person elected by shareholders at the annual meeting to direct company policies.

Discretionary Account: An account in which the customer gives the broker or someone else discretion, which may be complete or within specific limits, as to the purchase and sale of securities or commodities.

Discretionary Order: The customer specifies the stock or the commodity to be bought or sold, and the amount. His agent is free to act as to time and price.

Distribution: Selling, over a period of time, of a large block of stock without unduly depressing the market price.

Diversification: Spreading investments among different companies in different fields.

Dividend: The payment designated by the Board of Directors to be distributed pro rata among the shares outstanding.

Dollar Cost Averaging: A system of buying securities at regular intervals with a fixed amount of dollars invested over a considerable period of time, regardless of the prevailing prices of the securities.

Double Taxation: Short for Double Taxation of Dividends. The federal government taxes corporate profits once as corporate income; any part of the remaining profits distributed as dividends to stockholders is taxed again as income to the recipient stockholder.

Dow Theory: A theory of market analysis based upon the performance of the Dow Jones industrial and rail stock price averages.

Down Tick: (*See:* UP TICK)

Earnings Report: A statement—also called an income statement—issued by a company showing its earnings or losses over a given period.

Equipment Trust Certificate: A type of security, generally issued by a railroad, to pay for new equipment.

Equity: The ownership interest of common and preferred stockholders in a company. Also refers to excess of value of securities over the debit balance in a margin account.

Exchange Acquisition: A method of filling an order to buy a large block of stock on the floor of the Exchange. Under certain circumstances, a member-broker can facilitate the purchase of a block by soliciting orders to sell. All orders to sell the security are lumped together and offset with the buy order in the regular auction market. The price to the buyer may be on a net basis or on a commission basis.

Exchange Distribution: A method of disposing of large blocks of stock on the floor of the Stock Exchange. Under certain circumstances, a member-broker can facilitate the sale of a block of stock by soliciting and getting other member-brokers to solicit orders to buy. Individual buy orders are lumped together and crossed with the sell order in the regular auction market. A special commission is usually paid by the seller; ordinarily the buyer pays no commission.

Ex-dividend: A synonym for "without dividend." The buyer of a stock selling ex-dividend does not receive the recently declared dividend. Open buy and sell stop orders in a stock on the ex-dividend date are ordinarily reduced by the value of that dividend.

Ex-Rights: Without the rights.

Extra: The short form of "extra dividend." A dividend in the form of stock or cash in addition to the regular or usual dividend the company has been paying.

Face Value: The value of a bond that appears on the face of the bond, unless the value is otherwise specified by the issuing company; ordinarily, the amount the issuing company promises to pay at maturity.

Fiscal Year: A corporation's accounting year.

Fixed Charges: A company's expenses, such as bond interest, which it has agreed to pay whether or not earned, and which are deducted from income before earnings on equity capital are computed.

Flat: This term means a bond is being traded without any accrued interest included. It is applied to bonds that are in default of interest. "Flat" means that the market price is the full price. Income bonds, which pay interest only when earned, are usually traded flat. All other bonds are usually dealt in "and interest," the seller receiving the market price plus interest accrued since the last payment date. When applied to a stock loan, "flat" means without premium or interest. (*See:* SHORT SALE)

Floor: The huge trading area—about two-thirds the size of a football field—where stocks and bonds are bought and sold on the New York Stock Exchange.

Floor Broker: A member of the Stock Exchange who executes orders on the floor of the Exchange to buy or sell any listed stock.

Floor Trader: Any member of the Stock Exchange who trades on the floor for his own account.

Fluctuation: (*See:* POINT)

Formula Investing: A predetermined investment technique.

Free and Open Market: A market in which supply and demand are expressed without restraint in terms of price. Contrast with a controlled market in which supply, demand and price may all be regulated.

Funded Debt: Usually interest-bearing bonds of a company. Could include long-term bank loans. Does *not* include short-term loans, preferred or common stock.

General Mortgage Bond: A bond that is secured by a blanket mortgage on the company's property, but that is often outranked by one or more other mortgages.

Gilt-Edged: High-grade bond issued by a company that has demonstrated its ability to earn a comfortable profit over a period of years and pay its bondholders their interest without interruption.

Give Up: A term with two different meanings. For one, a member of the Exchange on the floor may act for a second member by executing an order for him with a third member. The first member tells the third member that he is acting on behalf of the second member and gives the second member's name rather than his own. For another, if you have an account with Doe & Company but you're in a town where Doe has no office, you go to another member firm, tell them you have an account with Doe & Company and would like to buy some stock. After verifying your account with Doe & Company, the firm may execute your order and tell the broker who sells the stock that the firm is acting on behalf of Doe & Company. They "give up" the name of Doe & Company to the selling broker. Or the firm may simply wire your order to Doe & Company who will execute it for you. In either case you pay only the regular commission.

Good Delivery: Certain basic qualifications must be met before a security sold on the Exchange may be delivered. The security must be in proper form to comply with the contract of sale and to transfer title by delivery to the purchaser.

Government Bonds: Obligations of the U. S. government, regarded as the highest-grade issues in existence.

Growth Stock: Stock of a company with prospects for future growth.

G.T.C. Order: "Good 'til cancelled." A customer's order to his broker to buy or sell securities at a specified price, the order to remain in effect until it is either executed or cancelled.

Guaranteed Bond: A bond that has interest or principal, or both, guaranteed by a company other than the issuer.

Guaranteed Stock: Usually, preferred stock on which dividends are guaranteed by another company.

Hedge: (*See:* ARBITRAGE, PUTS & CALLS, SELLING AGAINST THE BOX, SHORT SALE)

Holding Company: A corporation that owns the securities of another, in most cases with voting control.

Hypothecation: The pledging of securities as collateral for a loan.

Inactive Post: A trading post on the floor of the New York Stock Exchange where inactive securities are traded in units of 10 shares instead of the usual 100-share lots. Better known in the business as Post 30.

Inactive Stock: An issue traded on an exchange or in the over-the-counter market in which there is a relatively low volume of transactions.

In-and-Out: Purchase and sale of the same security within a short period—a day, week, even a month.

Income Bond: Generally income bonds promise to repay principal but to pay interest only when earned. In some cases unpaid interest on an income bond may accumulate as a claim against the corporation when the bond becomes due. An income bond may also be issued as a substitute for preferred stock.

Indenture: A written agreement under which bonds or debentures are issued, setting forth maturity date, interest rate, security, and other terms.

Index: A statistical yardstick expressed in terms of percentages of a base year or years. For instance, the Federal Reserve Board's index of industrial production is based on 1947–49 as 100.

Interest: Payments a borrower pays a lender for the use of his money.

Investment: The use of money for the purpose of making more money, to gain income or increase capital, or both.

Investment Banker: The middleman between the corporation issuing new securities and the public. The usual practice is for one or more investment bankers to buy outright from a corporation a new issue of stocks or bonds. The group forms a syndicate to sell the securities to individuals and institutions. Investment bankers also distribute very large blocks of stocks or bonds—perhaps held by an estate.

Investment Counselor: One who is professionally engaged in rendering investment advisory and supervisory services.

Investment Trust: A company which uses its capital to invest in other companies. There are two principal types: the closed-end, and the open-end or mutual fund.

Investor: An individual whose principal concerns in the purchase of a security are regular dividend income, safety of the original investment, and, if possible, capital appreciation.

Issue: Any of a company's securities, or the act of distributing such securities.

Legal List: A list of investments selected by various states in which certain institutions and fiduciaries, such as insurance companies and banks, may invest.

Leverage: The effect on the per share earnings of the common stock of a company when large sums must be paid for bond interest or preferred stock dividends, or both, before the common stock is entitled to share in earnings. When a company has common stock only, no leverage exists because all earnings are available for the common.

Liabilities: All the claims against a corporation: accounts and wages and salaries payable, dividends declared payable, accrued taxes payable, fixed or long-term liabilities such as mortgage bonds, debentures and bank loans.

Lien: A claim against property that has been pledged or mortgaged to secure the payment of a loan.

Limit Order: A customer's order to a securities broker to buy or sell at a specific price or better. The order can be executed only at that price or a better one.

Liquidation: The process of converting securities or other property into cash. The dissolution of a company, with cash remaining after sale of its assets and payment of all indebtedness being distributed to the shareholders.

Liquidity: The ability of the market in a particular security to absorb a reasonable amount of buying or selling at reasonable price changes.

Listed Stock: The stock of a company that is traded on a national securities exchange.

Load: The portion of the offering price of shares of open-end investment companies that covers sales commissions and all other costs of distribution.

Locked In: An investor is said to be locked in when he has a profit on a security he owns but does not sell because his profit would immediately become subject to the capital gains tax.

Long: Signifies ownership of securities. "I am long 100 U. S. Steel" means the speaker owns 100 shares.

Management: The Board of Directors, elected by the stockholders, and the officers of the corporation, appointed by the Board of Directors.

Manipulation: An illegal operation. Buying or selling a security for the purpose of creating false or misleading appearance of active trading or for the purpose of raising or depressing the price to induce purchase or sale by others.

Margin: The amount paid by the customer when he uses credit to buy a security, the balance being advanced by the broker.

Margin Call: A demand upon a customer to put up money or securities with the broker. The call is made when a purchase is made; also if a customer's equity in a margin account declines below a minimum standard set by the Exchange or by the firm.

Market Order: An order by a customer to a broker to buy or sell at the best price available when the order reaches the trading floor.

Market Price: In the case of a security, market price is usually considered the last reported price at which the stock or bond sold.

Matched and Lost: When two bids to buy the same stock are made on the trading floor simultaneously, and each bid is equal to or larger than the amount of stock offered, both bids are considered to be on an equal basis. So the two bidders flip a coin to decide who buys the stock. Also applies to offers to sell.

Maturity: The date on which a loan or a bond or debenture comes due and is to be paid off.

Member Corporation: A securities brokerage firm, organized as a corporation, with at least one member of the New York Stock Exchange who is a director and a holder of voting stock in the corporation.

Member Firm: A securities brokerage firm organized as a partnership and having at least one general partner who is a member of the New York Stock Exchange.

MIP: Monthly Investment Plan. A pay-as-you-go method of buying

New York Stock Exchange listed shares on a regular payment
plan for as little as $40 a month, or $40 every three months.

Mortgage Bond: A bond secured by a mortgage on a property.

Municipal Bond: A bond issued by a state or a political subdivision,
such as county, city, town or village. The term also designates
bonds issued by state agencies and authorities.

Mutual Fund: (*See:* INVESTMENT TRUST)

NASD: The National Association of Securities Dealers, Inc. An association of brokers and dealers in the over-the-counter securities
business.

Negotiable: Refers to a security, title to which, when properly endorsed
by the owner, is transferable by delivery.

Net Asset Value: A term usually used in connection with investment
trusts, meaning net asset value per share.

Net Change: The change in the price of a security from the closing
price on one day to the closing price on the following day on
which the stock is traded. The net change is ordinarily the last
figure in a stock price list. The mark + 1⅛ means up $1.25
a share from the last sale on the previous day the stock traded.

New Issue: A stock or bond sold by a corporation for the first time.

Non-Cumulative: A preferred stock on which unpaid dividends do not
accrue.

Odd Lot: An amount of stock less than the established 100-share unit
or 10-share unit of trading.

Odd-Lot Dealer: A member firm of the Exchange that buys and sells
odd lots of stock.

Off-Board: This term may refer to transactions over-the-counter in unlisted securities, or, in a special situation, to a transaction involving a block of listed shares that was not executed on a
national securities exchange.

Offer: The price at which a person is ready to sell.

Open Order: An order to buy or sell a security at a specified price;
remains in effect until executed or cancelled by the customer.

Option: A right to buy or sell specific securities or properties at a
specified price within a specified time.

Over-Bought: An opinion as to price levels. May refer to a security
which has had a sharp rise or to the market as a whole after
a period of vigorous buying, which, it may be argued, has left
prices "too high."

Over-Sold: An opinion—the reverse of over-bought. A single security or a market which, it is believed, has declined to an unreasonable level.

Over-the-Counter: A market for securities made up of securities dealers who may or may not be members of a securities exchange. Over-the-counter is mainly a market made over the telephone: the principal market for U. S. Government bonds, municipals, bank and insurance stocks. (*See:* NASD, OFF-BOARD)

Paper Profit: An unrealized profit on a security still held.

Par: In the case of a common share, par means a dollar amount assigned to the share by the company's charter. In the case of preferred shares and bonds, however, par often signifies the dollar value upon which dividends on preferred stocks, and interest on bonds, are figured.

Participating Preferred: A preferred stock that is entitled to its stated dividend and, also, to additional dividends on a specified basis upon payment of dividends on the common stock.

Passed Dividend: Omission of a regular or scheduled dividend.

Penny Stocks: Low-priced issues often highly speculative, selling at less than $1 a share.

Point: In the case of shares of stock, a point means $1. In the case of bonds a point means $10, since a bond is quoted as a percentage of $1,000. In the case of market averages, the word point means merely that and no more. If, for example, the Dow Jones industrial average rises from 470.25 to 471.25, it has risen a point. A point in the averages, however, is not equivalent to $1.

Portfolio: Holdings of securities by an individual or institution.

Preferred Stock: A class of stock with a claim on the company's earnings before payment may be made on the common stock and usually entitled to priority over common stock if company liquidates.

Premium: The amount by which a preferred stock or bond may sell above its par value. In the case of a new issue of bonds or stocks, premium is the amount the market price rises over the original selling price. Also refers to a charge sometimes made when a stock is borrowed to make delivery on a short sale. May refer, also, to redemption price of a bond or preferred stock if it is higher than face value or market price.

Primary Distribution: Also called primary offering. The original sale of a company's securities.

Principal: The person for whom a broker executes an order, or a dealer buying or selling for his own account. The term "principal" may also refer to a person's capital or to the face amount of a bond.

Prior Preferred: A preferred stock that usually takes precedence over other preferreds issued by the same company.

Professional: In the securities business, a student of the market or a person who makes a living buying and selling securities.

Profit Taking: Selling to take a profit, the process of converting paper profits into cash.

Prospectus: A circular that describes securities being offered for sale to the public. Required by the Securities Act of 1933.

Proxy: Written authorization given by a shareholder to someone else to represent him and vote his shares at a shareholders' meeting.

Proxy Statement: Information required by SEC to be given stockholders as a prerequisite to solicitation of proxies for a listed security.

Prudent Man Rule: An investment standard. In some states, the law requires that a fiduciary, such as a trustee, may invest the fund's money only in a list of securities designated by the state—the so-called legal list. In other states, the trustee may invest in a security if it is one that a prudent man of discretion and intelligence, who is seeking a reasonable income and preservation of capital, would buy.

Puts and Calls: Options that give the right to buy or sell a fixed amount of a certain stock at a specified price within a specified time. A put gives the holder the right to sell the stock; a call the right to buy the stock. Puts are purchased by those who think a stock may go down. Calls are purchased by those who think a stock may rise.

Quotation: Often shortened to "quote." The highest bid to buy and the lowest offer to sell a security in a given market at a given time.

Rally: A brisk rise following a decline in the general price level of the market, or in an individual stock.

Realizing: Same as Profit Taking.

Record Date: The date on which you must be registered on the books of a company as a shareholder in order to receive a declared dividend or, among other things, to vote on company affairs.

Redemption Price: The price at which a bond may be redeemed before maturity, at the option of the issuing company. Redemption value also applies to the price the company must pay to call in certain types of preferred stock.

Refinancing: Same as refunding. New securities are sold by a company and the money is used to retire existing securities.

Registered Bond: A bond that is registered on the books of the issuing company in the name of the owner.

Registered Representative: Present name for the older term "customers' man." Also known as "customers' broker."

Registrar: Usually a trust company or bank charged with the responsibility of preventing the issuance of more stock than authorized by a company.

Registration: Before a public offering may be made of new securities by a company, or of outstanding securities by controlling stockholders—through the mails or in interstate commerce—the securities must be registered under the Securities Act of 1933. Before a security may be admitted to dealings on a national securities exchange, it must be registered under the Securities Exchange Act of 1934.

Regular Way Delivery: Unless otherwise specified, securities (other than governments) sold on the New York Stock Exchange are to be delivered to the buying broker by the selling broker and payment made to the selling broker by the buying broker on the fourth business day after the transaction. Regular way delivery for government bonds is the following business day.

Regulation T: The federal regulation governing the amount of credit that may be advanced by brokers and dealers to customers for the purchase of securities.

Regulation U: The federal regulation governing the amount of credit that may be advanced by a bank to its customers for the purchase of securities.

Return: Same as Yield.

Rights: When a company wants to raise more funds by issuing additional securities, it may give its stockholders the opportunity, ahead of others, to buy the new securities in proportion to the number of shares each owns. The piece of paper evidencing this privilege is called a right.

Round Lot: A unit of trading or a multiple thereof.

Scrip: A certificate exchangeable for stock or cash before a specified date, after which it may have no value. Usually issued for fractions of shares in connection with a stock dividend or split or in reorganization of a company.

Seat: A traditional figure of speech for a membership on a securities or commodity exchange.

SEC: The Securities and Exchange Commission, established by Congress to help protect investors.

Secondary Distribution: Also known as secondary offering. The redistribution of a block of stock sometime after it has been sold by the issuing company. The sale is handled off the Exchange by a securities firm or group of firms, and the shares are usually offered at a fixed price which is related to the current market price of the stock.

Seller's Option: A special transaction on the Stock Exchange which gives the seller the right to deliver the stock or bond at any time within a specified period, ranging from not less than five business days to not more than 60 days.

Selling Against the Box: A method of protecting a paper profit. Let's say you own 100 shares of XYZ which has advanced in price, and you think the price may decline. So you sell 100 shares short, borrowing 100 shares to make delivery. You retain in your security box the 100 shares which you own. If XYZ declines, the profit on your short sale is exactly offset by the loss in the market value of the stock you own. If XYZ advances, the loss on your short sale is exactly offset by the profit in the market value of the stock you have retained. You can close out your short sale by buying 100 shares to return to the person from whom you borrowed, or you can send him the 100 shares which you own.

Serial Bond: An issue that matures in relatively small amounts at periodic stated intervals.

Short Sale: A person who believes a stock will decline and sells it though he does not own any has made a short sale.

Short Covering: Buying stock to return stock previously borrowed to make delivery on a short sale.

Short Position: Stocks sold short and not covered as of a particular date.

Sinking Fund: Money regularly set aside by a company to redeem its bonds or preferred stock.

Special Offering: Occasionally a large block of stock becomes available for sale which, due to its size and the market in that particular issue, calls for special handling. A notice is printed on the ticker tape announcing that the stock will be offered for sale on the floor of the Exchange at a fixed price.

Specialist: A member of the N. Y. Stock Exchange who assumes two responsibilities: First, to maintain an orderly market, insofar as reasonably practicable, in the stocks in which he is registered as a specialist; Second, the specialist acts as a broker's broker.

Special Bid: A method of filling an order to buy a large block of stock on the floor of the Exchange. In a Special Bid, the bidder for the block of stock will pay a special commission to the broker who represents him in making the purchase. The seller does not pay a commission. The Special Bid is made on the floor of the Exchange at a fixed price which may not be below the last sale of the security or the current bid in the regular market, whichever is higher. Member firms may sell this stock for customers directly to the buyer's broker during trading hours.

Specialist Block Purchase: Purchase by the specialist for his own account of a large block of stock outside the regular market on the Exchange.

Specialist Block Sale: Opposite of the Specialist Block Purchase.

Speculator: One who is willing to assume a relatively large risk in the hope of gain. His principal concern is to increase his capital rather than his dividend income.

Speculation: The employment of funds by a speculator. Safety of principal is a secondary factor.

Split: The division of the outstanding shares of a corporation into a larger number of shares. A 3-for-1 split by a company with 1 million shares outstanding would result in 3 million shares outstanding.

Stock Ahead: Sometimes an investor who has entered an order to buy or sell a stock at a certain price will see transactions at that price reported on the ticker tape while his own order has not been executed. The reason is that other buy and sell orders at the same price came in to the specialist ahead of his and had priority.

Stock Clearing Corporation: A subsidiary of the New York Stock Exchange which acts as a central agency for security deliveries and money payments between member firms of the Exchange.

Stock Dividend: A dividend paid in securities rather than cash.

Stockholder of Record: A stockholder whose name is registered on the books of the issuing corporation.

Stop Order: An order to buy or sell which becomes a market order as soon as the price of the stock reaches, or sells through, the price specified by the buyer or seller.

Stopped Stock: A service performed—in most cases by the specialist— for an order given him by a commission broker. Let's say XYZ just sold at $50 a share. Broker A comes along with an order to buy 100 shares at the market. The lowest offer is $50.50. Broker A believes he can do better for his client than $50.50, perhaps might get the stock at $50.25. But he doesn't want to take a chance that he'll miss the market—that is, the next sale might be $50.50 and the following one even higher. So he asks the specialist if he will stop 100 at ½ ($50.50). The specialist agrees. The specialist guarantees Broker A he will get 100 shares at 50½ if the stock sells at that price. In the meantime, if the specialist or Broker A succeeds in executing the order at $50.25, the stop is called off.

Street: The New York financial community concentrated in the Wall Street area.

Street Name: Securities held in the name of a broker instead of his customer's name are said to be carried in a "street name."

Switching: Selling one security and buying another.

Syndicate: A group of investment bankers who together underwrite and distribute a new issue of securities or a large block of an outstanding issue.

Tax Exempt Bonds: The securities of states, cities and other public authorities specified under federal law, the interest on which is either wholly or partly exempt from federal income taxes.

Technical Position: A term applied to the various internal factors affecting the market; opposed to external forces such as earnings, dividends, political considerations and general economic conditions. Some internal factors considered in appraising the market's technical position include the size of the short interest, whether the market has had a sustained advance or decline without interruption, a sharp advance or decline on small volume, and the amount of credit in use in the market.

Thin Market: A market in which there are comparatively few bids to buy or offers to sell or both. The phrase may apply to a single security or to the entire stock market.

Ticker: The instrument that prints prices and volume of security transactions in cities and towns throughout the U. S. within minutes after each trade on the floor.

Tips: Supposedly "inside" information on corporation affairs.

Trader: One who buys and sells for his own account for short-term profit.

Trading Floor: Same as Floor.

Trading Post: One of 18 horseshoe-shaped trading locations on the floor of the New York Stock Exchange at which stocks assigned to that location are bought and sold. About 75 stocks are traded at each post.

Transfer: This term may refer to two different operations. For one, the delivery of a stock certificate from the seller's broker to the buyer's broker and legal change of ownership, normally accomplished within a few days. For another, to record the change of ownership on the books of the corporation by the transfer agent.

Transfer Agent: A transfer agent keeps a record of the name of each registered share owner, his or her address, the number of shares owned, and sees that certificates presented to his office for transfer are properly canceled and new certificates issued in the name of the transferee.

Transfer Tax: A tax imposed by New York State, a few other states, and the federal government when a security is sold or transferred from one person to another. Paid by the seller.

Treasury Stock: Stock issued by a company but later reacquired. It may be held in the company's treasury indefinitely, reissued to the public, or retired.

Two-Dollar Broker: Members on the floor of the New York Stock Exchange who execute orders for other brokers having more business at that time than they can handle themselves, or for firms who do not have their Exchange member-partner on the floor. The term derives from the time when these members received $2 per hundred shares for executing such orders.

Turnover: The volume of business in a security or the entire market.

Underwriter: Same as investment banker.

Unlisted: A security not listed on a stock exchange.

Unlisted Trading Privileges: On some exchanges a stock may be traded at the request of a member without any prior application by the company itself.

Up Tick: A term used to designate a transaction made at a price higher than the preceding transaction. Also called "plus tick." A stock may be sold short only on an up tick, or on a "zero-plus" tick. A "zero-plus" tick is a term used for a transaction at the same price as the preceding trade but higher than the preceding different price.

Conversely, a down tick, or "minus" tick, is a term used to designate a transaction made at a price lower than the preceding trade. A "zero-minus" tick is a transaction made at the same price as the preceding sale but lower than the preceding different price.

Voting Right: The stockholder's right to vote his stock in the affairs of his company.

Warrant: A certificate giving the holder the right to purchase securities at a stipulated price within a specified time limit or perpetually.

When Issued: A short form of "when, as, and if issued." The term indicates a conditional transaction in a security authorized for issuance but not as yet actually issued.

Wire House: A member firm of the Stock Exchange with branch offices linked together by a communications network.

Working Control: Theoretically, ownership of 51 per cent of a company's voting stock is necessary to exercise control. In practice—and this is particularly true in case of a large corporation—effective control sometimes can be exerted through ownership, individually or by a group acting in concert, of less than 50 per cent.

Yield: Also known as return. The dividends or interest paid by a company expressed as a percentage of the current price—or, if you own the security, of the price you originally paid.

Index